Seven Years
on the Pacific Slope

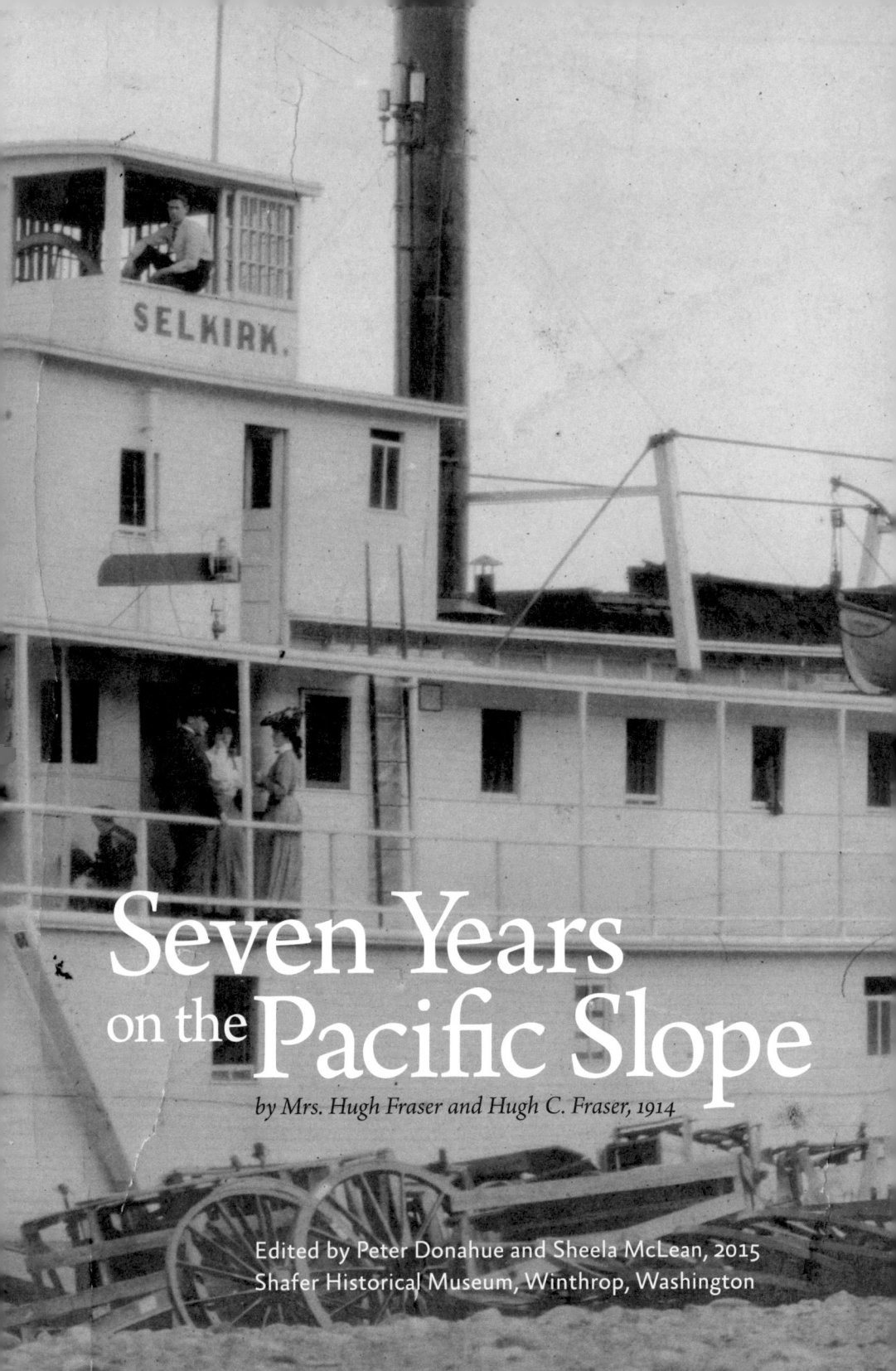

by Mrs. Hugh Fraser and Hugh C. Fraser, 1914

Edited by Peter Donahue and Sheela McLean, 2015
Shafer Historical Museum, Winthrop, Washington

Copyright © 2015 the Shafer Historical Museum

All rights reserved. No part of this publication may be reproduced or transmitted in any form or by any means, electronic or mechanical, including photocopy, recording, or any information storage or retrieval system, without permission in writing from the publisher.

Published by the Shafer Historical Museum, Winthrop, WA
www.shafermuseum.com

Library of Congress Control Number: 2015947314
ISBN 978-0-692-49475-2

Produced by Marquand Books, Inc., Seattle
www.marquand.com

Designed by Meghann Ney
Typeset in Arno Pro by Kestrel Rundle
Proofread by Barbara Bowen
Color management by iocolor, Seattle
Printed and bound in China by Artron Art Group

Contents

Introduction 7

Acknowledgments 11

Chapter 1   The Chinook State *13*

Chapter 2   The Far West at Close Range *19*

Chapter 3   A Neck of the Woods *29*

Chapter 4   Life and Ethics in the Methow *34*

Chapter 5   The "Nebrasky Outfit" *45*

Chapter 6   All About the Neighbours *56*

Chapter 7   The Spirit of Chance *63*

Chapter 8   The Canning Season *68*

Chapter 9   In a Forest Garden *76*

Chapter 10   Tragedy and Comedy *85*

Chapter 11   Happy-Go-Lucky *94*

Chapter 12   The Thoroughbred and His Cousins *100*

Chapter 13   Some Old Citizens and a New One *123*

Chapter 14   Feuds—Indigenous and Imported *132*

Chapter 15   Progress—By Leaps and Bounds! *141*

Chapter 16   A Prosperous Season *148*

Chapter 17   The Land Boom *159*

Chapter 18   Quite Another Story *165*

Chapter 19   Miner's Luck *175*

Chapter 20   The Unforeseen *189*

Chapter 21   Wedding Bells *196*

Chapter 22   God's Country *209*

Notes 213

List of People 220

Photo Credits 223

Peter Donahue

Introduction

Mary Crawford (Mrs. Hugh Fraser) was born in Italy in 1851. She came from a distinguished family. Her father was Thomas Crawford, a prominent American sculptor, best known today for the *Statue of Freedom*, atop the U.S. Capitol in Washington, D.C. Her mother was Louisa Cutler Ward, niece of Julia Ward Howe, the abolitionist and suffragist who penned "The Battle Hymn of the Republic." Her family, including three siblings, resided in Italy, and though she would attend boarding school in England and as an adult travel the world with her British diplomat husband, she always viewed Italy as her home.

She married Hugh Fraser in 1874 and for the next twenty years accompanied him on his diplomatic postings to China, Italy, Chile, and Japan. After his death in 1894, she wrote a number of volumes based on her experiences as a "diplomatist's wife," including several about Japan that remain notable for their detailed depiction of the country. In addition, like her novelist brother, Francis Marion Crawford, an acclaimed writer of historical and fantastical novels, Fraser published more than a dozen novels, also in the historical and fantastical mode.

Travel and writing were essential parts of Mary Crawford Fraser's life. By the time she came to Washington State, she had already trekked deep into the interior of China, helped establish an embassy in Tokyo, and published numerous books of fiction and nonfiction. So venturing into the rugged reaches of the Upper Methow Valley, and then writing about her adventures, was a challenge for which she was well prepared.

She came to the Methow Valley in 1906 to be with her youngest son, Hugh, a lieutenant in the British Army, who had been wounded in the Second Boer War in Africa (1899–1902). Hugh had been encouraged by Guy Waring, an acquaintance through the family's Boston ties, to move to the Methow to recover from his wounds and enjoy the quiet life of the valley. When Mrs. Fraser arrived, she immediately befriended Dick McLean, Waring's business nemesis. Shortly after her arrival, Mrs. Fraser and Hugh were joined in the Methow by her oldest son, John, known as "Jack," who receives only a few mentions in *Seven Years on the Pacific Slope*, and Katherine Lucy Wray, known as "Kitty," Hugh's bride-to-be, who figures prominently in the book.

Following her sojourn in the Methow Valley, which ended in 1912, Fraser moved to Spokane, where Hugh and Kitty had settled following their marriage in the Methow. After a brief residence in Spokane, all three returned to Italy. In 1914, news of the publication of *Seven Years* reached the valley, and then, with the start of the First World War, the Frasers returned to England. Hugh rejoined his regiment to fight in France, and in late 1915, Mrs. Fraser wrote to her friends in the Methow informing them that "My dear Hughie was killed in action in the beginning of August, and you will understand what that means to us all."

Fraser survived her son Hugh by several years, dying in 1922. It is unknown whether she remained in England or returned to Italy following the war. We do know that she continued to write. In a publishing career that spanned two decades, Fraser published more than thirty books. "I never found any vehicle for expression except in writing," she once remarked. "I was passionately in love with the science of language ever since I was a very little girl. A new derivation, a noble phrase or some fine old word rescued from oblivion, would go to my head like wine." Such love of language is evident in *Seven Years*.

Certainly, among early books about the Northwest, *Seven Years* is unusual. It is not a typical first-hand account of pioneer life in the vein of works by Ezra Meeker or Emily Inez Denny. Nor is it a report of exploration and adventure, aimed at an audience "back East," along the lines of Theodore Winthrop's *The Canoe and the Saddle*. Like the Methow Valley itself, *Seven Years* has its own set of characteristics. Foremost among these is what we think of as the author's outsider-insider perspective. Fraser came to the Methow from a life lived mainly in Europe and Asia. Her education, experiences, and sensibilities were decidedly different from those of anyone she encountered in the valley, including Guy Waring, whom she dubs a "Bostonian and Harvardian to the ends of his fingers." Nonetheless, interacting with the McLeans, Filers, and other pioneer families, she soon fit right in and before long was a fully accepted member of the community.

Community, after all, is a central theme of *Seven Years*. Fraser both observes and participates in the Methow community, particularly in and around the town of Winthrop. She is adept at noting mannerisms in individuals as well as generalizing about the community at large. She recounts the doings of the people around her, especially the antics of the McLeans, without judging or sensationalizing them. She recognizes when tragedy occurs, which it does, and respects people's sensitivities. Readers quickly see that Fraser genuinely cares about the people she portrays in the book.

And, if readers are familiar with the Methow Valley, they quickly see in reading *Seven Years* that the valley is much the same today as it was more than 100 years ago. There are still cougars, horses, orchards, alfalfa, irrigation ditches, and stunning scenery. There are still cold winters with plenty of snow and hot summers with wildfires. There are still farmers and ranchers, merchants and jobbers, loners and gossipers, cranks and eccentrics. Likewise, among locals there are still feuds, small and large, but these are always offset by the prevailing neighborliness, tolerance, and good humor of the community.

Readers can expect to find all of this and more in *Seven Years on the Pacific Slope*, which is why Sheela McLean and I took on this project. The idea for it came about after Sheela ran an excerpt from the book on *Methow Grist*, the online publication she edited from 2011 to 2013. Taken by the vivid description of the Methow in this short excerpt, I immediately obtained a copy of the out-of-print book. Two months later, I wrote a piece on it for *Columbia: The Magazine of Northwest History*, published by the Washington State Historical Society, and shortly after that, Sheela and I met for coffee and agreed there should be a new edition of *Seven Years on the Pacific Slope* available to everyone who loves the Methow Valley.

We also recognized that creating a new edition meant abridging and annotating the original since, as anyone who has tried to read it knows, the 1914 edition can be a slog. Without a doubt, Mrs. Hugh Fraser is a sharply observant, insightful chronicler of life in the Methow Valley. Her anecdotes are frequently hilarious, her prose often beautiful. Yet, the original *Seven Years* is laden with digressions, redundancies, and descriptive superfluities that diminish the work's better qualities. We are not alone in recognizing this aspect of Fraser's writing. Hugh Cortazzi, who edited and reissued one of Fraser's books about Japan in 1982, noted that she has "a certain Victorian tendency to overwrite." He added that, despite this tendency, "the author paints a picture of brilliant colour of life in Tokyo." The characterization applies just as well to *Seven Years* and the picture Fraser paints of life in the Methow. Indeed, Fraser's portrait of the Methow Valley is like none other—and it deserves to be read. Yet, for contemporary readers to fully appreciate *Seven Years*, it had to be edited.

To this end, Sheela and I have trimmed away roughly one-quarter of the original text to sharpen the book's focus on the Methow Valley. We also have included 133 endnotes to provide context for readers and identify the numerous people and places referred to in the book. In respect to Fraser's prose style, though, we felt it essential to preserve her unique voice, which is integral to her perspective on the valley. Therefore, with the exception of a handful of small edits for the sake of clarity, we did not alter her sentences. We also retained her British spellings.

Nonetheless, readers will readily see that Fraser's prose has certain idiosyncrasies. One of the more peculiar is her shifting use of personal pronouns. Though she speaks in the first person, she often uses the plural pronoun "we" while at the same time referring to herself and Hugh in the third person, especially when she adopts Hugh's perspective. This unevenness can be disorienting at times, so reader beware. She also changes people's names and/or gives them nicknames. For example, she calls herself the "Summer One" and her son Hugh the "Winter One," referring to the seasons in which each arrived in the valley. As for changing the names, examples include the McLeans, whom she renames the Mackenzies, and the Filers, who become the Tilers.

The issue of authorship is another point worth mentioning. The title page lists Hugh C. Fraser, her youngest son, as the co-author of *Seven Years*. Yet, it seems to us that the book was written by Mrs. Fraser alone. We conclude this based on the uniformity of the prose style. Many of the anecdotes she shares are second-hand, and it is likely that, in the sections putatively narrated by Hugh, she is simply recounting, through his perspective, events he related to her. Sharing the title page with him is likely a mother's deferential gesture, akin to her use of her marriage title and husband's full name. It was Mrs. Hugh Fraser, after all, who was the writer in the family—and whose presence presides over *Seven Years on the Pacific Slope*.

Acknowledgments

This project was a community effort. The book would never have come about without the strong support of the Board of Directors at the Shafer Historical Museum in Winthrop, an affiliate of the Okanogan County Historical Society. Our special thanks go to E. Richard Hart, chair of the museum's board, and Roxie Miller, who oversees the museum's finances. We also thank the Community Foundation of North Central Washington and the Moccasin Lake Foundation for their financial support of the project.

Several individuals have contributed to the painstaking effort of editing this book. Most of the endnotes are the monumental work of Barry George, whose research skills and knowledge of the Okanogan County Historical Society archives are unequalled. We also received enormous help from Karen West and Kit McLean, authors of *Bound for the Methow*, in selecting the photographs. In addition, Barry George, Karen West, Kit McLean, and Susan Donahue all provided invaluable editorial feedback on the manuscript and endnotes. We also were helped in the abridging process by Kegan Hovda, whose interest in history made him the ideal summer intern at the museum in 2014.

Finally, many current and former Methow Valley residents were consulted about the people and events in the book and the Methow Valley in general. These good people include Craig Boesel, Doug Devin, Elinore (Kent) Drake, Darrell "Duffy" Dufresne, Garry Dufresne, Tom Graves, Shirley (Palmer) Haase, Henry "Hank" Heckendorn, Walt Holcomb, Diana (Watts) Hottell, Hugh "Bill" Imes, Duane Kikendall, Rhonda Kikendall, Donna (Northcott) Martin, Karen Mathison, Rickard McLean, Vicki McLean, Jim Parrish, Darlene Pearson, Gerry (Heckendorn) Poor, Golda (McCain) Rosvall, Donna (Filer) Schulz, Larry Therriault, Judy (MacLellan) Tonseth, Frankie (Morse) Waller, and Don White. Thank you all.

Chapter 1

The Chinook State

Just twenty-five years ago, a rather irregular square, occupying the extreme northwest corner of the United States territory, was promoted, as "Washington," to the honour of being the twenty-ninth of the now existing forty-five States of the Union.[1] Its sixty-nine thousand square miles of rich, unexplored surface had been quarrelled over for many years, and it was only in 1846 that a boundary line was definitely drawn up and agreed upon by the High Contracting Litigants, Great Britain and the United States. It is a country which seems to have yielded unwillingly to the advancing tide of immigration, and this for natural reasons, since, beyond the towering barrier of the Rocky Mountains, which it shares with Idaho and Montana, it has a whole chain of its own, the Cascades; a procession of wild and formidable peaks which, parting from the great spine of the Rockies in Canada, shoots down through Washington and intersects it in a straight line almost to the southern boundary, forming a solid escarpment against incursions from the direction of the Pacific. It was a costly and complicated business to carry the railway through the Cascades to the beautiful port of Seattle on their further side, and even now, as my tale will show, snowslides in winter and forest fires in summer do away with any fear of monotony for the travellers on that line.

Between the Cascades and the Rockies proper, sheltered by both and enriched by uncounted ages of sun and rain, and snow as kindly and fostering as the dew, lies a district as large as England, where beautiful new cities have indeed sprung up, and there are townships by the hundred—very prosperous ones, too—but where, when I first visited it in 1905, there were over thirteen million acres of unappropriated land, of which eight million acres had not even been surveyed. The forests cover twenty-three and a half million acres of Washington—and there are no less than five full strong rivers that water and drain it royally.[2] The Columbia, the greatest of all, rushes down from Canada at the northeast corner, and then, after making, with the help of the tributary Okanogan, almost an island of the vast Indian Reservation called Colville, seems unwilling to leave the State, and twists and turns bewilderingly before it issues on the southern side and constitutes itself the boundary line between Washington and Oregon, for nearly three hundred miles, ere it tosses its travelled stream out into the Pacific Ocean.

If there is anyone among my readers who has heard year after year, through all the buzz and tumult of our modern life, the persistent call of great free spaces, ringing still through a hundred generations, of that desire of conquest which drove our ancestors from Europe to the new-born West—let him come over the Rockies into Washington and find content. To only a few comes the call. Here and there—to some restless, vigorous scion of an old stock, as a rule—but, once heard, it becomes an ache, a cry, a hunger, which it is good to heed and parlous to neglect. Some of us who hear it have first been driven through all that modern life has to give of show and colour, ambition, beauty, interest; but a day comes when all these things fall into a kind of dusty nothingness around us, and the entity we brought into the world refuses to be sustained by them any longer. Then—what? In such temperaments the sense of self-preservation is abnormally strong, and the same instinct that makes one rush to open the windows in some long closed, evil-smelling room drives them forth, scandalously careless of the opinion of friends and foes, to get what they need and *will* have, life in the raw.

Ah, the sweet wild health and strength of it! There is so much room that the cranks and the quitters do not really get in anybody's way except their own, and along that their neighbours watch them go, with large-minded and mostly silent compassion, knowing the hard conditions and that not all men are equal to them. Besides, life in the raw is full of surprises; the strongest may trip over some unexpected obstacle and find himself for a time among the stragglers and in need of pity. So one abstains from judging and learns to be indulgent and more ready to find excuses than condemnations.

And that is what we must ask from kind readers for the men and women spoken of in this book. They will find few wholly admirable— for these are all real living people, not characters manufactured to suit the reading public; also very few who are wholly to be condemned. There is generally some saving grace in our common humanity, after all. Even the least satisfactory had left everything behind, and faced the enormous West with all its huge, blind chances of good and ill; and it takes courage to do that; they had had the nerve to try; and, whatever the result, we may be sure Heaven loves a trier.

There are conflicting opinions even now on the value of that part of Washington State which forms a much elongated triangle between the frontiers of British Columbia on the north, and the Okanogan and Methow rivers, which empty themselves, within a few miles of one another, into the Columbia, on the South. The enthusiasts claim a splendid future for it; the pessimists declare that since the Great Northern Railway has found no use for it yet, it will live unstoried and "peter out" unmourned.[3] As I am among the enthusiasts I would remind our opponents that Daniel Webster, whom they as well as we rank among America's great statesmen, thus regarded the whole of the West. In Congress he fiercely opposed the acquisition of the Oregon Territory, which at that time embraced all the country now covered by the State of Washington, and over which America was quarrelling violently with Great Britain. Daniel Webster, in a famous speech, said, "What do we want with those barren wastes, this uninhabitable region filled with icebergs and mountains covered with eternal snow? Mr. President, I will not vote for the Government of the United States to spend one dollar to bring the Pacific coast a single foot nearer than it is today!"[4]

When one realises that if the United States had listened to Daniel Webster then, and to those who opposed the Louisiana Purchase later, Great Britain and France would now be owning vast territories—some of the richest on our Continent—within our own borders, one shivers retrospectively at the disasters avoided and rejoices at the enthusiasm which carried the hard-fought days. I think that all else being equal, it is better, more profitable, in the long run, to risk chances with the enthusiast than to sit down and croak with the pessimist.

In this book it has been necessary to give, as it were, two individual stories, which sometimes merge into one, sometimes take their separate ways. In no other fashion could the account of the place and our experiences there be made in any way complete. There are always, in primitive places, two little worlds, the one of the men, the other of the women. They have many points of contact, but the fact remains that women will open their hearts to a woman and men to a man in a fashion quite distinct from that which one sex will accord to the other. So, to give any true impression of the only bit remaining of the Far West, it was necessary that my son and I should describe things as they were shown to us individually. The result may be that we have both sometimes touched on the same event, but we trust that this will not be charged to us as repetition—since it only occurs where we witnessed reverse scenes and heard the different sides of a story. Of one thing, gentle reader, be sure—we are telling the truth. Some names have been changed, for obvious reasons; some stories that worked out slowly (as stories of human lives will) condensed into a continuous narrative; but facts, language, portraits are all as veraciously described as possible, and nothing has been set down in malice.

Many a time we have been asked in these long seven years, by old friends in the populous places, "Why on earth do you live in the Methow?" In answer to that question we say, "Because it is what its people call it, 'God's Country.' Because of the green glory of its summer mornings, the awesome beauty of its winter nights, the bloom of its unrifled soil; because our tired souls can breathe more freely under the vast circle of the Methow sky; because every star and tree and hilltop has become a landmark on a journey of rejuvenation for minds deafened by the warring noises of the world; because (perhaps, the strongest reason of all) the mental atmosphere of the 'Home Valley' is as untrammelled as its airs. There the only claim to respect is founded on character. The honest man and the worker, whether he be a struggling settler who has walked hundreds of miles to get there and then has set himself single-handed to conquer the wilderness, or a public-spirited citizen with a big bank account, is a prince among his peers. And the women—hats off, gentlemen!—are heroines of devotion and courage; because, in all this great world, swayed by the love of money and the baseness of snobbery, there is one—perhaps the only true—Republic, where a man is judged by what he is, not by what he has."

We were drawn to the Methow by a series of apparently unmeaning accidents and impulses which ended by crystallising into a chain and held four of us in the country for years.[5] My own count seven, but my younger son, he who writes this book with me, had preceded me by nearly two years. I was a little uncertain of his whereabouts when, one icy January morning in New York, I received a wire from Vancouver announcing that he would land at Seattle the next day. He was coming from the soft warmth of the East, and New York, that January, was a pneumonia factory, dangerous even to seasoned Yankees; so a wire flew back bidding him wait for instructions in Seattle, where an old friend of one of his uncles was requested to find a possible spot where he could pass the remainder of the winter. The friend was kind, but he gave not much thought to the matter, and finally sent off my son to another friend, the one hereafter mentioned in these pages as the "Owner."[6] The "Owner," kind in intention but not highly gifted with insight, was feeling cold and lonely, and at once became convinced that cold and loneliness and every kind of unnecessary hardship constituted the best recuperative treatment for a man who had been invalided out of the Army (after having gone through the entire three years of the South African war).[7]

"What you need, my dear boy," said the "Owner," "is hardening! You Englishmen take life too easy!"

The "Owner" professed to have had some trials and fatigues on first coming into the country seventeen years earlier, and though these were long past, the queer little streak of vengefulness that runs in the back of most people's heads made him like "to see the young ones at it." He never quite admitted this to himself, but he used to tell me frankly that, to his sorrow, he recognised a strong streak of the Puritan in his make-up, and this scourged him into hardnesses that the other man in him shuddered at secretly. But the Puritan held out, and, where circumstances supplied the power, could not resist acting as a "hanging Judge" to other people's frailties. So the boy had a pretty tough time at starting.

In the summer of that year, 1905, I was on my way to Japan from New York, and he came down to pass a couple of days with me in Seattle. I found him very thin and very quiet, but no word passed his lips that could make me feel anxious about his daily welfare and general contentment. It was a queer country up there, he said, but he had come to like it; the people were friendly and amusing, life presented no serious difficulties, and he was perfectly satisfied with it. A year later I returned, as I then thought, to spend a two months' holiday with Hughie and, when it should be ended, to go back to Japan, where much interesting work had been planned for me. But fate put up the shutters on work. For six months and more I battled with the misery known to brain-workers as "broken-head." My correspondence piled up unread—it gave me fever to read a letter. There was nothing for it but to give in and trust that rest in this strange, wild, peaceful place would cure the malady. It did, in time, but there remained from it such an overpowering horror of the old crowded life, where one elbows one's painful way through the din and the throng, that no cure known to civilisation could ever draw me back into it.

So the wilderness caught me and held me fast, as it was holding my son, and for another year and a half we two were there by ourselves, very happy, very interested, growing stronger and saner every day. But one thing was wanting to us—the presence of the other two, my eldest son and the very dear girl who was some day to become my daughter-in-law, a term at which we always laughed, seeing that for so many years she had filled for me the place of the daughter I never had; and at last she and Jack came too.[8] And for four or five years one very unusual bliss was granted to us; for each one the little brown house on the hill held the only persons in the world whose presence was necessary for happiness. "All I have and all I want, under my own roof," I used to say to myself when all was quiet and I went to lock the front door at night. Does anyone still wonder why we loved the Methow?

Chapter 2

The Far West at Close Range

Fate has a startling way of taking one at one's word—or a part of it—sometimes. I remember that, some nine or ten years ago, I was playing round in New York, very much pleased with myself, and things in general, when I received a letter from my eldest son, begging me to return to England, and describing, very charmingly, I must say, the delights of English rural life. In spite of published dates—and photographs—I was feeling at the time about twenty-five years old, and I replied by saying that I should die of boredom in the country in England, and by giving a list of the different homes I meant to have in the States, ending up with "a shanty on the Pacific Slope."

Not very long after I flung out that defiance I found the last item of it realised. Purely by accident, and much to my own surprise, the shanty had become my home; and a very real and interesting home too.

Hughie always calls me "The Summer One," because my first sight of the far Northwest was granted in the scorching days of August. I had come over from Japan, and landed in Seattle towards the end of July. Seattle and I were old acquaintances already, but the unknown interior to the North was all an unmapped problem, and I was quite in the dark as to the means of penetrating thither, when the standing luck of the vagabond came to my aid in the shape of a telephone call, informing me that the potentate referred to by the "Winter One" as the "Owner" was in Seattle at that moment and was coming to see me. Now the Owner's exploits as a pioneer were famous as far East as New York, where I had heard him spoken of as a dashing adventurer—in the honourable sense of the word—a man of iron will and amazing courage, who played with difficulties and rejoiced in dangers. We are all hopelessly conventional at heart, and I had pictured the popular hero to myself as a kind of glorified cowboy, big and broad, with a Homeric laugh, bright blue eyes, half a dozen pistols sticking out of his pockets and several yards of lasso draped round his person. (That I thought of "pistols" shows my utter greenness as to all things Western; a week after my arrival I had learnt to call them "guns.")

I was waiting in the entrance hall of the Butler Hotel[9] when a quiet-looking gentleman, dressed all in black and wearing large spectacles, slipped past me and disappeared inside the elevator. He carried a bottle of medicine in his hand, and I said to myself, "There goes a doctor! I suppose somebody is ill upstairs."

A few minutes afterwards I was informed that a visitor was waiting for me in the parlour, and I hastened thither to find that my "doctor" was no other than the magnate whose imaginary portrait had been so clearly painted on my mind, and who now stood before me as the gentlest, most unassuming of men, with a low voice and the general make-up of a Harvard professor. From that moment I realised that my valuations of things Western required readjustment. How kind and thoughtful you were, dear Owner! In the midst of heavy personal trouble you took me in hand, explained every stage of the long rough journey that lay before me, made out my timetable, told me what to do and what to avoid and "put me wise" to such things as my inexperience most needed to learn.

With all that, however, the journey proved almost too sensational for comfort. Leaving Seattle at 8 p.m., I expected to arrive at the railway terminus at two in the morning, but as a matter of fact we did not reach it 'til after four, the August time-table having omitted to take account of the forest fires which were raging at intervals along the road.[10] Hot as the night was, it was necessary to keep all the windows closed, and the sight of tract after tract of tall pines close to the line, flaming wildly, or writhing in what looked like human agony, in the last red glow of destruction, was rather terrifying. We had to go slowly sometimes, sometimes stop altogether, while the men went forward and cleared the rails of some wreck of burning timber that had fallen across them. Sometimes the reek of smoke was so thick that nothing else was to be seen 'til red tongues of flame leapt through and lit up the dark figures of men swinging axes and crowbars against the glare. Yet there was not the least excitement. My fellow-travellers scarcely glanced towards the windows, and both officials and axe-men had the calm, weary expression of tackling a tiresome job with which they were only too familiar.

So I kept silence, learning the first lesson of the Far West, the country of great silences, where it is a point of honour never to express surprise or fear. All my own also was my relief when in the grey dawn the heavily-laden transcontinental pulled in to something that looked like a station, and I and my belongings were tumbled out on a long unguarded platform where one or two lights blinked uncomfortably at the nascent day.[11]

Some other people had got out and I hastened to follow them, for it was necessary to find the Columbia River and get on board the steamer which was to carry me over the first part of the hundred-and-fifty-mile journey yet to be accomplished.[12] The river was reached at last, and I scrambled up the side of a toy steamer and found myself taken in charge by a friendly young man who appeared to run things generally and who evidently regarded me as a legitimate object of pity, for he got me a cup of tea and showed me to a stateroom—the size of a bandbox, but affording much peace and shelter to my weary body and mind.

Then came the long day on the river, past mile after mile of enormous walls of cliff rising sheer from the water, bare cruel masses of rock on which no blade of grass could find roothold. At last they sank away and the country spread in long gentle stretches, still green with alfalfa, towards a line of mountains on either side. It gave one a queer impression of past eternities to think that the stream, which was not a very wide or full one, had cut its way from the flats through the towering masses of rock I had been watching all the morning—and had done it in ages so remote that the work was accomplished before the first man trod the earth.

As the day wore on, the scenery changed and assumed a milder aspect, the hills receding enough to leave long rolling vistas of cultivated land, with little streams here and there emptying into the river where a clump of trees sheltered farmhouses and outbuildings. As I was watching one of these peaceful spots, the steamer turned round, with perfect deliberation, and started merrily back down stream. For several minutes nobody appeared to notice this act of insubordination, but at last a dinghy piled with rope was lowered, and two men rowed up towards some evil-looking rocks round which the water was dashing furiously. "What is the matter?" I asked. "The Rapids. Reckoned we could get past—water's low. No good," was the reply. Meanwhile the cables were twisted round a couple of snags ahead, a wheezy winch got to work, and after much labour the steamer was induced to turn her nose in the right direction and continue her journey.

That was necessarily a slow one, for it is only by the river that mails and freight can be distributed through all that lonely country. At one point, a most desolate spot, without a building in sight, we pulled up and waited while a bare-legged girl of ten or eleven, who had been lying flat on the edge of a steep cliff watching our approach, picked herself up and sauntered down a zigzag path to the beach. A small child followed her, and set up a howl at finding itself left behind. She went back for it, and, at the baby's pace, came to the water's edge, when a very thin and flabby mail-sack was pitched across to her. She was the postman! As we sheered off I saw her and the baby climb the height and disappear over the crest.

The sun was sinking when I, the only passenger for my port, was dropped with some few of my belongings at a real wharf, and I looked round, wondering what was to happen next, for there was not a soul in sight. Then, over the sandy dunes appeared a person in shirt sleeves—and very little else, the rest of his costume seeming to consist of patches and fringes—who gruffly advised me to go right ahead, assuring me that I should "hit the hotel" before long; and very glad I was when I did.[13]

I had to start so early the next morning that I do not think I fairly woke up until I found myself in the middle of the river and clinging for dear life to the side of a rig which threatened every instant to turn over in the current; the horses had given up the struggle and had doubled round already, half swimming in the stream, on whose turbulent bosom I caught sight—my last sight—of my best new umbrella sailing away, a black speck in the distance.[14] Somehow we reached the further bank, and then I took a good look at my driver—whom as yet I had merely heard addressing his horses, the river and the universe in general in language which can only be described as sulphuric. To find a boy of sixteen the possessor of such a vocabulary was a surprise which distracted my attention from immediate perils and discomforts for a time, but these soon claimed recognition, accompanied by some sinking of heart. Sixty miles or more of road lay before me; it was only six o'clock, but the sun was already scorching; the trail—it seemed scarcely more—ran like a switch-back of the craziest kind up and down angles of appalling acuteness, with cliffs above and precipices below, and I soon discovered that my boy driver was nearly insane with toothache and earache, and did not, for the moment, care a damn whether we pitched over or not. Our progress, in consequence, was distinctly sensational; he would not be bothered to hold the clumsy drag in place going down hill, and on the worst incline of all the cayuses[15] bolted so effectually that the impetus carried them and us halfway up the next ascent with no effort on their part. I thought it must all be a part of the "grand free life of the West," and held on in silence, frightened to death, but determined not to give myself away as a tenderfoot by voicing my fears.

Towards midday we pulled up at the half-way house for dinner,[16] and, sitting down at the rough table, I did start a little at the aspect of my opposite neighbour, a fine Western edition of a Corsican brigand, with a red beard and unkempt hair, a face of exceeding fierceness, and strange wild eyes which were fixed on me with unexplained persistence. I escaped from their scrutiny as soon as possible and, having found a tiny spot of shade in the moraine of tin cans which surrounded the lonely shack, was proceeding to soothe my nerves with a cigarette when, to my dismay, a gruff voice called to me and I turned, to see the brigand perched on the box seat of the stage—my driver for the rest of the day!

I confess that I felt in my coat pocket for my derringer as I settled down behind him, and I have never thought of that moment without laughing at myself pretty heartily. He turned out to be "The Preacher," an ardent Methodist with the gift of oratory.[17] He drove villainously, and his "fresh" team were hobbling skeletons; but he was quite kind through that long weary afternoon and showed much interest in me when he discovered that I was the mother of "Loo-tenant Fraser," with whom he declared he was on terms of the most friendly intimacy.

"That's where your son lives," said the Preacher, pointing through a cloud of dust to a low white cottage close to the river, "but he's running the creamery just now—maybe you won't find him here."[18]

He found me, however, for the moment we halted, a thin, very sunburnt apparition rushed out, and, in true British fashion, disguised his satisfaction at my arrival under a stream of reproaches for not letting him know when I was coming.

Never mind, in five minutes I had been made at home in the queer little domicile.[19] Hughie had brewed me some tea, I had propitiated him with a huge box of Melachrinos[20] which a Japanese friend had brought me at parting, and we sat there for a good hour exchanging our news. Then, as night was drawing on, it became necessary to move. Rooms had been engaged for me in the only house that had any to spare, but the old lady who kept them still had two days' "haying" to get through on her ranch, so the Owner's assistant kindly gave me his bedroom and slept among the mattresses and iron ware in a loft of the store.[21] For supper I was taken to the hotel, where every one welcomed me warmly for my son's sake, but which at that time had no sleeping accommodation except in a shed on the roof, reached from outside by a ladder. The supper was a gloomy meal, I must admit, some dozen men swallowing their food in dead silence—no one ever speaks at meals in the West—intent only on getting through with the business and out to the adjacent saloon as quickly as possible.

Two evenings later I was installed in the little brown house on the hill, where, though I little thought it then, I was to pass several years of my life.[22] The sun had sunk away behind the crags of Mount Gardner in the West and a big moon was rolling over the shoulder of a dark hill that towered in the background and jutted out like a rampart between us and the world I had left behind. We were on what is called a "bench" in the mountains, a space of flat ground stretching between one high shoulder and another. Behind, the hills rose in a steep screen, making a sharp outline against the sky, and below, the river, our own little river, ran, fringed with pine and alder,[23] through the rich valley bottom, to disappear in gleaming twists and zigzags among the canyons it had cut for itself, through the hills. Across the river the land rose again in terrace above terrace, all dark with fir-trees, 'til it reached a wide plateau surrounding and backed by range after range of rocky peaks, all looking very dim and ethereal in the flooding moonlight.[24] There was a little garden in front of the house, full just then of irises in bloom, their pale diaphanous petals fluttering noiselessly in the breeze that came down from the north. A roof or two showed far down in the valley, and off to the right I could just see the top of a big barn where I was told some "mighty nice neighbours" were living until they should find time to build a house. It was a lonely, silent world that I looked out upon, but it had one glory—the sky. That had never before seemed so near and yet so vast; the mountains had fallen back in a circle, like the petals of a flower from its heart, and the perfect round of the sky hung over the Valley, as utterly its own as if there were no other spot on earth for the sun to shine on or the darkness to brood over.

The air was divinely fresh, straight from Alaska, and with a quality of newness that one only gets in those empty northern regions. I found out all about it that first night. After seeing that I had all I wanted, my son ran down the hill to the creamery, where, in the warm weather, all the work had to be done at night, and my hostess, assuring me that I was perfectly safe by myself (there were no locks on any of the doors and no door at all to my bedroom), turned her back on me and disappeared down the road towards her ranch, promising to come back in time to cook my breakfast in the morning.

As everyone seemed to take the arrangement for granted I did the same, but I must say that to sleep entirely alone in a strange country in a house you have never seen by daylight—open to anyone who may choose to enter, and far out of call of any neighbour, is something of a trial even to seasoned nerves. I did attempt to explore the region behind the two front rooms, but as I found the way barred by piled furniture—and chairs and tables on their heads do look very hostile by candle-light—I retreated. My windows were close to the ground, and once during that rather long night some heavy animals who fought silently but furiously, with panting breaths and vicious bumps and hurls, had a grand battle on the porch. I don't know what they were—pigs or coyotes, I suppose—but I was very glad when the day dawned and I could creep out into the sweet-smelling front yard and greet the morning coming up cool and clear from the East!

Early as it was, a cloud of smoke was issuing from a stovepipe at the back of the house, and I found my old landlady actually engaged in getting my breakfast and her own. She had cooked that meal down at the ranch for the hired men who were getting in her hay, and had walked the two miles back, fasting, without a thought of fatigue, though she was nearer seventy than sixty.

She followed me back to the front of the house, enquiring into my tastes as to breakfast. Buckwheat cakes and fresh eggs sounded all right, but: "I guess you'd better come and make your tea yourself," she advised; "we don't go much on tea, me and Ed, and I believe you English ladies are particular about your tea. Yes, Ed's my son—the youngest of eleven I brought into this country fifteen years ago, and got no health—might die any minute, the doctor says—makes me awful anxious, but he's got to work![25] I don't believe honest work ever killed anybody even if they do turn blue, have spells, and get their left arm all queered up."

This seemed rather gruesome talk before breakfast. I tried to change the subject by admiring some trails of moonflowers that were climbing over the porch.

Naturally, the most vivid of all my impressions of the country were those I received in those first few months. To me, it spelt the world (as I knew it) backwards. It would be untrue to say that I did not get some violent shocks. The first came when I climbed down off the stage and the boy whom I had last seen in London looking typically "Parky,"[26] came out to greet me in rather battered overalls and a shirt open over a very sunburnt throat. The exterior aspect of his "shack" was rough enough, but the interior made me want to sit down and cry. Bare boards of the most ancient description on floor and walls, curtainless windows, a bed of unplaned lumber, a cracked stove and one small table, which served every purpose from eating to writing poetry—such were the quarters in which he declared he had been perfectly comfortable for some months—because compared to those he had occupied before, they appeared princely. His rations consisted of bacon, flour and coffee; bread he had not tasted for months. Only married men could obtain that luxury. The lonely ones mixed flour and water and a dash of baking powder together, dropped it in lumps into a baking tin rubbed with bacon rind, made a roaring fire and shoved the tin inside the oven. If they remembered to take it out inside of five minutes, the result was "hot biscuit," a thing one can eat when one is hungry and when it is hot—shutting one's eyes to the inevitable discomfort that will follow; but it is deadly and "sad" when cold. Milk was not known in my boy's menu, except when one of his beloved cats was ill and seemed to need it. Then he used to go and chop wood for somebody, to obtain a pint or so.

He had a friend who was always very glad to let Hughie work for him, but who was born with an overwhelming distaste not only for work, but also for parting with his money. So that these little "trades" were not always as remunerative as they should have been. The friend was a perfect specimen of the kind of Englishman who never should have been allowed to set foot on the western side of the Rockies. He was a naval man who had got himself invalided out of the service and was enjoying one of the pensions which seem to be so easy to get in the Navy.[27] I was so irritated at the way he made my son slave at nursing him and cooking for him while he, who was much more fit for work than Hughie, lay in bed rolled up in blankets and wailing that this was a hard cold world, that I "let fly" once or twice and had the satisfaction of listening to his reproaches for having come between two loving friends and broken up the ideal and precious conditions which had prevailed until my arrival. Apart from his overgrown instinct of self-preservation, the "Admiral," as Hugh's friend was usually called, could be a very pleasant companion, and he did a good deal to brighten my first months in the wilderness. He had been sent up to the Methow for his health, and was living in a tent on a bluff over the river, which ran very deep and dark just there, between high and precipitous rocks. The tent was in reality a moveable cottage, with lumber floor and roof and a brick chimney. Its sail-cloth walls could be made air-tight, and the "Admiral" used to close every lap and make such roaring fires in his stove that one nearly died of suffocation when one went to see him.

I used to find my house very small in the long mellow days of those Indian summers, and often betook myself to a delicious retreat in the loft of the barn. The furniture was the most luxurious in the world—delightfully perfumed alfalfa hay! I made a cosy seat in it and a rest for my writing pad; before me a great square opening gave me the whole out-of-doors to look at; I could see the entire valley, the stage-road and all the trails, and I was really in a fortress, for nobody could see me, and I never told anyone my secret.

It was not darkness but light that I used to seek in my secret chamber of the hay. Our scenery has a strange quality of coyness that makes it forbidding and dreary enough on grey, cold days; then the hills look inhospitable, the river is the colour of hungry steel, and the pines stand up in long processions, black and deathly, like mutes at a funeral. But there are days when every passing hour shows some new and perfect loveliness of colour and outline. I have an artist friend who spent two winters at the North Pole and one at the South Pole to paint the weird fire-and-ice beauty of the frozen realms. How I have wished he would come to the Methow, in late summer or early autumn, to paint the golds and greens, the peacock blues and bronze browns that make the Valley look, on a September afternoon, like a highway of jewels rippling over one another in the sun! The great cube-shaped haystacks raise their backs of humped gold, for all the world as if some giant in the mountains had been sweeping gold dust from his hidden mines down on the emerald velvet of the fields. Towards the "North Fork"[28] the river loses itself in a tangle of impenetrable forest shot through with quivering orange and red where the first touch of the frost has lingered too long. In the other direction a stream of sun-kissed azure twists in a hundred lovely turns, now broadening into a mirror wide and calm enough to reflect the mountains themselves, now narrowing between cliffs all hung with fir and shrubs. Towards night-fall a ribbon of white mist unrolls, exactly following the river's course, and hangs over it motionless, turning the peaks beyond into a fairy-land of mountains floating above the clouds. Up comes a great round moon over the shoulder of the hill behind my house, the mist curls away, and lo! there is no more gold, or green, or blue, but a silver waterway between folds of sable velvet.

Such colour and glory of colour I have indeed seen in other lands, but this one is, after all, most dear to me for its ethereal beauty of colourlessness, when the good mothering snow has laid its mantle of warm white velvet over all to keep out the frost and get the sleeping earth all ready for another spring. From the early morning, when the sun leaps up and makes the whole Valley glisten like a net of diamonds, 'til the South claims him, and his level rays turn the drifted whiteness into furrows of turquoise in the shade and running honey in the light, the winter day is one long draught of sparkling life. But the night! Who that has stood bare-headed, entranced, gazing at the silver and crimson splendours of the Aurora Borealis, leaping to the zenith, sinking back to the horizon to surge up the next instant and flood the ice-bound world with unearthly and terrible glory, can ever rail at the winter again? Standing on the uplift of the hilltop, one could almost catch at the huge stars that wing their mystic circle around the pole; the "Magnetic North" seems very near then. The faithful, the constant, the unmoving North Star is neighbour and friend as well as guide. The spiritual elation wrings one to pain—it is too acute. Then one is thankful if the scene changes and the stars pale, and the whole vast dome becomes a tent of dripping silver because a full moon, slow, majestic and familiar, heaves her white radiance over the hill and floods the winter night with a light as pure as peace, as reconciling as the pardon of many sins.

Chapter 3

A Neck of the Woods

It was a veritable "neck of the woods" into which Fate led us, mother and son, one in the depth of a semi-arctic winter, the other at the scorching height of the fierce season that is known as summer.[29] There is no half-way house between the seasons in the Northwest. Spring leaps full-fledged from the middle of winter, summer flings spring aside and withers it in passing. One day the hillsides are white, the next green, the next burnt umber. Autumn hurries past, trembling in its gorgeous robes, winter descends upon its heels and the world becomes a vast, silent threat. Cattle wander knee-deep in the snow, but without noise; stray sleds fly hither and thither, but as soundlessly as falls the snow upon which they travel. The little towns that serve as capitals to tracts of country as large as Holland stand out from the almost sickening whiteness of the earth, black and lonely—and silent. Such persons as are compelled to move from one pine-board shanty to another, do so at a run, their faces muffled: not a dog or a cat is abroad that can find a stove beside which to lie and dream.

The nature of the pioneer is a special thing, given to him and to him alone, for good and obvious reasons. If it were possible for him to live a settled life in a settled place, the frontiers of the States would never have passed Pennsylvania and the mountains of Virginia. East and West are not places, they are separate states of mind. In the East a man is suspected until he has proved, and proved abundantly, that he is above suspicion. In the West a man's qualities are taken for granted until he has proved that he does not possess them, and he rarely if ever gets a second chance if he has failed to meet the first test.

Though the barbed wire intersects the country and though the rancher has almost displaced the cowman, still the old spirit, the atmospherical inheritance from the great old days of the open range and the open town remain. "Kindness in another's troubles, courage in your own"—it is wonderful how some of these old nursery rhymes fit those dear, simple, golden-hearted, foulmouthed, sympathetic, unselfish, utterly fearless, utterly careless souls!

Well, when the Winter One disembarked at the river port, and left the dozen houses, saloon and hotel, that went by the name of a town, the stage driver put a lantern between his passenger's feet and wrapped him up as best he could in the rather scanty robes.[30]

"That's about all we can do in the Pullman line," he remarked. "I'd tie something over your ears if I was you. There's a wind along the river that 'ud skin a coyote!"

The passenger fell deeper and deeper into his dreams, the icy landscape ambled past him; except for a wind which curled through the robes and whistled past his ears, there seemed to be no great discomfort. Mile after mile passed, and the silence—as though the snow had buried sound beneath it, together with everything else—deepened and thickened. At last, as it seemed after hundreds of shivering years, the stage stopped, and the passenger, shaking himself out of his lethargy, stepped out of the stage and into a small store, the local post-office, while the driver disentangled the mail bags. Inside, a stout, kindly lady regarded him over the top of a huge pair of spectacles. She said nothing as he strode in and made for the stove, but as he came nearer, her gaze became keener and more fixed. Then, as he stripped off his gloves and held his hands out to the fire, she suddenly started forward and grasped at his arm. Still without a word, and pushing the spectacles up onto her nose, she examined the ear nearest to her, squinting with interest.

"Well, for the land's sake!" she exclaimed, "if you ain't got both your ears frozen! Keep still. Come away from the stove. Keep still!" she repeated, grasping his arm, "or you'll be liable to shake 'em off you! Get some snow!" she called to the driver, who was dragging in a pile of mail bags. "Drop those darned things and get some snow! This fellow's got his ears froze stiff!"

It was true, horribly true, and Frank gingerly but firmly buried them in snow and held them there, rubbing ever so gently, until the pains of the Inferno began to shoot through them, and the cold snow was as grateful as water to a soul in torment. When the ears had been thoroughly treated, and a length of flannel tied around them, it was discovered that four fingers had received a similar welcome from the morning air, so that, with one thing and another, it was all of an hour before the stage started again.

"That was the hell of a welcome to the Valley!" Frank remarked after a while.

It was a typical one, though, as the passenger discovered later.

The road, if road it could be called, was extremely narrow. Far below the remains of a little river tumbled along, and it was queer to think that all this massive miracle of rock should have been designed merely to enclose that tiny stream that ran through it. The whole effect was almost too gorgeous, and the passenger became drowsy with the study of it. The dim white ranges beyond shed the day slowly and clothed themselves in the awesome chastity of night, the everlasting silence crept down from the heights and settled on the Valley like a veil. The heavy lace-work of snow upon the pine branches fell back into the gloom, while the mountain and the river were folded up into the dark, and a pale, glittering star, like the frozen soul of maidenhood, came out over Goat Wall.[31]

Here and there, at long intervals, a stray light winked out of the pall, and the passenger wondered mentally what manner of people they were who could find it in their souls to live thus, miles from any fellow-creatures and cut off from any human intercourse, in this paralysing winter weather. In the summer, when the days, long as they were, were never long enough to finish the day's work, one could understand the attraction, or, rather, the spirit of those for whom the utter solitude has such an overpowering attraction. But now, when there was nothing at all to do save feed a few cattle and cut an occasional cord of wood?

Suddenly, a cluster of dots and flashes of light sprang out of the road ahead, in the midst of which a larger light showed, a sun, so to speak, around which the others moved and from which they drew their own. An undistinguishable word or two came from the bundle on the driver's seat, and the stage stopped, apparently in the middle of the road. It was only after a painful blinking of the eyes that the passenger made out a blur against the night and a needle or two of lamplight from behind blanketed windows.

When day came, Hugh peeped through his window and got a glimpse of the town, which looked like a field full of snow hummocks, the only indication of life coming from the stovepipes that stood out at every sort of angle, and the smoke that gathered and hung in the still, crystal air. The mountains gleamed dazzlingly in the background, the river forced itself through the fifteen-inch ice, and from below an odour of burnt bacon and soapsuds crept like a tired call to a useless day. It was the human surrender to the elements that struck the stranger so forcibly at first. No one made any show of resistance either indoors or out.

The men sat around the rusty stove and talked desultorily, keeping out of the women's way in a shamefaced manner and punctuating their casual remarks with a never-ceasing flow of tobacco juice into the box. It was just another day to get through with. Some, more energetic than the others, were cutting ice out of the river, some were loafing in the saloon, but all were waiting, as prisoners wait, for the snow to fly and the time of their release to arrive—passive, complete surrender!

They were mostly of German, French, and Dutch stock; stolid, set faces, like the snow-covered rocks by the river, but with a latent kindliness in them, a suggestion of charity and sympathy; and, though this did not appear until some instant word or action uncovered it, a desire to be understood, a wish to be liked, could any knowledgeable hand get under the wrappings that covered the treasures which they guarded so carefully from prying eyes, and of which they were as shy as a girl over her first love letter.

When the evening fell from the tooth's edge of Goat Wall, and swept down to them over the brown slopes of Mount Gardner, when the hush that followed penetrated to their labour-dulled consciousness and whispered that they had done another day's work; when the team was unhitched and they went slowly back to their cabins, leading one horse and driving another, when the dear hour of reward for work well done was theirs, and the world around them, from the dizzy heights where only wild goats could live, to the floor of the valley, was prone in adoration of its Maker, by no possibility could they tell for certain what the next day might hold. Perhaps they might be allowed to work in peace and quiet, but accident was waiting at every corner for them. Even a small accident might cause delay—and delay, in that climate, is fatal. The labour of months can be shriveled up in a week or drowned in half an hour, and, if a man's neighbours are five miles away and have their own fight to wage and their own wives and children to consider, all the neighbourliness and good will in the world are of little avail.

No one who has not actually seen it can have even the faintest idea of what the loneliness of one of those isolated homesteads is like. Conceive of a log or rough board dwelling, perhaps fifteen feet each way, perhaps less, and possibly eight feet high, with two small windows and one door, placed in the middle of an indifferently cleared half-dozen acres in the heart of dense pine forests. A trail leads in and out for a couple of miles, to be merged in a larger trail, which, in turn, arrives at a road. By these he must haul his supplies in the only vehicle which he possesses, a huge, heavy farm waggon, and, if he comes to grief and breaks a leg on the road, he will, if he is living alone, either have to find his way home by himself, or stay there until he dies. Even if he is married, he may remain there for forty-eight hours before his wife will leave the house to search for him if she has a calf or chickens on the place. The coyotes are never very far off, and they are always hungry. So it is with a beating heart that even the bravest woman sets forth on such an errand, for, to the possibility of an accident having befallen her man, there is always added the chance of meeting a cougar.

There is nothing very dangerous about cougars, to be sure. It is a large animal and of a sufficiently terrifying appearance; but the rule of forest and mountain life holds good with him—leave him alone and the odds are a thousand to one that he will leave you alone—live and let live. He may, however, happen to be feeling "mean," for animals have their days just like human beings, and, he would, in that case, be an ugly customer.

In the winter, in our time, there were at least five or six cases of men having frozen to death within a mile of town. The story in each case was the same. The man had left town as the night began to come down, the runners skidded, the cayuses kicked themselves and the sled to pieces; the driver was either pitched on his head, or killed in an attempt to straighten out the team—and a twisted body lay black against the blinding snow, with perhaps a dead cayuse near it, in the wreck of what had once been a cutter or sled. It is easy for a native to visualise the accident because, at one time or another, something of the sort has happened to all of us, and all of us ran the same risk at least twice a week, all through the winter.

Chapter 4

Life and Ethics in the Methow

Mrs. Tiler got rid of her hired men a few days after my arrival and came to cook and do for me generally in the house on the hill. Before she did so, however, I had, one evening, what would have been colloquially described as a "jar." I had got over my first nervousness at being left alone at night, and was, as usual, sitting close to my lamp, reading, when a heavy waggon came creaking along the road and stopped at the gate. Then shuffling footsteps came up the garden path and there was a heavy knock at the front door. I went to it rather unwillingly, and saw a tall man—it was too dark to make out anything of his face—who said gruffly, "I want to go upstairs and get my things."

"Your things!" I exclaimed. "What do you mean? Who are you?" and I held tightly on to the door handle, resolved not to let him get a foot inside.

But he came closer and his voice sounded threatening as he replied, "My things are all in those two upper rooms. I'm come to take 'em away. Didn't Mrs. Tiler tell you?"

Then I remembered that she had said something about the schoolmaster's having rented her upper rooms and left his furniture there when he went away. But what an hour to choose for removing it!

"It's all right," he insisted, "my name's Watson—Watson the schoolmaster.[32] Been getting my hay in—couldn't come before. You that English woman, ain't you? Heard you were boarding here. See, I've got the key—be as quick as I can—won't bother you long." He spoke in a curious, muffled way, and I thought he was drunk, a great injustice, as I learnt afterwards, he being one of the most sober of men.

The key convinced me; but even without it I could not have kept him out—he was determined to come in, and he was a big man. So I had to let him make his way to the upper floor, which I had never explored, and spend a couple of hours in the dead of night dragging boxes and furniture down the narrow stairs and out into the yard, leaving trails of dried hay all over the place, all the crockery having been packed up in it, ready for removal. Mrs. Tiler laughed heartily when I told her about my fright, the next day.

"That's just like Watson," she said, "that man never can do anything like other people! He's not been married long—took those upper rooms to bring his wife to—and tried to fit them up for housekeeping all on his lonesome! You never saw a man so phased. He bought everything at the store the day before the wedding, and brought it all up at once—cook-stove, kettles, bed, chairs and tables—enough to stock a hotel. He was awful worried his wife might find he'd forgotten something she wanted. He carried 'em all upstairs and dumped 'em down anyhow, and began hammering nails in wherever a nail 'ud go to hang things on. Then he forgot what he'd hammered 'em in for, and began laying out the cooking things and the china on the bed; and everything else was on the floor. Laura (that's my granddaughter)[33] went and peeped in and come running down again, laughing 'til she cried. 'Granma,' says she, 'Mr. Watson's sitting on the floor staring at them things as if he expected they'd fix themselves. You and me'll have to go up and lend a hand, or there won't be room for the bride to step, tomorrow!' So we went up—and the poor fellow made me want to cry, for all I was laughing, he looked that piteous. He'd got up from the floor and was running round with a frying-pan in his hand, trying which nail it looked best on. 'Run away and play, Schoolmaster,' I says to him, 'this ain't in your line. We'll fix it for you if you'll leave it to us.'"

Mrs. Tiler went on: "He brung his bride home next day, and she was real pleased. The boys give him the biggest shivaree we've had in the Valley. What's a shivaree? Why, when a feller brings his bride home his friends want to show they're glad to see her, so the crowd comes and brings the band and raises Cain for a bit in front of the house, and then the bride and groom has to come down and be congratulated and behave reciprocal—drinks and cigars for the men and candy for the boys."

At the end of a couple of months Mrs. Tiler went back to live at the ranch, and Hughie and I were left in possession of the cottage on the hilltop. Up to that time the dear old lady had given me her two front rooms, had fed and laundried me, all for the sum of one dollar a day, and had refused to take an extra cent for the many occasions when Hughie and his friend the "Admiral" had dropped in for dinner or supper. She "put me wise" to many things necessary for me to know about local ways, and she solemnly introduced me to the cream of Winthrop society. I remember it was in the early afternoon of a particularly scorching day, when I was sitting in a kimono with all the doors and windows open, that she entered my room with an expression of much importance and said, "Mrs. Hudson and Mrs. Hasketh have come to call on you.[34] Will it suit you to be presented to them now?" The phrase had a queer familiar ring about it—was I at Court again? Or was my landlady "joshing" me? I looked up at her and found her gazing at me in mournful and dignified earnest. "The ladies are in the dining room," she said. "I'll go and tell them you are coming directly."

I became as wax in her hands and followed meekly, and sat up pretty and answered the queerest questions about myself for some three-quarters of an hour, after which they departed. They had not smiled once during our interview.

"Lovely women," Mrs. Tiler remarked as they disappeared down the road; "they don't figger on payin' visits most times. Paid you a real nice compliment, they did."

Mrs. Tiler entered a good deal into our life in the first years in the Methow. Whatever was happening she was sure to turn up, and her dear old face under her bobbing black hood comes very often before me as my mind travels back to those days. One queer picture I can never forget. It was late one September night, very warm and still, but pitch dark, that I heard the strangest sounds of champing and rustling a little way from the house. Listening for a moment I located it in the field where Mrs. Tiler's fine crop of Indian corn was just ready to be gathered in. Something very big and hungry was having a grand time there. I flew upstairs and roused my landlady (with some difficulty, for she was very deaf), and she came tumbling down the stairs behind me with bare feet and a flannel petticoat thrown over her nightgown. We seized the stable lantern which I used instead of a candle, and went out together to investigate. I was dreadfully frightened and said I thought it might be a cougar!

"Cougar? Shucks!" she replied. "Cougars don't eat corn. Lay anything it's some of them blamed breachy heifers of Twickenham's again!"[35]

We stumbled on through the forest of corn that stood higher than our heads and grew in soft furrows into which we sank above the ankle. At every step the alarming crashings and snortings came nearer, and only where the lantern shed its narrow ray could one see an inch. Then, all of a sudden, close in front of me, a long brown nose pushed through the upstanding corn and smelt down at the lantern, and the gentle brown eyes of old Dolly stared reproachfully into mine, as if saying, "It's only me—can't you let me enjoy myself for once! There, catch me if you can!" and she turned, kicked up her heels and galloped away, cutting a fine swathe through the crop; and we followed, and caught her at last, and with much coaxing got her safely back into the barn again. Other people's horses used to get through the dilapidated fence now and then, and as the herbage close to the house was particularly green and tender, would come in the dead of night, with heavy, deliberate tread, to graze outside my room and take an occasional look in at the open windows—wondering, doubtless, whether my big bright lamp was a rising moon.

One night some colts invaded the grand new porch which we had built along the shady side for a summer sitting-room, and turned it into a kind of circus 'til they were driven off; but the cows were much cleverer and also more tiresome, for they discovered the ash-barrel on the kitchen porch, and came nightly to nose in it for cabbage leaves and lettuce and all the other tasty refuse that had collected during the day. There were seasons when fresh vegetables were a great luxury and very difficult to procure, and just at such a time a friend, whose ranch lay well to the sun, brought me a present of a good-sized packing-case filled with all the first fruits of the season. According to the queer, silent custom of the country, he had gone round and deposited his gift outside the kitchen door and slipped off again without saying a word. In the morning I found the remains of a kind of mayonnaise which the cows had left after making a grand feast of the precious things! We used to have the fences repaired periodically, the gates strengthened and barred, but nothing availed to keep the marauders out. They would tear up fence-posts, crawl through barbed wire, and, if very hungry, take the fence flying, as lightly as an Irish hunter takes a gate. Only once did I see retribution overtake one of the herd. A young heifer came past one morning, lowing piteously, and looking out to discover what was the matter, I saw that one horn was raw and bleeding from root to tip. The poor creature had got her head caught between the cracks of some planks, and in her wild efforts to get free had skinned the entire shell off the horn. We found it afterwards, on our side of the barn fence, a delicate, translucent thing without a crack in it. It must have hurt her terribly to tear it off.

We had so many cats that people called ours the cat-ranch, and some of them were terrible robbers, too, with very peculiar tastes. There was one disreputable-looking little creature, called Gwendolen Ermyntrude, the toughest thing in morals and manners that I have ever known. The boys said her home address was "Geranium Mews." Rather to my annoyance she had a large family, of which only one or two would have been spared her had not the grandmother of the tribe, a silky black darling called "Buffalora," instructed Gwendolen to hide them away, far under the house, where she herself always kept her nursery, and only bring them out when they were six weeks old and so pretty and lively that she knew no one would have the heart to drown them.

We had a gloriously mellow autumn that first year of my stay in the Methow, and it was only by the rapidly shortening days that one was warned of the winter's approach. Two important functions occur in that time of waiting. Hallowe'en, when a perfect Walpurgisnacht of mischief is let loose, and Thanksgiving Day, the only national feast in America, except the Fourth of July. Nobody has the slightest idea what Hallowe'en means or why it is celebrated, but the privilege is jealously preserved and fought for all over the West. My first awakening to the date came as I was half sliding, half walking, down the extremely steep road which leads into Winthrop at its far end, the road which every team coming down from the more northerly district must pass, to reach the town. It was growing dark and I was picking my way pretty carefully, when I was suddenly brought to a standstill by tumbling over a huge tree which lay right across the narrow road. I climbed over it patiently to find another and another beyond, a series of barriers hauled there with immense labour and trouble, in the hope of breaking some teamster's neck. The next morning Winthrop was in an uproar. As the teamsters had wisely kept away there were no broken bones, but somebody's chicken-house had been dumped into the river in company with somebody else's buggy— minus its wheels, which were discovered in a lonely wood a mile or so upstream. One man's barn had been broken open and cows and horses turned loose to run at will, and, worst of all in the way of adding fuel to old hatreds, the judge's boy and his boon companions had broken into

Dick Mackenzie's shack (the family was visiting some other members of the numerous clan), shot up the windows, torn the paper off the walls and generally wrecked the place.[36]

A sort of epidemic of lawlessness swept over our village now and then, and the hopeless weakness of the elders where their own children were concerned brought things to a pass which became quite intolerable once, when every boy in the place had got hold of firearms of one kind or another and let fly at anything in sight. I had a habit of walking up and down inside our front fence for half an hour at the end of the day when I felt too lazy to take a proper constitutional. There was a family, consisting of an absent father, a mother of weak intellect, and a crowd of young scallywags, who were camping that winter in a shack at the foot of our hill, and the figure of a lonely woman tramping up and down against the skyline proved too irresistible a target to be neglected. I was miles away in thought, as usual, when a queer something purred through the air over my head and there was a little tap on the roof of the house. I turned—fortunately—to look what had hit there, when another bullet, better aimed, sang past close to me; and then, glancing down the hill, I beheld one of the Martin boys carefully taking aim at me again, his eldest sister, a girl of fifteen, standing beside him and helping him to get the distance! Within twenty-four hours the judge had had his hat shot through, Sadie Lawrence had her hand in a sling, somebody else had all but lost a thumb; and even then it was only under the most severe pressure from my own family that the judge was induced to look up the statute which forbade children under fourteen to use firearms at all, and makes it felony for all and sundry to let them off within half a mile of human habitations and travelled roads.

I suppose a little lawlessness is inevitable in a huge new country, unpoliced and unguarded—though, after all, I am sure that there is really less of it in North Washington than there is in New York! It took occasionally the very irritating shape of borrowing one's properties without leave—really borrowing, for there was no intention of stealing, but some things took a long time to find their way home again. Hughie, when he came to live with me on the hill, had brought with him a particularly handy little cook-stove from his shack by the river. We had no use for it just at first, and in a couple of days it was known that it was standing on our kitchen porch, unemployed. Instantly we had half a dozen offers to try and induce us to "trade" it away, but Hughie refused to part with it 'til a man he knew came and asked the loan of it for a few days. He was going off somewhere else then, and would bring it back before he left. Of course there was no withstanding an appeal like that, and the man heaved the little stove into his waggon and went off with it. A day or two later he was away from home when a friend of his stopped to rest at his shack. Instantly the bright little stove caught his eye—so small, so handy, and evidently such a gallant cooker! Just what he wanted to take up to the mines! B⎯⎯ wouldn't mind lending it to him for six months—he was going away himself! Five minutes later the stove was safely bestowed in B⎯⎯'s friend's waggon, and the friend continued his journey to Slate Creek, twenty-five miles away, without leaving a word of explanation behind him. He brought it back the next year, and after some trouble (B⎯⎯ having left the country), discovered to whom it belonged and restored it to us.

Hughie's shack by the river was supposed to be haunted—chiefly because a certain unregenerate old man had died there. A poor ghost tramp could have found pleasanter places to hover around. In old times it had stood as good saleable land, but that was before the irrigation ditch had been carried along on the slope of the hill behind it. Where the ditch was cut through rock or banked up with slag it was solid enough, but in the frequent places where it had to be carried across hollows and depressions, the water was conveyed in wooden viaducts supported on trestles; these had to be kept in constant repair, and even at the best of times leaked plentifully; but they broke down completely every month or so, and then the rest of the slope below them, the stage road and all houses along the water's line were hopelessly flooded. The white cottage and its surroundings suffered most of all. A pretty old orchard at the back went on bearing a grand crop of apples all the same, but the rest became, when the ditch had been installed a few years, a morass of yellow mud close to the house, while its field developed into a real water-meadow, the prettiest bit on the whole road, with herbage so green and sweet that the cows and cayuses quarrelled for standing ground there and stood fetlock deep in ideal slush, through all the long summer days. There the first flowers of the valley bottom came up as soon as the snow had flown, and the crowd of upstanding white and yellow blossoms reminded one of the foreground of Fra Angelico's "Paradiso."

Ours seemed a rubbly inhospitable soil, yet the flowers, before the terrific summer sun had toasted everything to a crisp, were wonderfully beautiful. All through the State of Washington the syringa grows wild in the greatest profusion, and on warm days the perfume is almost too heavy on the air;[37] then the "choke-cherry" flings out its rich, white, cone-shaped tassels on every side, to turn later into a heavy blackish crimson berry which the school children and the cows devour indiscriminately and from which the industrious housewives make stores of jelly for the winter. The country has a rich delicate flora of its own which has not yet been catalogued and would repay the study. There is a huge yellow blossom, a cousin of the dock, which in April and May covers the hillsides so thickly that they are not green but gold, for miles.[38]

A more delicate and more lasting bloom is that of the so-called Montana or Pilot daisy. It is the first "old-timer" in the whole West; it did not belong there any more than the rest of us, but it is greatly honoured because of its history. When the first pioneers started to cross the plains and penetrated beyond the Rocky Mountains, they wanted to mark the trail for those who might come after them, and also, perhaps for themselves should they wish to return. It seemed an impossible task to plant sign-posts over the thousands of miles of trackless plains, where for weeks a man may ride in every direction towards an horizon unbroken by tree or hill. Then somebody—surely it must have been one of those sweet, brave women!—thought of sowing seed by the wayside as they went, and the hardy, faithful orange "daisy" that would grow in any soil, in any condition, was chosen as the sign. Sacks of the seed were piled on the last of the waggons, and through heat and cold, hunger and thirst, alternate heights of hope and abysses of despair, one faithful hand threw it out day after day, and now from East to West the Montana daisies smile and bloom along railway tracks and stage roads and lost trails, and have made the continent their own from the Ohio to the Pacific.

A less welcome immigrant is the dandelion, which burrows into alfalfa and grain like a sharp-toothed rabbit. The parvenu has become the curse of the farmer, its million feathered seedlings flying on every breeze to eat into and worry valuable crops. Another enemy of the rancher is the wild rose, which runs riot in every foot of spare land in the summer—beautiful to look at and shedding waves of sweetness on the air, but iron-rooted and nearly as hard to displace as sage-brush itself.

Oh, there are many sides to frontier life—but one learns to laugh at them and cope with them as one's neighbours do, in the end.

The unquestioning patience with which those same neighbours met the ever-recurring hardships and difficulties of their lives, the cheery spirit that never wailed or whined, but made the best of everything, struck me as worthy of great respect. Sometimes, indeed, a woman would tell you wistfully of the nice home broken up, of the furniture and carpets and "chiffoneers" which had filled her with pride in earlier years and which had to be left behind when the family moved West; but one and all took it for granted that if rough accommodations and tasks they would never have attempted at home came their way here, —why, the only thing was to laugh and put a good face on it, like all the rest of the world. New life in a new country serves as a wonderfully accurate sifter of the real from the false. Mere parlour tricks have no place in the general estimation of the folk who break new trails on this earth. Incidentally they are perfectly aware that they are sowing where they will probably not reap; that when they have worked hard and long enough, the civilisation which pushed them forth will eject them once more, and the railways and factories and the Syndicates will throng in and start making money regardless of the rights of the men who cut the first roads and battled to clear the forest and convert the wilderness into a garden. They believe hazily that their children will profit to a certain degree—that at least good prices will be given for the land they leave them; but that is not the moving force that sent them here and makes them work as they do. There is in it a touch—perhaps more than a touch—of the characteristic restlessness which becomes part of the make-up of our people, native or foreign born; but there is in every one of them a spark of that which may be called the genius of the conqueror, the nameless but imperious instinct to extend the dominion of humanity over its acknowledged birthright—every habitable spot on the face of the globe.[39]

What is all our culture and thought worth, compared to the work of men who add millions of acres to its wheat belt, who turn jungle into pasturage and water the desert 'til it blooms into life? I have felt sometimes that the heavy-footed, slow-witted men who dig twenty, thirty, a hundred miles of ditch to force some wild river to gentler uses are of infinitely more value to the general scheme of things than all the philosophers and writers put together.

I cannot get away from those irrigation ditches.[40] Nothing in the West impressed me more than the ingenuity and patience which has laid them, in long scientific lines, all over the country. The rainfall there is scanty, the ground, left to itself, hard and unyielding, although some ranchers who could command big sums of money for labour, have obtained satisfactory results on unirrigated land. But the ditches are the real sources of fertility, drawing off the superfluous torrents at the heads of rivers and distributing them according to necessity along a dozen different levels. We have two rivers in our Valley, the Twisp and the Methow,[41] neither very much to look at, fordable in a great many places, and scarcely anywhere broad or full enough to float a punt for a hundred yards without landing on rocks or shallows. Yet, working back and back up their courses in the higher hills between us and the coast, one long full waterway after another has been drawn from them and traverses the country at different levels on both sides of the valleys, carrying life and wealth on every ripple. What the labour has meant, the blasting of the rock, the building up on sandy places, the long, long viaducts thrown from steep to steep—only those silent, persistent workers know. Every man whose property came within the sphere of the crystal beneficence was assessed according to the acres he owned, and either in labour or cash paid up his assessment. To the owners of large ranches—of which perhaps only thirty or forty acres had yet been brought under cultivation—the enterprise cost fearfully dear, but nobody grumbled. The best experts were paid to make the survey, household expenses were reduced to a minimum, wives and daughters wore the same old clothes year after year with never a murmur, and at long last the stream was turned on at the head and came dancing down in heavenly coolness and abundance, to be used as each man wished, so many miner's inches of water to so many acres of land. Then began the individual work of leading it from the ditch itself in the different directions each farmer required, and these have to be changed so constantly that the work seems never to cease. Where the levels are varied, long private viaducts have to be erected, and shorter ones branch off from these, to be used as needed, and from every crack in the broad wooden channel, far overhead, little sheets of spray drip and glisten like a thin veil of diamonds,—intensifying the green below all along the course. A simple arrangement of sliding blocks cuts the water off or turns it on at the owner's will, and, where it is a question of irrigating the orchards, deep channels have to be dug and then filled up again when the fruit-bearers have drunk enough. Some of the orchards are big and old already, and a couple of days once in the season suffices for watering them, but the younger ones can drink less at a time and require it oftener.

Of all pretty sights, that of a well-watered alfalfa meadow is the prettiest. The stream plunges down into it and rushes hidden under the crowding green, which grows with such furious vigour that it becomes a solid mass, over a yard high and crowned with a froth of purple blossom most lovely to see. The verdure is dazzling, a liquid emerald, and it never fails from May 'til November. The moment one crop is cut another springs up, and there is no sweeter or richer food for cattle in the world. I remember standing with a rancher on his porch one September morning, looking down on the sea of waving greenness so incredibly bright and vivid in the sun.

"Is it not about time to cut it?" I enquired.

"I'm plumb sick of cutting alfalfa," my friend replied; "I have taken three crops off that field this year, and I haven't any use for more!"

Once sown it is hard to dislodge. A neighbour of ours took it into his head to plant wheat in what had been a ten-acre alfalfa meadow. We used to pass the place every time we drove down to Twisp. He ploughed and ploughed—and by the time he had got to the end of the field the alfalfa was springing up again at the other! In good years it sells for about seven dollars a ton, but once we had an alfalfa famine; the farmers had got something else into their heads and let the good crop wait. Heavy rain storms came and it was beaten to a pulp. Any morning in the late autumn of that year one would meet a string of cattle being driven away by buyers from the big towns on the coast. Alfalfa had gone up to fifteen dollars a ton, and there would have been nothing to feed the stock on 'til the spring. But it never happened again.

Chapter 5

The "Nebrasky Outfit"

Our cottage stands as a kind of half-way house between the world below us and the skyline far up behind. A trail, steep and rough, like a ladder set against the hill, leads from the front gate down to the irregular main road, which has every right to be rough, having run a good three thousand miles from the Atlantic coast to give up in despair in our mountains and turn into a mere foot trail within a short hundred of the Pacific. For some years now the immediate interest of life for us has centred along this last little section of it; every cabin roof has a meaning, every sputtering stove-pipe tells me its own story of what is going on within. Over there, an eighth of a mile back, the huge barn and the tiny dwelling mark the home of Judge Twickenham,[42] who owns or has owned almost all this land on the north side of the river. He does not belong to the "Nebrasky Outfit,"[43] which supplies most of the comedy of life for us, and of which the most typical member camps, rather spasmodically, in the cottage by the river, just where the road takes a twist and then makes hard for the three or four buildings which constitute the town. We call it a town, but in reality we are consumed with jealousy, because Twisp—nine miles further back, where our doctor has his chemist's shop and there is a real butcher, and a baker when flour is cheap and somebody feels like kneading bread for a spell—has managed by counting babies, chickens and pigs as inhabitants, to attain the requisite population for an independent township, and we are a long, long way from that distinction yet. That may be in part the fault of the Nebraska Outfit as represented by the Mackenzies, the leading member of that spirited clan having one evening "had words" with the Winthrop boys, while sitting round in the store waiting for the mail. The Winthrop humour is of the heavy kind, and Dick Mackenzie, the grandson of a British officer and a Hungarian gipsy, bore it, smiling lazily, for a bit, and then rose from the barrel on which he had been sitting and delivered himself of an ultimatum which will probably affect the whole future history of our end of Okanogan County. "All right, boys. I've had enough. You and your all-fired dust-heap can go to hell by yourselves. I'm going to have a town of my own." And he walked out. Two days afterwards the empty barn at the foot of our hill was opened as a store, and a mighty good one, too; no plate-glass fixings, of course, but a top-line in all the necessarys of life, not to speak of a barrel of "lemonade" always on tap behind the coal-oil tins. Dick's store throve and prospered mightily, and being half a mile nearer the down-valley folk than the other, intercepted legitimate trade to such an extent that Winthrop simply thirsted for his blood. But this was not the worst of it—for Winthrop. His five tall brothers and their families also shook the dust of the proud burgh from their feet,[44] and from that day Winthrop has waned and Heckendorn has waxed.[45]

    I know few men for whom I have more admiration and less respect than for gipsy Dick. As a companion he beats anyone I have ever met. His yarns are enthralling, his persuasiveness simply irresistible—his lies amazing—his laziness glorious, when he feels lazy, his enterprise really catching, when an idea strikes him. Our first long talk occurred a few mornings after my arrival. I was standing on the porch, looking at the landscape, when I heard something come bumping and scraping up our ladder-road, and a moment later Dick pulled round to the gate, driving a venerable one-eyed mare in a skew-wheeled buggy.

    "Here you are, Mrs. Fraser!" he called out triumphantly, "got just the thing for you! I heard the boys telling that you wanted a nice quiet horse and a light rig, and I was scared they'd be trying to trade you off some ornery cayuse that hadn't ought to come within forty miles of a lady—to say nothing of your being Hughie's mother—so I made up my mind to part with this little mare—gentle as a kitten she is and my kids ride her bare-backed, three at a time—rather'n have you put upon, that-a-ways! No, the buggy ain't so much to look at, I 'low, but the springs is sound, and when I paint up the outside and straighten them wheels, why, you'll feel as if you was riding in your favourite armchair! Come now, let me take you for a bit of a ride! You've sure got some trading to do down to Twisp—the ladies always have—I couldn't drive you to Winthrop—never set my foot in the darned place now, and the store just skins you—but Twisp's a real elegant town—Ben's wife'll be proud to give us dinner and she's a better cook than mine. There now, never mind about a hat, you just jump in and come along, and when I've driven you to Twisp and back—we'll do it in fifty minutes each way—why you'll say, 'Dick, there's your thirty dollars, and the rig and the mare's mine!' And dirt-cheap, too! What's that you say, ma'am? You won't buy a horse with one eye? Why, that's the best point about the mare for you—you ain't much of a hand at driving, I take it? Jest so. Now you see it's her left eye that's gone—providential, I call it, 'cause she can't see nothing to scare her that side, anyhow, and if she do kind of jib going down the Twisp grade she'll knock you into the hill and not over the cliff—see?"

"How about coming back, Mr. Mackenzie?" I asked. "She'll be blind on the wrong side, then!"

"Oh, you come back on the other side of the river, ma'am. It's as easy as fallin' off a log! Pretty road, all through the woods, nice and quiet. Come now, is it a trade?"

I had to explain that I made no "trades" without consulting Hughie, and that his wrath if I transgressed that agreement would be more than I could face. Dick saw the force of the argument and turned sorrowfully down the hill, but I learnt afterwards that I had risen vastly in his consideration for having stood firm against his allurements.

The winter passed, and when the spring came I had never yet spoken to Mrs. Dick. There is a rigid etiquette about visits in the Methow. The residents call on the newcomer, if they feel so disposed, and 'til they do, the newcomer keeps herself to herself. I had often passed Dick's shack on my way to the store (which of course was also the post-office) and a rather pretty picture showed within as the dusk came down and the hour for fetching the mail approached. In the summer the place looked squalid, but distinctly alive and interesting. Dick, himself, seemed to come and go somewhat fitfully, but a number of beds standing boldly out in the open, in every stage of make or unmake, served as romping grounds for a whole tribe of youngsters, three Airedale puppies, and a most insolent raven, who used to spit and swear at me as I came along. There was scarcely any glass in the windows, but the cook-stove always seemed to be at work, and whatever else was wanting in the happy-go-lucky establishment, it was evident that there was food in plenty, for the boys and girls were as handsome and rosy-cheeked as one could wish to see. I was given to understand that Mrs. Dick was not "feeling good," but would do herself the honour of calling as soon as she could climb the hill to my house; but that time did not come 'til the ensuing year. The winter drew on, the beds were taken indoors, the foot and a half of black stovepipe sticking up through the shingle vomited sparks and smoke day in, day out, but all I saw of Mrs. Dick was through her still open door when I used to slip past it on my way to and from the post-office at nightfall to fetch my mail.

And it was indeed a pretty picture that often showed then, in the square of light beyond the dark door-frame. A woman sitting at a cottage organ was playing and singing; her face was turned away, but the lamplight made a halo of her curiously fair hair. From the surrounding shadows the dark faces of three or four of the Mackenzie brothers showed picturesquely enough, as the men listened in rapt attention to the old revivalist hymn, while Dick, conspicuously occupying the only rocking chair, was stretched back at length, his arms above his head, staring at the ceiling, and certainly thinking less of "Meeting the dear ones 'cross Jordan's wide stream" than of his next horse-trade. On the floor, as near as possible to the cracked but red-hot stove, two or three little girls played silently with the puppies. The boys, scorning the family circle, were generally hovering round outside, plotting black mischief in whispers—they were perfect demons of mischief—and the river running on its cold way close behind the house and the wind sweeping down from the north over the big hills made accompaniment to the woman's singing. There was a queer careless happiness about it all that struck one as a new and rather pleasant note in human philosophy.

My first visit to the house, however, was a melancholy one. On a soft April evening, poor Dick came to our door with a very white face freely streaked with tears. "Do come down and see my wife," he said, "maybe you can do something. Mother Flanagan has been with her three days and the baby ain't born yet! It's just awful!"

As we raced down the hill together I asked why the doctor had not come. "Can't find him—the boys have been riding all over the county for him—nary sign of the man. Got a message to Brewster for Mackinley[46] —but it's a forty-mile ride and he can't be here before tomorrow. Damn all the doctors to hell—there—I didn't mean to swear before a lady— here we are—go right in!"

A house full of weeping women—the neighbours are all summoned on these occasions—a dead infant and a mother who seemed on the point of following it into eternity—as I have said, it was a melancholy introduction to the family, but in a few hours order had been restored, most of the neighbours had gone home and poor Mrs. Dick was resting comfortably. Then I turned my attention to "Mother Flanagan," who was sitting out in the kitchen, close to the stove, her winter coat drawn over her head, her face streaming with perspiration and tears, taking long pulls at her pipe, which I was glad to see, for she was evidently in need of its soothing influence. She was a strange old lady, reported to be a witch; she certainly looked like one, sitting there in clouds of smoke, with her deep-set black eyes and grim, hard mouth; but there was a very soft corner in her heart for suffering women and new-born babies, and she kept rocking to and fro, wailing to herself, "Five hundred of 'em I've helped into the world—five hundred—and this is the first I've lost! Oh my, oh my, oh my! Ain't it fierce?"

We got her to go home at last. There was nothing more for her to do, so she hobbled away in the darkness, leaning heavily on her crutch, towards the tiny cabin under the pine trees where she lived alone. And Dick's worst enemy, Judge Twickenham (with whom he had quarrelled about a dog two years before so bitterly that they had never spoken to each other since) made the cutest little white coffin for the baby, without saying a word; and his wife, who carried off the little girls to her own cabin, curled their hair and ironed their frocks and made them look "real sweet" for the funeral, which was quite a grand one, a funeral, even of a nameless babe, being an event that none of our people would ever miss. On this occasion it was considered more tactful not to have the Preacher make an oration over the grave, but all the other formalities were complied with, and a long string of buggies and waggons, crammed with women in their Sunday hats and best clothes, went winding up the hill to the cemetery on the "bench."[47]

I was a good deal in the Mackenzie shack for the next few days and, barring some anxiety about the sick woman, they were very amusing days indeed. The children were friendly, from fifteen-year-old Jim, the finest rough-rider for a hundred miles round, down to six-year-old Florence, who was furious with her parents for not "ordering a live baby from the store!" They all took me into their confidence most graciously. My favourite was the third boy, "Chan," who took upon himself to walk up the hill with me in the evening. He was ten years old, with a face like a moon, very fat, and as he confided to me, "born kinder short of breath" so that he saw no chance of taming "buckers" like his fortunate brother Jim.

The accommodation in the Mackenzie shack was, to put it mildly, restricted, so, during this time of trial, the three boys and their father slept on the counters at the store, Dick so troubled that he forgot to take off his boots for two or three nights and by the third day was hobbling round like Mother Flanagan. The kind-hearted enemy kept the two youngest girls most of the time, but the eldest, Ruth, aged eleven, had to stay at home and cook for the whole family, which was increased just then by the arrival of two sisters of Dick's from the old hunting-grounds "back in Nebrasky."[48]

Ruth grew up in the next few years to what is considered a marriageable age in that part of the world, fifteen. She seemed very uncertain about her status, one day wearing long skirts and having her hair elaborately done, and the next relapsing with boisterous relief into last year's pinafores and next to no skirts at all; in which costume I remember seeing her turning somersaults over the woodpile a month or two before she was married. I came to connect these variations of costume with the comings and goings of her young man. When Ira Van Piets[49] (a real Van Piets, if you please, of the old Knickerbocker stock) was due at the shack, with his double-seated buggy and his spanking team, Miss Ruth curled her hair and put on her one long frock and sat up and "talked pretty" like any town girl. But when Ira was reported to be hauling hay or working at his ploughing, his all but fiancée got her last innings of childhood and was even found playing with her small sister's dolls. Perhaps Ira heard of these pranks and thought he had been too precipitate, for he hung off for a time before winding up the preliminaries, and, although everybody knew that he and Ruth were "going together," he did not present her with an engagement ring. It was a sore point with her for a little while, and, after teasing her unmercifully about it, her fond parent, Dick Mackenzie, and his other self, Pete Malloy,[50] thought out a plan for bringing matters to a satisfactory conclusion and at the same time playing a monstrous practical joke on both the lovers.

The first thing that a Methow girl does when she has, even in her own mind, fixed on her future husband, is to collect feathers for her pillows. Long before Ira had screwed up his courage to the speaking point, Ruth had a huge bag of feathers tucked away under her bed, and her mother, sympathising with her daughter's legitimate aspirations, swelled the heap by feeding the family on chickens 'til there was scarcely a fowl left in the yard. Of course the thing was supposed to be a secret, for "getting feathers" is taken as announcing an engagement, and it doesn't do to say you are engaged to a man who hasn't yet asked you to marry him. Dick, poking round under the beds, when the women were out, for a jug of whisky which Ma had thought best to hide, came upon Ruth's treasure, pulled it forth, and with roars of laughter showed it to Pete, the amiable old-timer whom he always took into his house for the winter for the sake of his delightful company. Pete, a long thin man of wavering outline, like an unsuccessful pothook, with a crooked face of most attractive ugliness, stuck his great hands in his ragged pockets, threw back his head and roared too. Then these two worthies, having found the whisky jug under the pile of rough-dried washing in a corner, sat down to deliberate on the best method of "joshing" Ruth about her tardy swain, and of bringing the swain to the point. It was still early in the afternoon, they could catch the out-going mail, and the next day was Ira's birthday. Send him the feathers as a birthday present!

An hour or so later Pete edged into the store with a parcel under his arm, and handed it across the counter to the storekeeper, who was at the same time the postmaster. The latter took it, turned it over curiously (our postmaster took almost too benevolent an interest in everybody's affairs) and read aloud, "Ira Van Piets, Twisp—with a Happy Birthday from his loving friend Ruth Mackenzie."

"It's as big as a pumpkin and don't weigh wuth a cent!" he remarked. "What's inside, anyway?"

"Dunnow," replied Pete, as grave as a judge, "none of my business—nor yours neither, Tom.[51] Chuck it in the mail-sack and tell me what's to pay. Ruth's mighty anxious for Ira to get it to-morrow." To-morrow came, and Ira, with every other man in our county town, lounged into the Twisp post-office to see if there was anything for him. A huge parcel tied with many strings and profusely sealed with the coarse wax which women keep to close preserve bottles, was handed to him, and he turned pink with delight at reading the superscription. All his friends crowded round him as he sat down to open his prize. Half a dozen clasp-knives flew to help him cut the strings—and the next minute a cloud of feathers flew out, filled the place, and sent everybody out into the street, gasping for air and choking with laughter. When the public got its breath it expressed its admiration for the young lady's resource and courage. "Got it in the neck this time, Iry!" "Great girl, that." "Knows her own mind, don't she?" "What you hangin' fire so long for? Buck up, sonny, or I'll chip in and cut you out!" "She can cook, can't she? Then what in thunder you waitin' for?"

Thus admonished, Ira did make up his mind and acted with exemplary promptness. The next day, though it was in the middle of the spring ploughing, he put on his store clothes, paid a visit to the jeweller, and a couple of hours later drew up to Dick's shack at an avenue canter, with a forty-dollar diamond ring in his pocket. When it had been squeezed on to Ruth's fat third finger amid the admiring exclamations of her entire family, Ira remarked mendaciously, "I'd bought it already. You hadn't any kind of reason for sending me those feathers! Pretty hard on me! Opened the darned thing in the post-office. 'Low I'll never hear the last of it."

Indignant denial on Ruth's part, a splutter of laughter from Dick and Pete in the background—and the truth came to light. She cried for two days, poor little thing, and Pete and Dick felt so badly about it that they came to me with faces as long as your arm, to tell me the whole story and ask counsel as to what presents they could give the child to make up for their wickedness. Pete, who had dandled her on his knee, went and bought the handsomest clock he could find and was taken back into grace. Pa meant to do something first-rate in the way of pillows, but he forgot all about it long before the wedding, and suddenly waking up, on the morning of the great day, to a sense of his enormities, saddled a cayuse and rode away into the hills and never appeared at the function at all.

At this time I should have gone on to describe Ruth's wedding, but the truth is that there was a long wait, the bridegroom, for some reason, not having arrived, and the bride refusing to leave her own house until he should fetch her. I went over to chat with her during these rather trying moments of delay, and found her all alone, but for the puppies and the raven, in the living-room, the place bearing evidences of hasty breakfasts taken on benches and packing-cases, the little rooms opening out of it a whirl of confusion after the best clothes had been pulled out and donned, and Ruth, quite pale and a picture of prettiness in her white frock and blue ribbons, standing mournfully beside the cold stove and staring into space.

"Cheer up, Ruthie," I said, "Ira will be coming along in a minute!"

"I don't care if he doesn't!" she replied moodily; "he's half an hour late, and he ought to have been on time!"

Time was usually a negligible quantity in that household, so, thinking I could prove to her somehow that it was only a few minutes past eleven, I looked round for the family time-keeper, a wheezy old alarm clock that usually stood on the sewing machine. It was there now, face downwards.

"Somebody has upset the clock," I remarked, stretching out my hand to right it.

But Ruth screamed, "Don't do that! It won't go any more unless it's on its stomach!"

Then I sat down and laughed. It was so like the tribe to have a timepiece they couldn't see and yet insisted on keeping going!

She was rather displeased at my mirth and moved to the door, which stood opposite the road, showing a pretty vista of autumn colouring and mellow sunshine without. Suddenly there was a rumble of wheels on the bridge, and Ruth retreated to the furthest corner of the room, her eyes shining and her cheeks aflame.

"That's him!" she whispered. "He's driving a lick, too! Say, is my hair all right? Alice done it, but I couldn't find the glass to see it myself!"

I had only time to nod reassurance, for Ira was already at the door, calling to us to come out—he couldn't leave the team. Mighty handsome the young fellow looked, sitting up there in the sunshine, with his fair hair and blue eyes so like Ruth's own. As he reached down a hand to help her up he explained breathlessly that his Jersey heifer had selected that morning to stray five miles off on the range, and he had not dared to come away before he had tracked and brought her back to the barn.

"Might never have seen her again, you know!"—which was true enough, many a valuable animal having been lost in that way.

A moment later we were all inside Granma's parlour,[52] and the bride and bridegroom were standing up, very shy and red-faced, listening to "a few words" from the good man who had undertaken to act as parson for the occasion. It was not our erratic friend, the red-bearded Preacher. Times had changed since I had come into the Valley five years earlier, and Mr. F____, a quiet, honest butter-maker, who had started a religion of his own "down to Twisp," spoke excellent American and gave the young couple at least one piece of very good advice. "Life has rough sides as well as smooth," he said (none of the particular party present were likely to contradict that, and the older members of it nodded their heads sagely), "a hundred annoying things will happen and you'll get mad sometimes—sure enough, but I do pray and beseech you to promise me you'll never get mad both together! One at a time does very little harm—but two is destruction!"[53]

Then he made Ira produce the ring and put it on Ruth's finger, after which he told them and us that they were man and wife and asked Almighty God to bless them. "And now," he said, turning to the audience, "congratulations are in order!"

This was quite unexpected, and the circle stood unbroken, feet frozen to the ground and each one looking at his neighbour imploringly to give him a lead. Nobody seemed to know what form "congratulations" were expected to take, so I whispered in Mrs. Dick's ear, "Go and kiss Ruth! You must be the first!"

She stared at me for an instant in dismay. I might have been suggesting that she should fly through the ceiling. Then she dashed across to the bride, gave her a little peck on her cheek and collapsed into the nearest chair. Who had ever heard of a Mackenzie kissing anybody? But they all had to do it. Mr. F____ was relentless and would not even let off Chan, who tried to slink into a corner and escape making his first experiment in public. I think "Dave," Granma's enormously stout second husband, was the only one who had the presence of mind to mutter something about "puttin' on the pertaties" and sidle off into the kitchen before his turn came.

There was quite a royal feast laid out in that bright, clean apartment (everything round Granma was always bright and clean)—and when it was ended, Ruth and Ira climbed into the smart double buggy and set off for Twisp at a spanking pace, so as to get over the grades before the darkness fell. And now, for them, was to come the cream of the day, in the shape of a practical joke! Ira had been chuckling over it for weeks. None of his folks had been told the date of the wedding, and had not the slightest idea of what had been taking place that morning. He and Ruth were going to surprise Mother Van Piets and the girls!

The joke, I heard afterwards, was a great success. The family roared with laughter when the young people walked in and introduced themselves as "Mr. and Mrs. Van Piets." Mother was surprised, all right, so surprised that it was impossible to make room for them in the crowded house, and, when bedtime came, gave them her blessing, a lantern and a blanket, and sent them—perfectly contented and smiling—to pass their wedding night in the barn!

Chapter 6

All About the Neighbours

"It does seem queer to see Ruth with a baby!" said Mrs. Dick. "I can't hardly believe it is nearly a year since she was married, can you?"

"Time flies pretty fast with us busy people," I replied. "There—sit down and take a rest before we start on the cakes!"

Mrs. Dick rubbed some of the flour off her hands and found a seat. She had come up to bake a batch of pies and cakes for me in view of certain expected visitors the next day. The whole house smelt of fruit and hot pastry, and a perfect garden of pies, peach and apple and custard, was spread out to cool on the kitchen table. Mrs. Dick leant forward and gingerly touched each with the tip of a finger to test the success of the pastry, and leant back with a sigh of satisfaction.

"Guess I'd better put the pies away now and start in on the cakes. Say, we'd ought to have had some huckleberry pies! Don't you folks like huckleberries?"

I was not enthusiastic on this point, having been fed on huckleberry pie for a fortnight once, when I got stranded in the heart of the pie-belt—up in Maine. So I murmured something about their not growing in our vicinity.

"No, there ain't many round here," Mrs. Dick assented; "you want to go up towards Slate Creek to find them real thick. We went camping up there one summer, a whole crowd of us, the men went hunting, and we women, with the children, we picked huckleberries for nearly a week, 'til we had tubfuls to bring home. We used to move round from one place to another—and one night we had the worst kind of a scare! We didn't exactly know where we meant to camp, but just as it was getting dark we came on an old empty cabin in the woods. The men took a look in at the door and came back pretty quick to where we was waiting, and said, 'Come on, girls, you and the kids'll be snug inside there, and we'll sleep in the open and keep the coyotes off!' Well, we came to the door and took a look in, too. My, you never saw such a dirty old place! 'Not for ours, boys,' we said, 'you go inside and we and the children'll sleep here. We ain't afraid of the coyotes.' Well, they growled a bit, but when they saw our minds were made up, they gave in, and went and lay down inside, taking all the guns with them—*that* mean, they were! We got our bedding down in a nice ring—it was good and dry under the pine trees—and put all our buckets of huckleberries in the middle, and pretty soon everybody was asleep. It must have been about midnight I woke up, feeling as if something queer was happening. The moon was high—a good full moon—shining down through the branches on that ring of bedding laid out so tasteful and jest full of women and children, sound asleep and snoring—and sitting in the very middle, dipping into our buckets and eating our huckleberries as hard as he could, was a big brown bear! I let out one screech—and then all the rest woke up and screeched, too—you never heard such yells—and the bear gave a great gruntin' snort and kicked the buckets over and made for the woods, and the men came tumbling over each other out of the cabin door, and asked us what in hell was the matter—and when we told 'em, they raced off after the bear, shootin' as they ran—but he got away from them and I was glad! Poor thing, he'd only come after the huckleberries! And when the men got back we was all inside the cabin with the door shut, and they got their way, after all, and slept outside!"

At this point it was absolutely necessary to start making the cakes, as Mrs. Dick explained that she wanted to be at home when the children came back from school. That was the gayest hour of the day in our part of the world. For half an hour or so after school was over, highroads and by-roads were swarming with youngsters big and little; those who lived at a distance only stopped to do some errand at the store and then dived away at a great pace to get home before dark, while those whose parents, as our local paper put it, "were occupying their town residences," cleared up all the questions that had arisen in school hours, in the old way, in the open road. The big boys "scrapped," the big girls hung round applauding their favourites, and the little ones romped backwards and forwards like puppies on their first walk. We were rich in children. Long families are the rule in those parts, and no prettier or more heartening sight could be desired than that of these crowds of bright healthy children, full of life and fun, pouring out of the white schoolhouse on the hill,[54] as the clock struck four. Many of them rode to school, and it was one of the pleasures of the morning to see them canter past our gate, often two on one horse, their lunch-pails clanking at the saddle-bow, all racing along to be in time. Dutch Bob,[55] who lived behind us on the hills, had two fair-haired daughters, tall, well-grown girls with beautiful figures, whom it was his pride to mount on the best horses money could buy. No half-broken cayuses for them, but great spanking chestnuts, over sixteen hands, with glossy coats and arched necks. The girls rode cross-saddle, as women mostly do in that country, in their short walking skirts to which they gave such a deft turn as they flew up into the saddle. In summer, they were bareheaded, the sun taking their pretty golden hair; as the autumn drew on, a pink or blue scarf encircled the rosy faces and threw streamers out on the wind behind them; but when the snow came there was no more riding. Then the great horses appeared no more; a younger brother drove Dutch Bob's girls to and from school in a big sleigh with two sure-footed little bays, and they picked up all the other children they could on the way and brought them along. All day long the space under the pine-trees round the schoolhouse was full of tethered ponies, waiting patiently for going-home time; in good weather the various rigs lay round in the open, but when it was stormy they were housed in the school shed 'til it was time to hitch up and take to the road again. The children who had no ponies thought nothing of walking two or three miles each morning and evening in the spring and autumn terms, but during the winter that was not possible—they could not plough through the snow. So a kind of omnibus sleigh started from down the valley in the morning and took them back at the end of the day, a noisy crowd, hanging on any way they could all over the vehicle and the good-natured driver, rolling off and jumping on again and snowballing each other and him as they went. In summer, of course, there was no school, the bigger children being all needed to help in the fields and orchards, so that the scholars had an excellent opportunity of forgetting what little they had learnt in the preceding terms.

In the last years of our stay the population had so increased that it was necessary to have three schoolhouses for the different grades,[56] and the competition for the teachers' places became very keen indeed. Each house upheld its own teacher and nourished a bitter enmity against those of the other two. As I had little friends in all three, the inside politics of the system were freely confided to me, as well as all the intrigues and irritations attendant on the appointments. Somehow the only male instructor, who of course handled the top grade, had made himself most unpopular with both parents and children.

"He's vulgar, that's what he is," Mrs. Dick declared, as I was sitting in her kitchen one day—"you go outside, children, I got something to tell Mrs. Fraser."

The children obeyed—and instantly put their heads in at the window to listen. Remembering the rather lurid language in which the natives were accustomed to conduct their affairs, I thought something terrible was coming. Mrs. Dick glanced at the crowding heads at the window and went on in a sepulchral whisper, "What do you suppose he said in school this morning? He was talking about the Pilgrim Fathers, and what an awful mean time they had of it, and he said 'they stuck it out as long as they could!' Stuck it out! Ain't that a nice refined way to talk to children? Right down vulgar! He ain't fit to be a schoolmaster. Watson was a heap better—he used to bolt from the school to the poolroom the minute school was over—that's true, and let the youngsters nearly kill each other scrappin' in recess—but he could talk elegant, like a schoolmaster should!"[57]

This excess of fastidiousness as to diction spread to the other parents, and on the next election of teachers, when we all went and cast our votes, poor Mr. S, who really knew something, was voted down,[58] and the pool-loving Watson installed in his place.

There was something rather pathetic about Mrs. Dick. One felt that she ought to have had better luck. Married, like her mother and her sisters, at fifteen, by the time she was thirty-three she had borne seven or eight children, was in broken health, had lost most of her beauty and all her hopes of ever realizing woman's dream, the possessing of a nice little home of her own. But there was one quality she had never lost—indeed it seemed to gain strength from her misfortunes—her brave spirit, which, I am sure, was given her as a regard for her blind devoted, fanatical loyalty to Dick.

Her sister Louise declared that Dick had bewitched Sarah. But Louise had not got at the root of the matter at all. Sarah was not the only person who could not resist Dick's queer, all-subduing charm. When he wanted to be good he was so very, very good, and, with all his unsatisfactory qualities, he had something great in him. To be his friend once was to be his friend forever; some tiny favour conferred would earn his silent gratitude for years; little things that others would not have thought of twice were stored up in his memory and bore harvest in neighbourly service for which he steadily refused any remuneration. It was great-heartedness, one could not but acknowledge that. With all his roughness and ingrained idleness, this landless backwoodsman was almost a grand seigneur. His keen sense of humour made him kin to all that is best in this silly old world; the very character of the people who hated him most bitterly was a recommendation in my eyes.

Dick's store was just at the foot of our ladder hill,[59] and for some days I had been interested in watching an addition he was making to it, a double-storied extension at the back, the lower part of which was to serve as a spilling-over space for his growing business, and the upper room as the hall for the meeting of the Mehalahs, the chief woman's lodge in our district.[60] On the night in question the Mehalahs had held their first festival there, and made a roaring fire in their new heater stove. They must have been very preoccupied with their ceremonial, for they confessed afterwards that they had quite forgotten to place a sheet of metal under the stove as well as to put in the thick layer of ashes which is necessary to keep its iron bottom from being burnt through. Also, they had all gone home and left the fire burning, a thing nobody in his senses ever does in that country of framework buildings. It must have been going on for ten o'clock when I stepped out on our porch to look at the night, as I usually did more than once in an evening. The white world sleeping in deathlike silence under the huge icy stars was a sight too sublime to miss.

But that night I scarcely glanced at it, for, even as I came out, I saw the door of Dick's upper room, which was approached by an outside staircase, thrown open, revealing a furnace of red flame inside. For an instant the dark figure of a man showed against it—then he flew down the stairs and tore away down the road in the direction of the Mackenzie shack. I turned and screamed into our passage, "Dick's alight!" I heard Hughie make one movement—he was plunging into his waders—and the next instant he leapt past me without a word and rushed down the hill, hatless, in shirt sleeves, to the rescue. There was no use in my following him—the men would not have let me come near the place—so I too got into my waders and somehow dug my way through three feet of snow to the house of our model neighbour. Every pair of hands down there to help in removing the stock would mean hundreds of dollars to poor Dick. By this time the flames had burst through the roof, but they had not yet reached the lower part, and as I went plunging along, falling at every other step, I glanced down and saw three or four black forms rushing in and out of the store, carrying heavy loads and dumping them in the snow on the other side of the trail. Only three or four! If I could rouse Mr. H and his boys there would be at least three more—and the salvage was becoming a matter of minutes.[61] When the fire reached the explosives there would be one great roar and all would be over.

Well, I stood before that house for ten minutes, calling for help at the top of my voice—and a frightened woman can scream like nothing else on earth—the coyotes aren't in it with her—but good neighbour H and his whole family lay low. Neither light nor answering sound came from that tightly closed building, and at last I gave it up, and came back crying like a baby. It is awful to see a man ruined before one's eyes. The next morning I learnt that they had all been standing on the back porch, which I could not reach through the locked gate, calmly watching the conflagration. With the morning something like contrition visited the head of the family; he came and offered the loan of a hundred dollars towards making good poor Dick's loss. But the offer was refused. It was a mere drop in the bucket compared to what instant help would have effected, and Dick wanted no charity which did not spring from sympathy. The one man who really worked hard with him and Hughie that night, at the risk of being blown up or overwhelmed by the blazing roof, was the man who had first discovered the fire, a connection of one of the Mehalahs, who had thought it wise to look in after their departure, and he was one of Dick's most bitter enemies ever since a quarrel about the one subject which can never be overlooked or forgotten—the invariable, inevitable dog!

There were some queer scenes that night. Close to the store was a big barn where Dick had a round dozen of horses. His own youngsters, Jim and Bill, tumbled out of bed at the first alarm, and, without waiting for orders, rushed to the barn, sprang on their own cayuses, and drove the whole neighing, snorting, frightened mob down the Valley, far out of the zone of danger. There they mounted guard over them and kept them together, all but the old mule, a fine great fellow who considered himself a member of the family, and who used to share Dick's tobacco with him, solemnly biting off a piece of twist and chewing it with his big teeth 'til his old muzzle was all a swamp of tobacco juice, when he would spit like any rancher and then start all over again. He got away from the boys that night, sneaked up the hill by some roundabout trail, and came trotting past me as I stood there—almost trotted over me in his eagerness to get down to his own people again. Just at that moment the explosion came—a roar followed by a fearful stench of gunpowder and a flare that filled the sky—and I was too wildly anxious about my son and the others to note what became of old "Senator"; but they told me afterwards that he got down all right and joined the group of weeping women and children who were camped in the snow watching the men. They got out all the machinery and a good lot of the canned goods, but the tobacco—some four hundred dollars' worth—was at the back of the store, and the fire had worked down to within speaking distance of the kerosene tins when they remembered it. The roof was almost gone when Dick started back after his tobacco, threatening to shoot the other men if they dared to accompany him, but poor Mrs. Dick flung herself on her husband and held him with both arms, screaming wildly that he would get killed and that she would not let him go. He disengaged himself quite gently, and then, picking her up in his arms, carried her some twenty yards off and set her down in a snowdrift, where she could take no harm; but when he returned the store had blown up and all was over.

With morning light I went down to his shack to condole, but I found that condolences were quite out of place. Dick, very streaky and ragged, was standing by the cook stove, his eyes shining, his best smile on, waving his pipe triumphantly and discoursing about his amazing luck.

"What is there to grouch over?" he cried; "ain't we all here, with nary a scratch or a scald, the whole gang safe—from me down to Florence and the store cat? Just think of it—a flare-up of that size and not so much as a broken bone among us! Damn the losses—I got my family, and the kids saved the horses! What in thunder could I ask more?"

I was so overcome that I began to quote Scripture and quoted it wrong. "Good for you, Dick! The Lord loveth a cheerful loser!!"

"That so?" said the Mackenzie. "Glad to hear it. Sarey, ain't you goin' to get Mrs. Fraser a cup of tea?"

Chapter 7

The Spirit of Chance

After the fire, Dick's good humor continued unabated throughout the day; when some strayed cayuses had been found, and Sarah, who had been terribly upset, restored to her usual equanimity, he took himself up to the saloon. Bill, in the meantime, boylike, found an irresistible attraction in the ruins and, towards twilight, went across again to dig among them by himself. As he told us afterwards, he was kicking about among the debris of scrap-iron that had once been hardware and stores and cans, when, in the dim light, his eye was attracted to a white object that seemed to stick up conspicuously against the universal black, and he cleared a way towards it over a heap of wreckage. Then he looked again—and started. It was like the skeleton of a hand—horribly like! Bill was not a nervous child, but he found it impossible to approach any closer, and equally impossible, in the grip of a morbid fascination, to retire. Cold and white, fleshless and grisly, the fingers pointed up to the skies reproachfully, as though asking a question. The evening grew darker and darker; as the light disappeared Bill began to get uncomfortable, and icy trickles ran down his spine as he gazed at that dreadful hand. Then he fled, precipitately and shamelessly.

He found the family at supper, and Dick, now in the highest of spirits, rallied his son about the colour of his face and the twitching of his hands as he attempted to roll the food into his mouth. But though Bill's horrid secret made him feel very superior, he was not yet equal to speaking about it, so he bore with his father until his little stomach's needs were satisfied, and he had wheedled a cigarette paper and some tobacco out of his parent.

"You ain't caught a chill, Bill, have you?" his mother asked. "You're shiverin' all over!"

"Chill, hell!" replied Bill, inhaling rapidly. "I ain't got nothin'—but—say, pop—there wasn't no one burnt last night, was there?" he asked.

"Nary—there wasn't any reason for none of 'em gettin' hurt, either," Dick reminded him. "Why?"

"I dunno. I just asked." Bill relapsed into his cigarette and continued to inhale, a mysterious light in his eyes. He was warm, now; he was fed. He was, in short, beginning to enjoy his thoughts enormously. Jim, he knew, would not fail to notice it, and Jim knew nothing about the hand! He gloated to himself.

"Whatchyer grinnin' at?" his brother asked. "Anythin' funny in me—yes, you are, too!" he added, without waiting for the certain reply.

"It's my own damn mouth," retorted Bill. "If I want to stretch it I will. Go sit on yerself!"

"It don't need stretchin'!" remarked Jim calmly. "I didn't want you to hurt yourself, that's all."

"Well, it'll get it," replied Bill tersely, and then their father interfered.

"This is all the house we got now, fellers," he said, "and we'll need it to sleep in. If you want to scrap, run outdoors."

Bill only grinned again and repeated his previous question.

"I've told you once already," said his father with a little impatience, "and I don't give a damn if they was anyone hurt—it was a accident, anyway—seein' only five men were inside at all."

"And they all come out?"

Even Dick began to be slightly exasperated.

"Hell, yes! ain't I said so? What's got you, anyway?" he demanded.

"Nothin'—can't a fellow ask a question?"

"Aw, cough it out, Bill," his mother adjured him wearily. "Cough it out and you'll feel better."

Bill got to his feet.

"Well," he remarked, "you say they all come out, but somebody sure stayed—"

"Whatchyer mean?" Dick demanded, rising also. "Whatchyer talkin' about—"

"I seen somethin' in the back of the store, that looked awful queer to me—however, you say they all—"

"Cut it out!" Dick cried, snatching at his hat and making for the door. "You come and—"

"Bill!" his mother clutched at his arm. "You tell me this minute—" but Bill slipped out of her grasp and ran after his father, who, red-faced and now thoroughly frightened, was poking among the debris with a lantern, while Jim, like a small and energetic terrier, was hovering at his heels, his mind full of delicious horrors.

Cautiously, as though expecting the skeleton hand to rise up and smite him, Bill led the way to where the bony fingers pointed up to the skies.

"Someone stayed, all right, you see," he whispered, emboldened by the presence of the others.

"Gee!" murmured Jim, peering over his shoulder. "Gee! He's got burnt to a crisp, ain't he?"

Dick said nothing at all, but with clumsily reverent fingers began to clear away the heap under which the skeleton lay.

"Who could it be?" he muttered as he pulled and tugged, "who in thunder could it be? I ain't heard that no one was missing! Who could it be?"

At last, after infinite pains, the whole body was brought to light and, as it lay there, white and hideous in the rays of the lantern, Dick shook his head.

"That's the queerest thing," he said aloud to himself, "the thing's complete—it's too damn complete. Why, there ain't a bone missing—yes there is, too—" he bent down and examined it more closely where a rib dangled painfully from the backbone. "Why—hell!" he shouted, "it's wired together! Come on, fellers," he said to his sons, "let's get her out o' here; it's a frame-up, that thing!"

It was an ingenious one, though, for it was a bona-fide skeleton, and though of a very respectable antiquity, it was in a good state of preservation—what remained of it. Every joint was carefully wired. It was evidently designed to last. But what could it be? He certainly had never brought it into the place, nor had he ever seen it before. It was some time before the solution of the puzzle presented itself, and then Dick slapped his knee and roared with profane laughter.

"It's them Daughters of Mehalah!" he yelled with mirth. "This is one of their parlour ornaments! Well, of all the—"

If the skeleton had never served any useful purpose before, it dissipated the last shadow of gloom in the Mackenzie cabin, for Dick and the boys brought it back and fixed it to the front of their house where all the passers-by could see it. Then Dick tied a huge cardboard placard to its chest, "The women got at me!" it read. "Please take me home!"

The "Daughters" never forgave Dick for that; and it was a long time before the "Brotherhood" forgave him either. They could have stood almost anything, but humour at the expense of the sacred skeleton was sacreligious and wicked.

About this time there entered much into our lives the old Englishman, Mr. Hasketh.[62] The British instinct for feudalism had lingered in his spirit through forty years of exile from his beloved Essex, and when we settled in the Methow, he, beginning by doing odd jobs about the house, became, in a short while, something like a permanency. We wondered at first how he contrived this, but we found out later. He would not finish a job. He was always ready to start one, and ready, too, to carry it to a certain length—generally, about two days' work short of completion. By that time he was heartily sick of it and was looking about him for something else to do. This, the conditions being what they were in a frame-house which we were trying to make as habitable as possible for human beings, was never a difficult thing to find. If it were not to be found, he would invent something, and begin on it instantly, without saying a word to us about it. Then there would be two jobs in the house, neither of which could be abandoned while they were half finished, and before we had time to turn round, the house, the attic, the kitchen, the porches, and the garden—for he was a very good gardener—were little more than a series of irregular outlines, enclosing Mr. Hasketh's sporadic activities.

Of course he became a habit after a while, as he had intended to become from the beginning. He began one May to build a chimney for us, in the "annex" which he had been constructing the winter before. Now we needed the "annex" badly, and he had for once finished a job within three months of the time he had set himself. In October he added a few more bricks to the chimney, and then the mortar froze. Taking this, evidently, as an omen, he abandoned the chimney for the warmer and more varied occupation of papering the dining-room, which done, he left the paper, the paste, the brushes in the little hall and set himself to making a doorway. All attempts at bringing him back to the paper, which was littering the whole entrance, and for which three other rooms were crying, were met with "Just as soon as I've got this job done—it won't take me any time, now. I'm an Essex man, Mrs. Fraser; I like to finish one thing before beginning another. I'm nearly through with this door now."

We succeeded at last in pinning him down to a day for the papering, and, the night before, he made his preparations, which consisted in taking every door within reach off its hinges and putting the boards and trestles exactly where everybody had to pass to come in and out of the dining-room and the kitchen.

"I'll be round at seven," he said, as he went out at the back door. "Good-night—now you won't move anything, will you?"

We promised cheerfully, and he departed, singing an old English song, of which he was very fond, to himself.

We were about early the next morning, intending if he attempted his usual maneuvers, to head him off and bring him back to the paper by force, if necessary. It was a cold morning, too, a very cold morning, as we who ran around lighting the stoves remember. Seven o'clock came, and the quarter arrived, but no sign of Mr. Hasketh.

Then, as we began to speculate, somewhat hopefully, for we had other things to do, on the chances of his having been kept at home, a sharp rapping sounded from outside and we opened the back door, peering through a crack. At first nothing was to be seen, but the tapping continued, and then the Winter One, glimpsing a grey sweater in the dark recesses of the wood-shed, ran out.

He was not mistaken. Mr. Hasketh was perched upon a beam of the shed, three or four planks were already ripped off, and his face, rosy with honest perspiration, shone in the new sunlight.

"I didn't like the look of this roof!" he called down. "It seemed to me to be sinking. I've got the waggon there," he waved towards the road, "and just as soon as I get these planks off I'll drive down to the mill and get some lumber. Why," he added, "this thing might come down on you while you were cutting up wood. It's in an awful state. Got any coffee?"

It was well into March before the rooms got papered, and the chimney was completed, with two hours' work, eighteen months later!

Chapter 8

The Canning Season

We were very popular people all through the summer, on account of our berry patch, which produced far more fruit than we could ever use ourselves. The currants and raspberries and gooseberries proved an overwhelming attraction to all the children of the place, and there were few mornings when some little fair heads were not bobbing up and down among the bushes and the murmur of chatter and the tinkle of berry pails were not borne to my ears. The first showing of gooseberries (the earliest of the berries)—little pale green balls on a sparsely leafed branch—was always the herald for a train of knocks at the front door. "Please, Mother says, may we pick on half shares? She'll put up yours for you if you like!"

This is the recognised trade in berries, for the picking of them is a slow, wearisome process, none too highly paid by taking half the produce. The "putting up" consists in preserving and sealing in glass jars for winter consumption. People who can have vegetables and fruit all the year round have no idea of the craving for green food that possesses those who live under the snow for five months at a time. One year, when the spring had been bad and late, and the stores had run out of canned vegetables, we actually boiled and ate the first potato tops that came up—and were properly poisoned for our pains!

As I have said, green gooseberries open the canning season, sometime in May, for they must be secured before the seeds harden. The strawberries come next, then the raspberries, and all the "canable" vegetables, ending up with a perfect carnival of apricots, peaches and plums that carries the glorious excitement right on 'til the end of September. Then deep pits are dug, and the cabbages and potatoes and carrots are buried in five feet of earth, to lie 'til some touch of thaw makes it safe to open them in the first days of March, a good two months still before anything eatable can rise above the ground. Then the most acceptable gift, more welcome than the hothouse flowers that people in other countries are sending one another as Easter gifts, is a big head of cabbage, smelling of the good brown earth—a green globe, ragged outside, like a beggar saint, but white and juicy to its untouched core!

Later, the new rich soil produces such an amazing abundance of fruits and vegetables that everybody, down to the pigs, can eat no more, and, for lack of transport facilities, they lie round in heaps or rot in the fields. But, before that, the good housewives have their cellars stocked for six months ahead with "Mason" or "Economy" jars, crammed with fruit and pickles, and it is only the shiftless ones whose table will be wanting in preserves all winter long. Some of my friends used to put up as many as five hundred quarts of stuff, and thought nothing of buying sugar by the hundred pounds at a time. It was quite an experience to visit their kitchens in the height of the canning season. As there is no school in summer, the whole family, down to the three-year-olds, would be sitting round, cleaning and preparing the fruit, eating hard most of the time, and spilling about so prodigiously that the whole kitchen looked and smelt like the inside of a jam pot, while huge cauldrons of fruit bubbled on the stove and sent clouds of perfumed steam right up to the rafters. Naturally some of the ordinary household tasks are a little scamped at this time, and the men groan bitterly over the upset and discomfort it all entails.

One day I found our friend the Judge sitting on top of his barnyard gate, looking down the Valley as gloomily as if it were peopled with creditors. A surly nod was all I got in answer to my greeting, and I stopped, surprised, for he generally met me with a cheery smile.

"Anything wrong with the folks?" I enquired, glancing towards the cottage across the road. It looked as busy and gay as usual; the "clothes spider," a kind of merry-go-round of cords and poles, was twisting like a windmill, with the many coloured family wardrobe flapping noisily; the two fat white geese were paddling in the ditch, the hens and chickens were all over the place and only kept from going into the house by the old black dog, dean of all the dogs in the Valley, so old that nobody could remember when he was born, but a sporting coyote-killer still. The only threatening note came from the stovepipe sticking up through the shingles; it was vomiting smoke and sparks like a mimic Vesuvius.

"They have got some pitch-pine in the stove," I remarked. "Aren't you afraid they will burn the house down?"

"Don't care if they do," he replied; "twould stop the canning, anyhow. It's just plain hell when the women get canning! Not a chair you can sit down upon, vittles never on time—Maw down with headache, sure's you live, tomorrow, and that young scamp Clarence fillin' himself with fruit and sugar so's he'll be bawlin' all night! Enough to drive a man to the bug-house! I'd go and get drunk, only them skunks has busted up the saloon—doggarn their ornery hides!"

"We don't do any canning," I said, "we are much too lazy, and besides, our men won't stand for it. Come up to our place and have a chat with the boys!"

"Miss Kitty there?" he enquired, brightening up.

"Sure! She'll be glad to see you!"

He scrambled down off the gate and we sauntered up the hill together.

"Dunnow's I ever saw such a girl as Kitty for cheering folks up," said the Judge, as we approached my house; "there ain't a man this side of Carlton wouldn't walk ten miles for a talk with her. She's a ray of sunshine, that's what she is. Always a joke and a laugh—and her pretty face and her dinky hats—say, she's just a picture! See the hat she made for my girl for the Fourth of July? Classy? Wasn't one to touch it down to the Oration in the Grove.[63] Cost me a lot, that hat did. Maw said I must buy Vi'let a dress to match—and me with six hundred and fifty dollars assessment to pay on the new irrigation ditch! I had to sell a yearling—that red and white one of Jersey Bessie's—to get Vi'let the dress, all along of Kitty's hat! But the women folk was pleased. S'pose that's all they think a man's there for. Say! I'll come and fix up this gate of yours when I get round to it. Them hinges don't hold for shucks, and you can't expect the critters not to come in if the gate's open."

This was a delicate way of apologising for a little contretemps earlier in the season, when eleven of the Judge's cows broke down our fence and ate up a whole field of Indian corn in the night.

A few minutes later the good man was installed on the porch, a drink to his hand, a box of "Pedro" ready for his pipe at his elbow, and Kitty, with a kitchen apron over her pretty frock, smiling down at him and asking him to stay to supper.

"Why, I don't care if I do!" he drawled, in the tone which means perfect satisfaction—"take me in my working clothes?" and he glanced at his muddy boots and straw-spangled overalls rather shamefacedly.

"Take you anyway we can get you, you old dear!" said Kitty. "There's a fresh boiled ham and one of my salads, and Mother's made a chocolate cream."

"That's good enough for me," he responded; "I always tell people you folks know how to treat a man white! Say, it's mighty queer your coming to live in this house. It was mine first—sold it to old man Parsons and he gave me another hundred dollars for the spring. Springs was valuable in those days. There wasn't a ditch this side of the river, and most people had to haul their water in barrels same as Beehardt does now, way up on the bench behind here.[64] Then Parsons wanted to quit, and he sold the place to Mrs. Tiler. It reached way over to the schoolhouse then, but he said it warn't right to sell it to one party alone—the spring was enough for two families, and it ought to be split up. That's why Hudson has the other half of the water-ground up there—"[65]

"I wish to goodness he hadn't!" Hughie exclaimed; "he's water mad! He has dug half a dozen tunnels into the hill and he irrigates 'til his place is a lake and ours is a swamp! He will ruin those young fruit trees!"

"Hudson is a good man and he stands high up in the Brotherhood," said the Judge, setting down his glass, "but he's got one vice—he can't stop working! When there's nothing else to do he'll undo what he's done and do it all over again, just to keep going. Seen the loads of fertiliser he hauled last week? Three a day for six days! Fertiliser! Eighteen loads for new land that's bursting with richness! and he won't let it take breath to cough up the stuff he wants of it! Got no patience with such loonies, I haven't! They call me lazy—ah, yes, they do—I know. I don't plough a furrow more than I have to, to keep us in grub and trade to the store for groceries, but I'm milking seventeen cows, and the tester at the creamery 'lows more butter-fat to my cream than anybody else's, and I'm good and satisfied. And when people buy land from me they don't get stuff that's swamped and choked 'til it's like a dirty sponge. No, sir, and I don't aim to sell it all and quit like some fellows do. That's what makes them tear it to pieces to get all they can out of it while they're on it, and they don't care a red for the chap that's coming after them. 'It'll last my time,' they say, 'and the devil take the rest!'—which, between you and me, he most generally does. Well, that ain't my way of thinking. Eighty acres of my best, and the house and barn, is all Maw's[66]—deeded to her out an' out, I can't touch it if I try—and when they take me to the bone-yard, Maw'll see that Clarence can't touch it, neither, more'n to make a livin' for the family off it.[67] 'Course I sell the town lots down there, but no more'n two to one party, and that party has to build—he can't make a ranch out of a hundred foot square, can he? It's buildings I want—a fine town. Got it all surveyed and drawn up in blue print, and it's called Heckendorn. It's growing now, ain't it? Six new houses this year and good 'uns, too. I tell you, in two or three years more, Waring's old Winthrop he's so stuck on won't be in the same class with Heckendorn. *We'll* get the school and *we'll* get the post-office, and when the railway comes *we'll* get the depot, right here, and Winthrop'll be wiped out! Looks like six bits in a mudhole now, 'longside of this!"

We all regarded the Judge in silent respect when he had finished his peroration. The truth of some of it was but too patent.

"Well done, Gene," said Jack,[68] "you speak the words of wisdom. You ought to go and tell some of that to Grantley and get him to print it in his paper.[69] The ranchers are just murdering the land round here and somebody ought to stop them."

"It won't be Grantley," replied the Judge. "First place, Grantley don't care anymore about the land than he do about the ranchers. He's there to boom it for the Land Estate Company and *they're* there to buy it low and sell it high to greenhorns out East, and fill their own dirty pockets and clear, 'fore they get lynched. Anyway, I'm outs with Grantley. We ain't spoken since Christmas. He treated me yaller and I ain't forgiven him!"

"Oh, there must be a mistake!" I cried. "He is the kindest man on earth and he has a fine ranch of his own, and of course he takes an interest in the land! He and his wife run the ranch and the printing-press singlehanded, and the 'News' is a very well-run paper!"

"Think so?" drawled Gene; "well, I don't! What d'you suppose Grantley did to me? I was trading, down to Twisp, Christmas week, *twice*—and he never so much as put it in the paper! 'Local News,' indeed! Pretty local news! 'Miss Selina Scaraway give a fashionable tea to her schoolmates Satterday. Five gallons of ice-cream was *con*soomed by the young ladies. Everybody had a most enjoyable time and doctor says they'll be round again 'fore long.' 'Abe Sourdough been into the city this noon lookin' for his bride as was due by the stage last night, which he'd paid her fare from Leavensford, Kansas. Driver Charlie says she jumped off at Gold Creek and got kissed by a drummer as was waitin' for her in brown clothes with a license stickin' out of his pocket. Find another, Abe,—and pick on a home-grown one this time!' That's the sort of local news Grantley prints—and here's *me*, a prominent citizen, takes the trouble to bring my best team over the grades to their all-fired old town and pay 'em the compliment of tradin' at their robber stores, real neighbourly, and he never says a word about me! I'm through with Grantley,—ain't no further use for him and his rag. I told him so, too. Stepped into the office the day after New Year. S'pose I felt glum enough, and Grantley give me one look and skips behind the printing-press. 'Hello, Judge,' says he, from behind the trays, 'ain't the world treatin' you right? Seem down on your luck this morning.' Then I let him have it good! An' I kept my hand behind me—holdin' nothin' wuss than a poke of candy for Violet, but he thought 'twas a gun—seen 'em in the office 'fore now, I guess—and he 'pologised and said 'twas an oversight and he hadn't meant no offence, and the next week he gives a column and a half to me and my family and my fine public spirit—never read such a yarn! But I ain't any more use for Grantley. I'm through with him!"

 The night had fallen, supper was over, and we were still sitting round the table listening to Gene's descriptions of early days in the Valley, when there came a sharp tap at the front door. I opened it and was confronted by Mrs. Twickenham, a kind, easy-going woman as I had known her, but evidently in no easy-going mood just now. The prophesied headache had anticipated the schedule, and her head was tightly bound up in the red handkerchief she always wore at such times; her eyes were blazing with anger. Violet showed a pale scared face over her mother's shoulder; and now, through the open door, came a hideous chorus of yells and barks from the direction of their place. The next instant our own dogs had leapt out into the night, screaming with excitement, and Gene's wife swept down me past the passage and stood, like accusing Fate, before her dismayed husband.

 "You come home this minute, Mr. Twickenham," she commanded; "the devil's broke loose there—and you sitting here drinking whisky and leaving your wife and children to be all eat up by wild beasts!"

 The Judge got to his feet, shaking in every limb. The din seemed to fill all the air. "What in blazes is it?" he asked. "Can't you speak, Vi'let?"

 Violet was trembling, too. "It's a great black thing," she stammered, "come tearin' down the hill straight into the yard—butted into the clothes mill and sent that flyin'—jumped over the well—raced round the house—screamin' and snortin'—the dogs went after it and it kicked 'em into the ditch an' I believe it's eatin' Clarence now! Come home, Paw—it's the devil, sure enough!"

Our boys had got down their Winchesters and flown down the road, and the Judge followed, his wife and daughter clinging to him and dragging him along. Kitty and I looked at each other across the deserted table, and then Kitty laughed aloud.

"It's Chapman's black bull on the rampage again," she said. "They won't tie him up! Last week he walked into Laura Dibb's kitchen when she was canning peaches, and smashed everything in the place![70] She's been in bed with the fright ever since. Those people are too bad!"

"He's gone this time," I told her. "Hark! The dogs are chasing him right down the Valley! He'll get to Twisp just in time for breakfast."

We went out on the porch together and looked at the night, the strange dark silver of the northern night. Across the Valley the enormous hills rose shoulder to shoulder, ethereal yet stern, under the stars. There was a touch of frost in the air, and from far, far away the hunting cry of the dogs came back to us on the wind. Behind Luther's Hill a waning moon, distorted and of deathly brilliance, was creeping up the sky, and the river below was one trailing shroud of thick white mist.[71] From the peaks behind us, where Lake Perigin lies, a mystic tarn in its mountain cup, came the long keen howl of a coyote out for prey.[72] We shivered and turned indoors. There are nights when the Valley is not good.

The autumn came early that year. The first snow struck us in mid-October, and two weeks later came a fall which buried the fences up to the third wire and laid the pall of silence over all the land. It was the silence that lay most heavily on one through those endless winters, a silence of death, muffling every sound connected with human life and making the rare night cry of some starving beast a thing of terror. They came very near in those frozen months, the creatures seeking food. One night, when everyone but myself had been in bed for hours, I heard a queer, heavy stumbling against the front gate—which was left just open enough to allow human beings to sidle through, while large animals could not pass; there was no moving it after the drifts had formed. I listened, thinking somebody might be coming in, but after a little shuffling the sound ceased and I went on with my writing. The next morning we found the tracks of a huge bear, and, dancing along beside them the delicate hoof prints of a deer. I fancy the deer had come first and the bear was loping along in chase of him. It was strange to mark every day the fresh coyote tracks over the pathless snow—little pointed prints, set in long straight lines, one exactly before the other, Indian fashion. You could never believe it was a four-footed creature that had made those unerring "Jacob's ladders," as even and single as if marked with a walking stick, uphill and down dale, from heights where the snow could barely cling, to the new-fallen whiteness by the garden gate. The trappers say that the coyote only runs like that when he is out to kill. I saw one once. They are the shiest, wariest creatures imaginable and rarely show themselves by day, but this was on a rainy autumn afternoon and in a very lonely part of the country. He was a longheaded, slender-limbed creature, of a pale moon-grey, a shadow of an animal, like an emaciated wolf, and he turned and stood still to look at me with such a strange glance of fear and defiance that it struck one like a pang. So he stood for a full minute, facing the terror he took me for, then there was a flash through the bracken and he was gone. They never attack human beings, so I was not frightened, only sorry for the evil-living, hunted thing. The government pays a dollar for every head brought in, but there are great numbers roaming the country still, and no smaller animal is safe from their attacks.[73]

The bears are rarer but much more alarming. One woman I knew shot a little black one in her own back yard. There is generally a loaded rifle hanging up in the kitchen or the barn, and many of the women are first-rate shots. These are born, not made. A German friend of ours, a gentle, emotional creature, who cries if she thinks she has offended one and who never handled a gun 'til she came to the Valley a year or two ago, carried off all the prizes at a shooting match where our best men were competing. Our own Kitty is a marvel. She hits the bull's-eye almost every time, and Hughie—instructor of musketry—says he has nothing to teach her!

Chapter 9

In a Forest Garden

It was August, and scorching hot. We had touched a hundred and twenty in the shade.[74] The whole Valley was filled with the smell of burning wood, and the air was all a dark blue with the "smother" of the forest fires that were raging twenty miles away, between Mazama and Slate Creek. Over there hung a red flare, ugly enough by day and terrifying at night, and the wind was blowing our way. At the hottest hour of all the hot afternoon I heard the gate click, and "Loo-ise," Mrs. Dick's sister, came staggering up the path, hatless and scarlet, and subsided into a rocker in a corner of the dining-room.[75]

"Hello!" I remarked, "you look all in! What have you been doing now? Digging fence-posts again? You'll get a sunstroke if you're not more careful!"

"No, 'tain't fence-posts this time," she replied, "but you've hit it; I'm all in but my shoe-strings! Got a reg'lar peach of a headache."

"What else do you expect?" said Kitty sternly. Kitty was brought up in a North Country rectory and has a very authoritative way with her. "It is sheer madness to come out at this time of day without a hat. Of course you've got a headache!"

Loo-ise lay back in her chair and rolled her eyes up to the ceiling. "You don' know what you're talking about, Kitty! This ain't a sun headache. No, sir, it's a powder headache. I've had 'em before when I've had to fool round with dynamite, and I know!"

"Dynamite!" we exclaimed in a breath. "You don't mean to say you people keep dynamite in the house?"

"Course we do! Asa got a lot off a man for a bad debt two years ago, and it comes in handy clearin' stumps and workin' at the ditch. What you look so scared for?"

"Now, Mrs. Larkins," I began severely, "we've got to talk seriously. Asa's away freighting, I understand? Well, we can't wait for him. We must get that horrid dynamite out of the house and off your place before tonight. It's sheer madness to have it lying round loose like that.

The children may be playing with it at this moment, and it will go off at a touch just because it is old. Asa shouldn't have had it up there at all."

Asa's wife grew yet more scarlet, and turned on me with flashing eyes. "Asy knows what he's about, bet your life he does—and if anybody says a word against him! Do you mean to say he don't care for his wife and family a darned lot more than you do? Do you think he left the stuff there a-purpose to kill us all?"

"No, of course not! He brought it up and then forgot all about it. And he'll be angry enough when he finds out that you have been meddling with it! Where have you stowed it, anyway?"

"Come out on your back porch and I'll show you," she replied sulkily, and as we went through to the kitchen she explained, "It was out in the shed on top of some potatoes, and it was all right 'til just lately, and then it began to come through the sacking in kind of sticky shreds—and it got in my way, so I've hung it up outside—there." We were out on the porch by this time, and she pointed to her cottage far up on a bench of the hill. "See that bundle against the wall? That's it—can't do a bit of harm—you see that for yourself!"

What we saw was a large sack, hanging from the low eaves about a foot away from the house wall. A most welcome breeze had arisen and was blowing down from the hills, and it was taking the terror sideways, swinging it vigorously parallel with the wall. Mrs. Asa contemplated the sight with satisfaction.

"It was considerable of a pull for me to get it up there," she remarked, "but I done it! The cartridges is just behind, tucked in under the eaves, all handy for Asy when he wants 'em."

I groaned, but Kitty—our Dresden China Kitty whom all these good people worship—laid a hand on our friend's shoulder and turned her round so as to look her straight in the eyes. "Mrs. Larkins," she said very sternly, "if the wind changes a point and that sack swings against the wall instead of in front of it, do you know what will happen? The house and the children and the barn, and all your stock, will be blown into Canada, and there won't be enough left to show which way they went! You go straight home and bring the children down here, while I go and find a man to take the dynamite a mile away and bury it. Run along—I'm going after the Judge. He has handled the stuff before and won't hurt himself."

Kitty conquered, as she always does. The Judge is one of her devoted slaves, and at her word he hitched up his team, got the explosives away—and hauled them home in triumph. I hear this evening that he has suddenly remembered that Asa got them for *him*! Dynamite is always treasure-trove to the pioneer, and the Judge is going to hold on to his prize—"you bet!"

One of the queer features of this country is that everybody seems to have lived everywhere at one time or another. The Larkins' house, a long climb up from our place, had changed hands several times before my arrival, and I think they got it by the ever dubious method of "relinquishment." However, they have held to it stubbornly, and in another year or so hope to prove up. If hard work alone could make for success, the Larkins family should be tremendously prosperous, but both the parents have a very weak side where the children are concerned, and they cannot be called prosperous yet. Most of the people here spoil their children hopelessly—but there is another and a better weakness in the rancher's character, which keeps him poor, and that is his imagination. These good people, who are up against the hardest kind of conditions from year's end to year's end, whose whole time and strength must be devoted to the effort of dragging a living out of the land at all costs, find solace in things as far removed as possible from the relentless grind of their everyday lives, and, crazy as their actions in this way may look to an outsider, I verily believe that these extravagances go far to preserve their health of mind—in some cases their reason itself. I wonder if Mr. Edison ever dreams what the gramophone has meant to the dwellers in shaky little houses lost in the folds of the tremendous hills, five or six miles from the nearest neighbour—a distance which, during some four or five months of the year, when the snow obliterates the trails, might just as well be fifty or sixty as far as any intercourse is concerned!

Talking of gramophones reminds me of one that I listened to in the course of a queer and pleasant experience "up Mazama way" one summer. It came about in this wise. The dear old Englishman, Mr. Hasketh, carpenter, builder, nursery gardener and many other things, began to talk to me one day about a friend of his, one Brunton, who lived all alone on a timber claim at the foot of Mount Gardner, and who had made himself a most beautiful garden in the heart of the woods. "You ought to see it," said Hasketh, "it will be in its glory now. Will you come up with us to his place when we go next week? It means staying the night—but you won't mind that?"

It seemed to me possible that Mr. Brunton might mind having an extra guest "wished" on him without warning, but I was told that he was a great reader and had often expressed a desire to talk with me; so, on the day appointed the Haskeths, husband and wife, came to fetch me in their huge waggon, which Mrs. Hasketh, who had a gay spirit, always called "the automobile." When it appeared I thought there would hardly be room for me in it, for it contained a mattress, bedding, pillows, a sack of potatoes, a mountain of fresh vegetables, and all the nice things that Mrs. Hasketh had baked and cooked to lighten the strain of entertaining our party.

"There's lots of room!" she cried; "we're going to pick up Mrs. Hill after this! There, give me your hand and put your foot on the hub—so!"

When we had picked up the postmaster's wife[76] and her specialised contributions to Mr. Brunton's housekeeping, the Haskeths' "Studebaker" could not have taken anything larger than a kitten for extra fare; but it was explained to me that this was all for our advantage, as the more heavily a waggon was loaded the more steadily it would travel over the kind of roads that we must traverse. I had done very little waggon-travelling at that time and had rather dreaded the experience, but I found it quite pleasant to go loitering along at almost a foot's pace, over what was new country to me. Our little hamlet lies very prettily and most inconveniently in a kind of pocket formed by the north and south fork of the Methow River; behind it, along the north fork, the rocks rise on both sides of the stream in great cliffs, so sheer that scarcely anything can find a roothold on them; dark and narrow is the river's way between the enclosing walls, and the road to Desolation Hill and the No-man's land beyond has to make great curves and twists away from the river to be a road at all.[77] But along the south fork the mountains are more indulgent, at least for a few miles, and the stream winds between rich stretches of pasture, bordered with osiers and lovely tangles of Virginia creeper and clematis, and widens out every now and then into little lakes thick with bulrushes and swarming with wild fowl. Beyond the fields were great belts of forest, pine and cotton trees[78] covering a perfect jungle of undergrowth through which neither Indian nor white man has attempted to cut a way as yet. The cotton trees are of little value, except for light fencing and fuel, but there is a moment in the early summer when they beautify everything, tossing out their white floating gossamers, light as eiderdown, almost impalpable and invisible taken one by one, but in those masses veiling the air with a filmy rain that catches the light and lightens the shade, and lies on all the roads thick and soft and white, like new fallen snow.

That was all over on the September day of which I was speaking, but the autumn tints had begun to glorify the woods with splashes of crimson and orange against which the pines stood like black sullen sentinels, refusing to deck themselves for Nature's carnival and prophesying of the dark long winter to come. But they are so faithful, the good stubborn pines! When everything around them is rioting greenly, or blushing red with the first frost, they do look black; but when all the other trees are mere inky skeletons against the snow, the pines show green, a dark, dark green indeed, but green all the same, dear constant things, keeping up one's faith in Mother Earth while she takes her five months' sleep.

As we travelled on that day and came at last to where only the pines would grow, one realised that, left to themselves, they come to their best and foster a delicate vegetation in their shade, sparse and thin but very beautiful. We crossed six or seven fords, and with each the climate seemed to change, the air to grow fresher and purer. It was a great relief, for the heat in the Valley had been very oppressive for days past. Towards one o'clock we halted by a broad stream for dinner, and then the fire was built among the pebbles, the kettle hung on the forked sticks in true gipsy fashion, and the thin blue smoke went curling up among the trees in those delicate bubbling grey-blue spirals that can only form in the stillest air. The horses were unhitched and given their dinner, too, and then they all wandered into the water and drank daintily, raising their heads and looking round them as if they too could appreciate the clear air and lovely scenery. The most serious task we had was that of extinguishing the fire, every last spark of which had to be religiously stamped out before we left it, for the forest fires, once started, work fearful devastation in the thick old woods, and they are almost invariably started by careless campers.

At last we all climbed into the waggon again, and from that time travelled as straight as we could through the pathless woods, twisting and turning a hundred times between the trees, but making progress, since there is next to no undergrowth where only pines will grow. Underfoot the deep brown mould of pine-needles muffled all sound and had thrown up a thin crop of fine soft grass, and the wind coming to us through the canyons of the last hills between us and the Sound sang its soft sibilant song in the branches, the song that is caught in the seashell and that the sea has sung to the shore. Driving along the lower roads where big pines are scarce, thinking of everything under the sun except trees, that low but commanding dirge has made me pull up suddenly sometimes and look round for the sea; I could have sworn I heard the roll of breakers on some unseen shore. And at last I would look up instead of around, and there was the giant bole upholding the great green harp that had been making that music for a hundred years!

The afternoon was mellowing already when we came to a level space, and I saw through the copper and gold of the tree trunks a square, barely an acre in extent, but an acre all of flowers, a hothouse spilt out in the open air, fenced on every side by tall pines and having for frame and background vistas of fairy woodland melting away in fainter and fainter tints of green and gold 'til they faded into the blue-grey shadows of the hills beyond. But the jewelled riot of that mountain garden looked as if it could never fade; the sweet peas ran in long lines three feet thick and waist-high, one woof of pink and lilac and white and crimson. There was a stretch of double poppies as tall as myself, of every shade, from blood-red and purple-black to white that would have put the snow to shame, fringed fritillated globes that filled the air with their mysterious sleepy perfume. Roses and pansies and heliotrope filled all the beds, and over the white log cabin which stood in the centre grew masses of a pale rose-coloured creeper with flowers that might have been twin sisters to the cherry blossoms of Japan. Two small square windows looked our way, and these were almost hidden by great bushes of "golden-glow," its pale yellow spheres as big as dahlias. The whole suggested some dazzling burst of sunshine, captured to the ground.

"Hullo!" came a cheery voice from within. "Say! Just stay outside a minute—been cleaning up for the ladies—and my bread'll burn if I don't take it out!"

We had scrambled down and come close to the window, through which floated the pleasant aroma of freshly baked bread, and I caught a glimpse of a tall figure scooting about inside, handling a broom with frantic energy. Then Mr. Brunton came out, broom and all, and made us welcome.

"I started tidying up hours ago," he said; "I just aimed to have the place spick-and-span for you folks, but every blamed thing that could happen did happen today—the cook-stove busted itself and I had to tinker it up—and my sponge (dough) got cold and I had to knead it twice—and my cat got into a mix-up with a coyote and I had to go after 'em with a gun—and a stranger has been in and tried to make me trade him my mine for a second-hand sewing machine and a baby carriage—wonder he didn't try to trade me a wife! These drummers have got gall![79] And by the time I could look at the kitchen floor—well, I just had to take a hoe to it—so things ain't exactly as I aimed to have them, but I'm mighty glad to see you and I hope you'll make the best of 'em as they are!"

This, I found, was a long speech for our host, and having delivered it he turned back to his bread and relapsed into the taciturnity that grows on lonely bachelors in these wilds. But my companions seemed to understand the situation and took command of it at once.

"Now, Mr. Brunton," said little Mrs. Hasketh, "you just go and talk to Mr. Hasketh, outside. You ain't goin' to do another thing in this house 'til we clear out tomorrow. Mrs. Hill and me'll see to supper and washing up and breakfast in the morning. Ain't that so, Mrs. Hill?"

"Sure!" replied the postmaster's wife, "you needn't even tell us where things are. We'll find what we want, all right. Mrs. Fraser here is going to look at the flowers—the kitchen's too small for three women—and think up a nice piece for her next book. Run along, Mrs. Fraser—guess you ain't much of a cook, anyway!"

"Have it your own way," I said meekly; "I can't compete with such artists as you and Mrs. Hasketh, but I did make the sausage rolls!"

"And mighty good they were—we'll put the rest on for supper. Now, clear!"

"Say!" Mr. Brunton's head popped in at the window. "Did you bring them records? That's right!" as Mrs. Hasketh pointed to a box which she had nursed on her lap for sixteen miles or so; "I've been figgerin' on them for a party—I get in all the kids for miles round, Saturday afternoons, and I've about busted all the records I got with the machine. Them kids do love the music!"

We saw that a little later when a young woman from a farm three miles away sauntered into the garden with her small boy, a silent, big-eyed child, who looked wistfully towards the horn of the gramophone in the corner.

"Right away, sonny!" said Mr. Brunton; "you can go and sit outside, and I'll take the music upstairs and play it to you from the window. This place is too small," he explained in answer to my questioning look; "it's a powerful loud gramophone, and it don't get a chance in here."

The cabin, all of logs, carefully whitewashed, without and within, consisted only of two rooms, a kitchen below and a bedroom above. The latter had a window at each end, and in one of them the gramophone was installed, and then the first of the new records was let loose. Powerful! It was thunderous. It brayed like a whole brass band, a shameless polka that set the roof shaking and caused a sudden flight of birds from all the trees around. Before I followed the birds I glanced at the little boy, sitting on the grass, holding tight on to his mother's hand, his eyes shining, his whole face suffused with delight. Then I wandered as far away as I could wander, through the woods and up the steep hillside towards the mine, through deep grass and ferns and Michaelmas daisies, and when I had put a quarter of a mile between myself and the source of the noise it mellowed down to a faint dance tune, very pleasant to hear in the green solitude.

There was a grand supper in the white kitchen, and when all the dishes had been washed up and put in place we went out on the porch and prepared to "swop yarns" while the twilight came down.

The men slept on the hay in the barn that night and we three women shared the raftered garret upstairs. I persuaded my companions to take possession of the bed—the kind bodies wanted to give it to me—and let me sleep on the mattress we had brought, the necessity of which I understood now. I put it close to the north window, which opened almost level with the floor, and I got my head on the window ledge and spent most of the night looking at the stars. They always look huge in that clear northern air, great pulsing diamonds that seem to be drawing nearer earth as one gazes at them. The world was very still and the song of the pines most sweet and constant; the forest spread for miles around, and I lay in its very heart, with star-lit vaults above and the dim dewy garden below. There are nights when it is worthwhile to leave out sleep, and that was one of them. Each hour brought some lovelier change in the woods, and in the fathomless sky where, far as the eye could reach, the stars crowded, fainter and ever fainter, 'til they merged into the infinite depth that is neither light nor darkness but a breathing mystery through which the great planets swing on their god-set courses, and the constellations whirl in obedient splendour round the immutable dear North Star.

Who could sleep with all that to gaze on and think about? The best hour of all my night in the clearing in the woods was the last before dawn. A cold thin breeze came down from Alaska, moving the tree tops and setting the flower bells swinging for an instant. Then it went on down the Valley, and there was a whisper in the woods—just a whisper, as if little heads had come out from under soft wings to ask if it was time to wake up, and then snuggled back again into the down. No, it was night still, the last, sleepiest, sweetest hour of it; but it was withdrawing all the same. The indescribable, nameless change that brings back the colour to the rose and the outline to the hill, the breathless pause that calls silence into sound and death to life—it had come, and the trees and the flowers knew it before ever a bird had chirped. Then with a rush came day. The hills grew black against grey, purple against sleepy saffron and chrysoprase that suddenly blushed to rose and flamed in orange at last, to clear, pure new-born blue as the sun leapt up in the East and shot his laughing gold down the answering green of the Valley. The miracle of morning once more!

Chapter 10

Tragedy and Comedy

Tragedy stalked through our midst sometimes, unveiled and undisguised. The pressure of the tremendous surroundings induced melancholy as an ocean casts its atmospherical sadness inland with its rain and its wind. The contemplative nature is a peculiar one, and it is not to be acquired. To mechanically active temperaments, enforced and unrelieved contemplation is an agony. It is even worse for a mind that has had no training, and which, once sunk in the rut of despondency, has no means within itself to find relief. One must, as we say, lift oneself up by one's own boot-straps, at times, and that takes a good deal of practice.

One poor fellow we knew, who gave up the struggle against the scenery, laid down his pack almost as soon as he had picked it up. For weeks he had hung about the landing place of the cage, slung on ropes, that transported people across the river;[80] he was always ready to answer a smile, but rarely a word. He would sit, staring at the merciless hills, light struggling pitifully with the descending dark in his eyes. Some said there was a girl in the case, but one who saw him thus day after day, always in the same place, his gaze always upon the same hills, knew better. For he had seen it before, and he had been through the dark places of that same journey himself. Besides, the child was no more than seventeen or eighteen. He knew nothing of the reasons of life nor of the Giver. He felt himself already half buried in the pit of the Valley, and the skies held for him nothing at all.

So, one morning, having walked into the village with his father,—who, if he had any heart or sight at all, must have seen this coming for months and who, yet, did not move a finger to help him!—they went together into the saloon; the boy drank a glass of beer, went out into the woodshed, and—shot himself through the head.[81] The Winter One was at the creamery when it happened, and, hearing a single shot—always a bad sign—hastened in the direction from which it had come. In the open country, of course, he would have paid no attention to it, but in the town! He had had a prophetic disquietude of the spirit, that morning, too, so he ran.

There was no difficulty in locating the scene of the trouble, for a crowd was already gathered: a very still crowd, that neither moved, nor spoke above a whisper. Edging his way through, he saw, lying face downwards, one arm thrown out as if in self-protection, his friend; but nobody offered to so much as straighten the poor body out. The Winter One stooped down, turned it over and closed the poor glazed eyes. "Lend me a hand, somebody," he said. "And let's take him across to the hall. We can't leave him lying in the street here."

But though the murmured words that came from the crowd were sympathetic, no one stirred, and the Winter One stood up. On the hill, in front of his house, stood the old German—he of Metz—looking down, and the Winter One shouted up to him, waving an imploring hand. The old soldier hastened down swiftly.[82]

"Vat is? Vat is?" he asked, elbowing his way in with comfortable haste. "Ach du lieber!" he exclaimed when he saw. "Veil, veil!" he went on a moment later. "Vat are ve all vaiting for? Vy don't you bick it up and take it across?"

But the others backed away. They could do most things that circumstances demanded of them, but handle a dead body—not if they could help it. So the Winter One and the veteran lifted him up between them and bore him across, followed by the rest, among whom was the boy's father, crying and sobbing and wringing his hands. One does not want to be brutal, but at that moment the Winter One could have hit him. It is so like that kind to make the life of youth miserable, and then to howl in public when the inevitable has happened!

Having done what they could and sent the father home in charge of two willing but uncomfortable consolers, the veteran and the Winter One adjourned to the Duck Brand for a drink. In spite of an ample experience of such things, the latter felt that this was a moment for strong waters.

The Duck Brand was full and doing a good business, for that time of the morning, but it was oppressed and silent. The bartender,[83] a good little man, red-haired, with very bright blue eyes, and always dressed in funereal black, was shaky too, and was filling the glasses with a somewhat unsteady hand—he had been the first to see the body in the woodshed.

He was proud of his place and rightly, for, as has already been said, it was a model. The two last comers drank in silence and rested their elbows on the bar, while the quiet and the oppression grew thicker and thicker.

Then, just as, like a rain-cloud, it had reached the point where it must burst or spill itself, a rig drove up to the door and, a moment later, a "drummer" entered, linen-coated, hard-hatted, bustling and genial.

"Howdy, gentlemen!" he said, looking around him. "Anybody feel like something?"

The crowd's interest in life revived a little and they approached the bar, throwing back their shoulders and attempting to speak naturally to one another.

"Beer for mine!" said the drummer. "Nothing but beer, this weather!" There was a stir, as he spoke, and the Mackenzie came round and caught the sleeve of his coat.

"Don't drink that beer," he said with mysterious vehemence. "Don't touch it—take whisky—but don't go near that beer."

The bartender's eyes flashed with righteous wrath and he glared at Dick Mackenzie.

"Whatcher mean?" he demanded. "What's eatin' you? What the hell's wrong with my beer?" We thought for a moment that he was going to spring over the bar.

"I dunno," replied the Mackenzie. "I'm no druggist. I'm just tellin' him for his own good."

"Come on," said the drummer. "Spit it out. What is the matter with it?"

The crowd behind listened with suspense. The Duck Brand beer was generally excellent.

"I tell you I dunno," reiterated the Mackenzie; "but a feller came in here this morning—and he drank a glass of it—just one—and . . ." He paused dramatically.

"Well," the drummer demanded. "What happened?"

"As I tell you," went on Dick, "I don't know a thing about the beer—I never drink it, I'm no Dutchman! But the man I'm tellin' you about—he drank one glass, and then he went out back and shot himself!"

The main occupation of such of the manhood of the little village as felt the need of occupation was the saw-mill, instituted, if one was to believe the owner of it, from a benevolent desire to give work to the deserving. That was not the generally accepted story, though, and it is to be feared that benevolence, as usually happens, was compelled to be its own reward. After a study of the question from both sides, the Winter One came to the conclusion that on the Owner's part it was something of a hobby,[84] on the other a desire to save up a few dollars against the chance of getting married in the spring—for the men who worked in it were all young and all unmarried except the foreman, and his need of money could be easily traced to the bright and exceedingly orderly little saloon.

Now the Owner had arrived there from the heart of New England. He was Bostonian and Harvardian to the ends of his fingers and he had laboured long and incessantly to plant a seed of order in the mental habits of the countryside. With him, order had, in the first place, been a religion, but ten years had turned the religion into a fad, and twenty-five had developed a "crank"!

There was no quarrel with that in itself. Every "oldtimer" was a crank, but the necessity for getting along with the others helped to smother the little individual obsessions, and the life of range and lumber camp had given each some of the colour of his neighbours, so that to one another they did not appear to be so very mad. The Owner of the sawmill lived very much by himself, and his "crankinesses" were those of a scholar and a gentleman; so that he seemed, from the common point of view, to be very mad indeed.

The engine of the sawmill had been bought second-hand, and such parts as were past hope had been replaced by new ones; but the boiler, the faithful, over-worked, old boiler remained. Putting new wine into old bottles is not "a marker" to surrounding an old boiler with entirely new machinery, and the result, as far as the sawmill went, was that the crew was laid off for two days a week, until, as shall be told presently, the boiler gave up in despair one sunny afternoon and surrendered, with a hiccough.

The mill had stood originally in the pine woods, some five miles off, and the reasons for moving it down were never very comprehensible, even when most carefully explained.[85] This may have been due to the half-hypnotic influence exercised by the Owner over the minds of some of his employees. In the eyes of some he could do no wrong; they accepted everything as the workings of a superior mind, and the less intelligible was the thing the firmer became their assurance. In view of others he could do nothing right, and nothing that he said or did could, by any possibility, have a good reason behind it. Since he himself seldom or never condescended to explain, but merely ordered a thing to be done, there was fuel for both sides. One could not help thinking, after awhile, that he, personally, enjoyed being suspected of madness and that he relished dislike, for he cultivated it. The best-natured, most delightful of men, he lived in a continual terror of being found out; he repressed the warm, human side of himself ruthlessly because it was human, and because it did not fit the man he had evolved from the excellent material of his own soul and heart, whom he had endowed with every attribute of roughness and harshness which he disliked in others, but which he admired in his own creation, and to whom he had given his own name and the temporary use of his own body for a dwelling place. It was a Jekyll and Hyde affair, save that the real man had never quite surrendered, but maintained a desultory struggle with the other, the success of which depended, in a large measure, upon the weather, the condition of business, and the company in which he happened to find himself.

He—the real man—prided himself upon a strict sense of justice, but the other, at the same time, refused to consider evidence, and suborned judge and jury. Common sense was the be-all and end-all of one, but the whisperings of the other twisted the point of view out of focus. With all that, he was the kindliest of men and the best of friends, and one thinks of him with nothing but the purest affection.

To return to the mill. The end came suddenly, but not unexpectedly. During the morning the crew had been left to themselves, and when midday came it was discovered that the output for the five morning hours exceeded all records. Not a hitch, not a breakdown had occurred; it approached the ideal. This, at dinner time, was reported to the Owner, and he smiled and nodded delightedly when the foreman brought him the news. Then he looked out of the window by the side of his desk, and the Winter One, sitting at a little distance, saw that his eyes had grown dreamy behind the gold-rimmed spectacles. Presently the dinner bell rang from down the street, and with something like a sigh, the Owner rose, blinking at the sunlight on the snow. The Winter One was not then familiar with the symptoms, and, seeing the growing wistfulness of the other's expression, imagined that his thoughts had been led, in one way or another, to the land of his yearning and the blue waters of the Newport shore. He felt sorry for him, and made no attempt to break through the circle of silence which the other had built around himself.

Dinner is not a time for conversation in those parts; and the Winter One, not yet accustomed to the hot biscuit, meat and potato diet, or to the fearful heat of the stoves, did not wait very long, but escaped into the open as speedily as possible. It was like jumping from a boiling bath into an icy sea, and it was a moment or two before he could recover his breath.

While he was still gasping, he heard the door behind him open, and the Owner appeared, tying a red bandanna tightly round his ears. His eyes were alight now, as they travelled up the street in the direction of the mill, and he started off briskly, his hands deep in his pockets. Neither to the right nor to the left did the potentate turn, but made straight for the mill that stood by the side of the half-frozen river, a thin coil of smoke arising from the engine-room chimney. The air was full of the sweet smell of pine lumber, and so still was the midday that the cracking of the snow on the roofs sounded like the snapping of dog whips.

A danger sign hung conspicuously at the top of the mill steps, so the Winter One, finding the sun warm and the lower step fairly dry, sat himself down. The sound of moving footsteps came from the interior, with, now and then, a muffled sound and the "flap" of planks being turned over. It was early yet, and the crew were still filling themselves against the five-hour interval before supper, so that the place was undisturbed by anything save the crooning of the river, the soft, occasional hissing of the idle engines, and the tiny, insect-like sounds, of which such places are always full—snow dripping from a corner of the roof, thousands of green planks swelling and shifting, and the steel rails of the hand car expanding by the millionth of an inch at a time in the sun.

The tramp of returning feet aroused him and he clambered out of the way; but he had not gone far when a smile—it was the smile he saw first, even before he saw the face—arrested him, and a pleasant, rather indistinct voice suggested that he should come and keep warm in the engine-room.

"Come right in," the newcomer went on, and the shyness which first attracted the Winter One, the shyest of men, vanished in a laugh. "If the Boss comes I'll tell him you're helping stoke! I don't reckon he'll be down here, anyway. He ain't been here for a week or more!"

"He's in there now," said the Winter One, as the other opened the door. "He's been moving about in there for twenty minutes or more."

"The hell he has!"

The door was shut with a crash, and Charlie—as the Winter One came to call him within a week—opened the firebox and pushed in armfuls of odds and ends of wood, examined the pressure, tried the water and sat down.

"They're going to put up some chutes for the sawdust," he remarked presently, "and load them onto *her*, atop of everything else." He nodded towards the boiler. "And she's hauling just about her limit now!"

The Winter One replied with vague sympathy, and Charlie bit off a piece of tobacco.

"That's him clambering about on the roof, now," he said. "It's a wonder he couldn't leave the place alone when he don't know a planer from a ripsaw; but no, he just can't! I'll bet a dollar we don't saw a couple of hundred feet this afternoon! Oh well, I don't care—I'll get paid just the same."

He was right; the Owner had one of his attacks of order that afternoon, and the knowledge that so much work had been done in his absence was annoying him extremely, nothing like it having ever been accomplished at any time when he was present. It was, in a fashion, a slur upon his self-esteem. He was perfectly certain in his own mind that it had been an accident, but the annoyance remained. He would now so arrange things in the mill, so organise the men's energies, that the good work might continue—but with his assistance.

But the mill was in a frightfully untidy condition, and good work could not exist side by side with disorder, so the first thing which he resolved to do was to tidy up a little bit. There were ten or eleven men in the crew and they were paid at the rate of from two and a half to three and a half dollars a day; for the next four hours the entire energies of all were turned to moving planks, and boxes, and tool chests from one side of the mill to the other. But the engine did not cease to be fed, for nobody could say when the Boss might tire of his present occupation, remove himself, and allow real work to be resumed.

In the engine-room Charlie dozed, the Winter One dozed. Footsteps clattered in the mill, voices swore, and a continuous rumble of falling objects and scraping planks came from above. At last, as the outlines of the mountains began to become obscure and the mounds of houses were being wrapped up in the dark purple veiling of the dusk, the Owner left, and, with his leaving, an austere and cynical star came into sight, like a mocking message of hope. Charlie snapped the door of the fire-box shut.

"Can you beat it?" he asked of the gloom. "Of all the—"

His voice stopped like a broken banjo string, and he leaned over, standing up on the tips of his toes. Some six inches above his head, the steam gauge gleamed against the pale light thrown up from the snow under the window. Diving into his pocket, he lit a match and glanced at the gauge once more.

Quietly, as an evening sea breeze ruffles through the wheat, there came from his half-open mouth, in something just above a whisper, a medley of language so appalling, that the Winter One, old soldier though he was, sat in a kind of trance, unwilling to disturb.

With one last sibilant malediction that rose from the level of the rest and soared above it until it disappeared by infinitesimal degrees into space, Charlie turned and flung open the door.

"She always was a—old—" he said. "She never had no more sense than a Siwash![86] Come on, get out of here before she cuts loose! She's gone plain bughouse! I ain't goin' to stop an' argue with her!"

"Hi!" he yelled, when we found ourselves outside. "Hi! Fellers! Get out from under! Happened? What happened?" he shouted, as an indistinct voice bellowed the question. "The hell boiler's goin'!—Get out from under! She's carryin' a hundred and fifty more now than she's got any right to—and she's goin' up five pounds a second! Goodnight all!"

Half an hour later the engine expert of the village was routed out of the saloon and guided down to the scene. He shook his head mournfully.

"Engines?" he gurgled. "What you think you know about any bloody engines? Not a thing—not a—thing. Where'd ye keep the safety valve—up on roof?" He stared unbelievingly. "Never heard of such a thing. Get up and open her! Engines!" he chuckled with happy laughter.

Then Charlie it was who remembered that the Owner had been walking about on the roof just before he left. True to his instincts, he had been unable to keep himself away from the neighbourhood of the safety valve, which, in some fashion known only to himself, he had contrived to shut with his foot, and in such a fashion that two strong men had to take alternate tricks with a monkey wrench for over half an hour before it was opened again.

But the poor old boiler had given up the struggle in despair long before that. She had not exploded; as Charlie remarked afterwards, she had acted like a perfect lady; she had merely cracked, shifted, and disengaged herself from the surrounding machinery.

Chapter 11
Happy-Go-Lucky

One particular and ever-present danger in the winter was that from the chimneys of our cottage, which had a habit of catching fire about once a month. It did not seem to make any difference whether we cleaned them out or not, they would go off—always at supper time—just the same. At first we used to be rather frightened, and not without reason, because it does not take much to start old shingles into a blaze, even if they are a little wet, and our roof was so sloped that the snow never stayed on it for very long. The sun was hot, too, so that once the snow was off, it dried up very quickly.

The first time this happened, the old German veteran, who had been doing some carpentering for us, rushed back when he was half way home, and burst into the house.

"Shut your stofe, good people," he cried. "Your place is firing!"

It was a good medium-sized blaze, that one, and it brought up quite a crowd from the village. Just as it was getting low, some one of the onlookers suggested salt on the fire. The Comrade[87] and all of us rushed into the kitchen, snatching up a bag of what seemed to be salt, and threw it on the offending stove, bag and all.

The damper was turned off in the stovepipe and the draught shut off so that the wood-coal was smouldering harmlessly when the bag arrived in its embrace. There it lay subdued for a while, waiting 'til the door should be closed and the room empty.

A moment later the watchers outside, whom the family had joined, from prudential reasons, saw the dispirited flames rally smartly and shoot up ten feet above the roof, spouting sparks, while inside, a roar like that of a landslide came from the room on the left of the passage.

When we got to it the stove was glowing redly, and some genius suggested pouring water on the top of it. A bucket was brought in on the run, and one stood, holding it at the ready, while another, with a crowbar, pulled off the stove lid.

Down went the water like a ferret into a rabbit hole. As the flames leaped out under the encouragement of the air, a series of horrible hisses, punctuated by sparks, emerged from the brown fog, and the stove-lid slid with a clang into the mess.

It was an hour and more before the wreck of the room was even partially cleaned up.

"Well," said we, later. "The blamed old thing won't go off again for a week or two, anyway. We're that much to the good."

"Kitty!" said Mother[88] to the Comrade next morning, "I cannot find that saltpetre for curing the beef.[89] What on earth has become of it?"

"Was it—was it in a bag? Oh, my goodness, that must have been what went into the stove!"

The fireworks seemed to be accounted for.

A fortnight later the kitchen chimney went off while we were at supper, but there was snow on the roof and, though we felt anxious, we felt no very wild alarm.

"Well," said we, "that ought to do the chimney for quite a while."

We had not taken into account, though, the quality of the firewood with which our friend, Mr. Kelly, had been supplying us.

"That's good wood," he had said, wiping his mouth. "You folks have treated me white and I'll do the same by you."

Beyond short-weighting us by something like a rick in the cord, he did, as he understood it. The wood was not only good, it was enthusiastic. It burnt quickly and thickly. It could choke up a good-sized range in three days, and a chimney in three weeks, for it was not three weeks later that the front chimney caught again. The first we heard of it was from the Lord of the Manor, who walked into the dining-room without knocking and informed us that he had seen the blaze from his store half a mile away.

We shut down the stoves; but he must have thought us singularly apathetic, for he suggested climbing on to the roof and pouring water down.

"It won't do any good—and nobody could stick on that roof, anyway," we told him. "Sit down and have a drink. That chimney's haunted. It'll give over when it gets tired."

"Are you going to sit here?" he demanded, "and let the house burn over your heads?"

"It won't," we answered him. "Let it alone—if we monkey with it, it will only irritate it—and we're insured, anyhow. Let it alone."

It burnt itself out quite peacefully, as we had hoped it would, but we must have injured its spirits by our lack of interest, for it did not repeat the performance until well into the spring.

One year, before Mother's arrival, just when the snows began to go and the damp, sweet "bunch grass" leapt out of the ground, the Winter One departed to the top of a place known as Desolation Hill, where for some months he lived in company with a young man from Seattle, who, finding nothing but hard work in that city, had emigrated into the open country, bringing with him a delicate lung and a profound assurance of his own capacity to live comfortably with half the toil of the less cultivated native. The idea is a very common one; nearly everybody who arrives from the pavements is possessed with it, and we have watched, with a pity that dared not express itself for fear of giving offence, the struggles of several different "outfits" in its throes.

It reminded one of the angler coming to unknown waters with rods, and dry flies, and wet flies, and silk and gut, and heaven knows what besides, and the small native with a stick and a piece of string and a bent pin. One could foretell with absolute certainty what was going to happen, one knew every stage of exaltation and depression through which the self-immolated victim was going to pass, and one had to sit and listen with cheerful sympathy to the tale of pleasant ways abandoned, of friends left behind, of chances returned to the "discard," of hopes for the future—if one has heard it once, one has heard it twenty times, and the end was always the same.

The Winter One's companion, whom we will call B., had the affliction badly, and was, besides, handicapped with an imagination like a toy balloon. Even when the toil of the moment and its necessities held it to earth, it strained wildly at the string and it fluttered madly in the stillest air.

His ambition, for a while, was to fit into the colour scheme, and though the Winter One pointed out that the scheme was complete anyway, that the utter neglect of every sort of mind prop which he might possess would not make him any the better farmer, and that his neighbours were making a living out of the ground in spite of their ways of thought and living and not because of them, he persevered, tearing his hands open wide because gloves—which everybody else did use, by the way—were effeminate; trading and re-trading until he could not have told, himself, what belonged to him, and hurling himself at every day more grimly and more grubbily than at the last.

He began the spring with three horses, pretty good little cayuses, two of them were—the third was a souvenir. The two cayuses he traded off for his ploughing, so that when the time came for "cultivating" his corn, he had to pay four and a half dollars a day to the same man to whom he had traded his team; and he lost in cash about sixty dollars over the two transactions. He never kept any very accurate accounts, though. He had a wealthy stepfather in Seattle, so that the knowledge of his loss, if he ever had any, did not worry him very greatly.

It was seven miles or more from Desolation Hill to the village which we called Town, and, once a week, one of the two dwellers on the summit would make a pilgrimage for mail and supplies. The rare loveliness of that road as it wound down the side of the river, through stretches of pine wood, haunts the memory to this day. It was like passing through a park, and even the cabins and farm yards, some of which occupied the middle of the road, lost their squalor and their dreary ugliness in the setting, and hardly startled the eye at all.

Of all the sad and helpless-looking objects, a frame cottage, with its discoloured boards, its tiny windows, its weather-worn shingles, is one of the most melancholy. A log cabin, whatever may be its disadvantages as a place in which to live—and they are many—is at least picturesque as an object in the scenery. It falls to pieces gracefully too; a frame "shack" in decay looks like the incarnation of shiftless despair.

For any desiring solitude and space and peace, these stretches of pine wood and quaking-asp, between the trail and the dainty little river, would be a haven. But only a very strong mind can support the complete solitude for any length of time, and a moment arrives when peace becomes a burden and space a nightmare. To hear the same sounds—and only those same sounds—day after day and night after night, to see the same objects and nothing but those objects alone, always alone—indoors and out of doors for week after week, and not surrender the mentality to the surroundings, is difficult even for the strongest; for others it is all but impossible. The great world recedes into the half-light, and its doings have no more interest for one than the activities of the inhabitants of Mars. If the whole earth were at strife, the wheat would continue to grow, and nothing beyond the Columbia is half as important as the chances of rain and the future of the corn. Today is today, tomorrow is tomorrow and next year is next year. "Let her buck!" is the motto of the whole country.

Does an accident happen to any neighbor? Lightning never hits in the same place twice. Has a bridge been condemned? Well, one more trip over it cannot make any great difference to its stability, and it's too much trouble to go around, anyhow. Why worry? If it is bound to happen it is bound to happen, and nothing that one can do will prevent it. A man has got to take a certain amount of risk every time that he takes six horses and a trail waggon over roads where it is sometimes difficult to maneuver a buggy and a team. A little worse risk here and there will not make any particular difference.

In the course of the seventy odd miles between the head of the valley and the river there are three bridges; and a loaded freight waggon with four horses—in one case a trail waggon and eight—has at one time or another dropped through all of them; and, though the condition had been well known for months beforehand, it had never occurred to anyone to have them mended until then. When, at last, they were mended, do you imagine that they were rebuilt? Not much! They were just patched up. A native of these parts takes a far greater pride in the manufacture of an ingenious make-shift than he does in a complete piece of work.

The attitude of the County Commissioners was typical, too. Having inspected the bridge and found it to be in a thoroughly dangerous condition, they "condemned" it, placed a notice at each end informing the world of the fact and hurried back to the county seat. Weeks and months went by, but the bridge remained unaltered and the notices at each end grew dimmer and dimmer. It was the only bridge that crossed the river for ten miles in one direction and fifteen in another, and the traffic over it continued merrily until the inevitable occurred, and a freighter returning from the river with a ton or more of freight dropped through it one autumn afternoon. Of course he was not injured, and his horses, save for a few cuts and bruises, came to no harm, for such is the way of fate in her dealings with such folk; but one of the waggons dropped fifty feet into the river, and he, having been pitched out, was flying through the air when a protruding spike caught him by the seat of his trousers and held him, hanging over space. He was saved by the strength of his overalls and nothing else.

Chapter 12

The Thoroughbred and His Cousins

It has already been said that anything purchasable by the mere signing of a name can be sold in the West, and at prices which make one blink. At one time, a society was formed for the betterment of our local breed of horses, a most worthy object, as all will agree. A cayuse, to be sure, does not "mix" well. His is a breed evolved by necessity, and his qualities are exactly those needed in the countries in which he is found. He is small and he has no "bone" to speak of; his temper is too well known to need explanation; but he can outwork two ordinary horses, he can carry a load of two hundred and fifty pounds all day without fatigue, and he can thrive on food that would kill his Eastern brother, while he is doing it. He can climb like a cat and live through a blizzard. Who will say there is no plan in the scheme of creation?

But cross him with a softer and heavier breed, and most of those qualities disappear—as we discovered later, but not until we had paid, among us, a good many thousand dollars for the knowledge.

We knew all about cayuses, and we knew nothing at all about any other breed of horse; but our native cock-sureness forbade the serious entertainment of such a suggestion, and when it was made, with all tact and caution, we did not receive it kindly—in fact we dismissed it instantly, arguing that a horse was a horse, and that a cayuse and a Percheron were, fundamentally, identical.

Robinson, in league with some importers, introduced to our attention a splendid black animal with a pedigree stretching back into the early mists of time.[90] Why is it that people who profess to disregard the value of a pedigree in a human being, desire it so keenly and boast of it so proudly in an animal? His price was only three thousand dollars—in bankable notes—at six and twelve months—no cash required at all, and he was paraded daily, up and down the main road, decked in ribbons and loaded with ginger.

"Stock companies" were something of a fad with us in those days. We had worked hard for years and were fast beginning to reap some of the rewards of our virtue. Some of us had lost fingers in planing machines, most of us had broken arms or legs, nearly all had been frozen at one time or another, and all had been scorched to a dusky brown—but we were getting on. Mortgages were being paid off. Organs, gramophones and pianos were trickling in, houses were being built with ornamental windows and balconies, and it was beginning to look as though the land which we had reclaimed might, some day, be of considerable value. We were pleased with ourselves, and, besides, it was the paradise time between the windy, rugged spring and the brooding melancholy of the summer.

The head and front of the Percheron Company was one Robinson, who, with the English naval officer aforementioned, had started a creamery. He was a most amiable person, with violent likes and dislikes, and a temper which, when roused, was exceedingly difficult to grapple with. The one sure way to soothe it was to sympathise with him; but one had to handle one's sympathy carefully, because after a few hours of indulgence, it had a habit of forgetting its origin and fastening itself upon anything that lay to hand. As a partner he was impossible. Without a grievance he seemed to find it impossible to work, and, with one, to co-operate. He was effusive and suspicious, genial and sulky by turns: nor was there any known way of finding out which of his moods would come next, or why.

He flung himself into the business of organising the Percheron Company whole-heartedly—so whole-heartedly, in fact, that his partner had to pay a man to do most of his work for a month.

"Three thousand dollars!" he exclaimed almost contemptuously. "Why, to hear you, one would think these folks around us was paupers! It's worth it, too—say, don't you know that horse'll pay for himself in three years!"

"Maybe," was the patient answer. "But why should he have to do it six times over?"

"Whatcher talking about?" he demanded. "Six times over? Do you mean to tell me you don't think he's worth three thousand?"

"I sure do. He's worth about twelve-fifty to anyone that could use him. I've seen better horses than him," his informant went on, "much better horses, go for two hundred and fifty to three hundred pounds!"

"Ah, go wan!" he replied. "I ain't got time for joshin'. I'm busy."

"If you ain't now, you soon will be," replied the other, "paying for him."

"Some folk," Robinson shouted after him, "ain't got any public spirit at all!"

It was a fortnight later that the speaker saw the Percheron again. He looked dingy. The ribbons, which still adorned his mane and tail, were draggled, and he looked about him with the puzzled politeness of a cultivated gentleman who has lost his way in a slum.

"He wouldn't hurt for a brush," said one, sitting on the creamery steps. "And I'd have those things out of his hair, before they have his hair out. Where's he living now?"

"Over at Ed's. He looks all right to me," replied Robinson. "You always got to have a grouch on somethin', ain't you?"

"I haven't got a grouch! I'm just sorry for him, that's all."

"You ain't got no call to be sorry for him. Ed treats him like he was one of his own children!"

"Maybe he'd rather be treated like a valuable horse. I know I would."

Robinson was called back to the interior at that moment, and, when he came out again, was full of wrath against his partner, who had incensed him by a complaint on the subject of the use of lye, inside the churn.

"A busy man like me—a fellow that's usin' his brains all the time! The two buckets was side by side. It won't hurt the blame old churn, anyways. That fellow's got a mean streak in him—you know that. Oh, you won't say so, 'cause you're too damn good-natured, but you know it. If he thinks I'm goin' to stand for bein' damned and cussed all over my own plant!"

"On whose half of the plant does the churn stand?" the other asked.

"Oh hell, Colonel!" he grinned in spite of his anger.

"But I tell you, that fellow's gettin' entirely too fresh."

"Well, go and swat him with a paddle—or go and ask to see the monthly accounts. You can get your own back over them."

"I could. And if it wasn't for the locoed way he keeps 'em, I'd do it. He's got 'em to now that we owe everything we own and we own everything we owe. Double entry or some such damn foolishness, he calls it. I don't know half the time which way we're running."

It developed that Ed's idea of grooming a horse was to let him roll in the yard, and that his notion of exercise was an hour's walking whenever he happened to think about it. Like all the rest of us, the Percheron ceased to care after a little while and his dissipated appearance ceased to trouble him. But the stockholders began to wake up to their troubles before long, and, as one of them said, they had to work harder than they had worked in years to pay off their notes and wait in patience for their problematical profits.

"There ain't goin' to be no Christmas in our family, this year," one of them announced gloomily. "That fool horse has got it!"

When the colts began to arrive, however, their spirits rose again.

"That 'lil' horse," said one of our friends, speaking of a colt unborn, "will be worth a hundred and fifty dollars to us as soon as he stands up."

The expression was in general use, the whole expression, amount and all. And when a colt actually did stand up, the stock of the company shot up several points—as measured by the value of an old shotgun, a saddle and what had once been a buggy, which were traded for half a share.

But the 'lil' horses that did stand up were the exceptions. They were too tired, as a rule, after the tremendous exertion of being born of mothers little larger than themselves, to live for long after they came.

"There's a hoodoo on that horse," remarked Robinson, after an experience of this sort. "I ain't ever heard of anythin' like it. That mare of mine never had a day's sickness in her life—and the colt didn't live for five minutes!"

The Percheron was there still the other day, apparently as much a part of the countryside as anyone else in it, slouching about in the mud as though he had been born to it.

Science and humanitarianism have discovered various ways of dealing with refractory horses, and many and widely advertised are the "cures"; but it is doubtful whether any of them can show better or simpler results than could a couple of hours' acquaintance with the Mackenzie family. Most "tamers" approach a horse delicately, as an intricate problem—or at least, they pretend to. Dick approached horses as a jovial acquaintance, who, while thoroughly understanding and sympathising with their moods, was bent upon showing them how good a thing is virtue.

"Cussed?" he would say. "I'll bet you'd be cussed if you'd had his bringing up. A cayuse that's been treated like a coyote from the time he first had a halter on him's like a kid that's been reared on lickings!"

The first thing, in Dick's system, and the most important, was to convince the animal, both of his own helplessness and Dick's good will. He was not to be spurred or beaten: he was to be put either under a saddle or in a very heavy cart with an "old and patient" horse of three times his own weight and be allowed to try and fight himself loose. Half an hour of this would quiet anything that was not a confirmed "outlaw" when he would be taken out and made much of and turned into the yard for a couple of hours to discuss his experiences with the other horses. Then he would be put in again.

Sometimes the "patient" would have to be tied up to a hitching rack sideways and secured there by a rope passing round his chest and hind legs: that done, he would be left to his own devices for half an hour, when a sack would be placed over his eyes. Jim or Bill would climb cautiously onto his bare back, the rope would be loosened and the sack taken off. The two boys would take turn and turn about, the one who "stuck" the longest getting a quarter of a dollar after each round. Three minutes was the record for very pronounced cases; Jim held it, and Bill, try as he would, was never able to equal it, though he was, as Dick said, the best horseman of the two.

When a horse is five or six years old, of course, he is practically incurable as far as bucking is concerned. He may become a good and useful horse and do his work nobly; he may eat out of your hand and be safe for a child to touch, but he will buck when he feels like it—which is to say, whenever he is given a chance.

One such we had. A little bay, willing and good-tempered, with a mild and affectionate eye, but he could buck himself out of almost any saddle we could put upon him. Hughie, knowing his little ways, would jam his head almost against the horn of the saddle, whilst mounting, and keep him "short" for half an hour afterwards. Once, though, starting from the house, he turned for a moment to catch some message; the next second the reins were pulled out of his hand, the cayuse had got his head away downhill, and that time he bucked until he untied the cinch—untied it! a double knot of hard leather, and deposited his rider, in the saddle, on a heap of rocks.

1. Mrs. Hugh Fraser

2. Hugh C. Fraser, her son, in his British Army uniform.

3. The steamboat "Columbia" idles at the Pateros landing.

4. Frank Witte drives a stagecoach down the east side of the Methow River towards Twisp.

5. A creamery sat above the Methow River near where the Methow Conservancy is today.

6. A bird's-eye view of Winthrop circa 1912.

110

7. Heckendorn family members stand in their canning house, in Heckendorn, which was later incorporated into Winthrop.

8. The Methow Trading Company store in Winthrop was built by Guy Waring in 1904.

9. Two gentlemen stand waist-high in an alfalfa field in the Methow Valley on May 30, 1911.

10. A modest white school house stood on Castle Avenue near today's Shafer Historical Museum.

11. Ethyl Haase, who taught all grades in different locations in the Methow Valley, used a sleigh in winter and a saddle horse in summer.

12. The Duck Brand Saloon, today's Winthrop Town Hall, in 1905.

13. Guy Waring's sawmill operated in Winthrop until 1907.

14. This Winthrop bridge collapsed in February of 1912.

15. Harry Greene, one of the first residents of Winthrop, was Guy Waring's step-son.

16. Farmers used derricks to stack hay in the Methow Valley.

17. Guy Waring, right, was the main founder of the town of Winthrop. The man on the left is unidentified.

Then the little brute trotted back to Mother, who, too horrified to move, had witnessed the feat from the garden gate, and tried to put his muzzle on her shoulder!

As far as sitting a buck—always supposing that the saddle remains to sit in—it is not so difficult as people suppose, once the knack of it has been caught. Everybody knows how perfectly impossible it seems to waltz properly, or even at all, when one is just beginning to learn. Sometimes one will muddle along for months and years, and then, suddenly, one finds oneself dancing well—one has caught the trick of it. It is just the same with bucking. One gets thrown again and again; it seems as though one would never be able to control one's balance as the cayuse's head disappears underneath one and the "see-saw" begins. And then, one morning, one finds oneself swaying backwards and forwards as though on springs, lightly and naturally, one's legs and body working together without a jerk.

"Pitching" is another affair. Nobody can feel thoroughly comfortable on a horse that knows how to pitch and that means it. One has seen men get off after one of these bouts with the blood coming out of their ears. Then there is the "end for end," a mad, dervish-like affair, and the "sunfishering," a rotary movement, with all four legs outspread, which few horses can accomplish successfully. It is the hallmark of the genuine article.

In the Mackenzie family a child was given a horse almost as soon as it had cut its teeth, but Dad kept a sort of sovereignty still over the "kids'" cayuses and had a tiresome way of trading them off without asking their owners' permission. The only one who had managed to keep her own horse was Florence, the youngest, a child with eyes of the loveliest blue I ever saw, and long golden curls that made a halo round her angel face. But Florence was not all angel; three-quarters of her composition consisted of tomboy. Next above her in age was Alice, a real beauty of intensely aristocratic type, tall and slim, with exquisite hands and feet, and a way of holding her head that made one want to call her "your Highness." But Alice was also a child of nature, and in the summer mornings she and Florence used to come regularly up to our gate, and call to me to come and see how fine "Eve" was looking. Eve was the pony, a vicious chestnut, a kicker and bucker if ever there was one, but as docile as a kitten when her little mistresses were astride of her shining back and four small feet were pounding her sides with all their might. They looked so pretty, the two little maids, dressed like boys in blue jean overalls, their hair flying in the sun and wind and their eyes shining like little stars with the sheer joy of living!

Florence would have made her fortune as a trick rider in one of the shows; there was nothing she could not do on or with Eve. One morning, when she was about eight years old, her men folk were lounging round the yard, and Dick, who had just got an offer for the pony from a venturesome drummer, told Florence he thought she had better have a gentler mount—Eve was too much of a handful for her, in his opinion. "Oh, is she?" said Florence. "Come here, Eve!" The cayuse approached and stood waiting. "Put your head down—so—stand still!" Florence turned round, and, reaching up behind her, took a firm hold of Eve's ears, gave a spring, turned a clean somersault backwards over the pony's head and landed astride on its back. Then she slid down, and came and stood before her father with flashing eyes.

"Can you do that, Dad?" she asked.

"Ain't going to try, kid. Guess you can ride Eve, all right," was his reply. They were not demonstrative in that family, but lazy old Dick, leaning up against the fence, with his hands in his pockets, had tears of joy in his eyes as he looked down on this true scion of his horse-breaking race.[91]

Chapter 13

Some Old Citizens and a New One

Two little villages, divided by a road of perhaps half a mile in length, constituted the headquarters of the upper valley.[92] Each had its store, its blacksmith's shop, and its ten or twelve dwelling houses, but the store of one was a big, plate-glass, show-window concern, long and broad and spacious, conducted by the owner of the sawmill, and, in its polish and respectability it shone among its surroundings like a "good deed in a naughty world." The other was more typical of the country. It was large, too, but it was not spacious, and its proprietor, Dick Mackenzie, was the country itself—a nomad, a born horse-trader, a master of the rather complicated dialect of the Slope, with a heart of gold, an hypnotic tongue, and an active and usually perfect understanding of the mind of the person with whom he happened to find himself. For example, coming of a winter's evening into his store, one would find him with half a dozen other men, around the stove, telling yarns that might have melted the snow on the porch, in language which kept his audience—experts themselves—in a continuous tremor of half unwilling admiration—but language to warm your hands by! Talking to us, he contrived a friendly, neighbourly note without the suggestion of any ornamentation, yet his humour never dulled, nor did he ever appear to be putting any kind of restraint upon himself. He would have made a good politician if he had ever turned himself to it, and had it been possible for him to set himself to any serious occupation in life, or to resist the promptings of his heart, and of that sense of humour which could never help laughing and making others laugh at either his dearest friend or his worst enemy, when either came under his eyes.

Dick's gipsy gifts and his talent for horse flesh came from his grandmother, of whom he used to boast, as an Egyptian or Hungarian Princess. His grandfather, he used to say, had been concerned in some rising in Canada and had slid over the frontier in a hay waggon. It was a long story that he used to tell about it, but the details have become rather misty, varying as they did with the condition of Dick's imagination.

The Winter One, finding himself in company with Dick Mackenzie, in the street of the village one Sunday morning, offered in jest to bet him a dollar that he could not trade the next man who crossed the bridge out of the team he was driving, before the latter started home again.

"Trade him out of his team?" said Dick. "Why, say, I'd trade him out of his wife and family if I hadn't got my own."

We moved up to the Bridge road and settled ourselves comfortably, while Dick stared at the river, making a mental inventory of the animals, guns, odds and ends of horses and broken-down waggons and buggies that he had at his disposal.

Presently, from beyond the trees, came the creak and sound of runners and the padding of horses' feet. Dick shifted the tobacco in his mouth and spat reflectively. Nearer and nearer came the sleigh, but neither by word nor movement did Dick betray any interest in its arrival. At the end of the bridge the horses were pulled up into a walk and came towards us, thudding softly. Still Dick did not move, but his eye travelled over the horses, speculatively. They were a team of sorrels, young, sound, of a good weight with more to come.

"Howdy, gentlemen," said the driver as he passed, and we returned the greeting; but not until the waggon was halted and the team tied up near the saloon, did Dick uncurl his legs and drop to the ground.

"You're out a dollar, Dick," the Winter One laughed. "You couldn't trade Jenkins out of that team in a coon's age."

"Not?"

That was all he said, and we slouched up to the hitching rack.

"Well, well," cried the owner of the team, as we came up. "Will you look who's here? Why ain't you workin', Dick?"

Disregarding the allusion to his known dislike of labour, Dick bent a little as though to examine a hock.

"Because God sends you and your friends to save me the trouble," he said presently, stooping still further.

"I'll bet you never found me any labour-savin' device, you old son of," the other retorted with a touch of warmth. "What are you starin' at?"

"I dunnow," replied Dick equably. "There's moments when it looks like a horse, but I dunnow. What would you say it was, Professor?" he addressed the Winter One.

The Winter One refused to be drawn into the argument, though, and the owner of the team laughed.

"You don't see one often enough to know one when you do," he said.

"I see a spavin often enough to know one when I meet one," was the even-tempered retort, and a guffaw from the onlookers who had collected announced the first drawing of blood in the contest.[93]

"Spavin!" The other's face grew red, a fact which Dick noticed with delight. "You don't know a spavin from a can of beans! Spavin!"

"All right." Dick pushed his hands into his pockets. "All right. Don't get mad about it. Maybe it's only a birth-mark. I never seed a birth-mark quite like that, and I don't reckon anybody else ever did—but the world's full of curiosities."

"Down your way it is," the other countered, and the laugh that followed restored his good humour, for a minute later, after winking at the crowd, he continued.

"Want to trade?" he asked.

"I ain't got anything I'd want to trade for either of those. I got a few cayuses—but—" Dick shook his head.

"Come on," said the other, keeping up the joke. "Let's hear about them."

"Well, there ain't anythin' else to do this morning. Jim—Bill!" Dick called without turning his head. "Go down to the barn and bring up anythin' you can find down there."

The boys, who had been waiting close behind their father, on the back of a patient cayuse, were half-way down the road before the sentence was completed.

Dick began as leisurely as ever to walk round the team, only, now, something of proprietorship had crept into his manner. He looked at their mouths, examined their feet, tried their eyes, all without a word. This silence was becoming almost oppressive by the time that the two boys returned, driving a mob of horses before them. These they turned neatly in front of the saloon, when they pulled back and sat like two small, battered sentries on guard, just beyond reach of any straying heel.

Dick closed one eye as he looked the herd over and then turned to the other party.

With Dick's first words, the storekeeper in him took the place of the horse-trader and the same expression of friendly innocence with which he was wont to force upon an unwilling customer something for which he had no possible use, came into his round, red face.

His adversary was not so ready an artist, though, and the presence of the spectators was making him feel both nervous and self-important. He chaffed Dick loudly and addressed the audience in jovial tones, but the audience kept its impassive neutrality. A horse-trade is like a fight between two men. The code forbids any interference from outside. Dick's pleasant good-humour was like a suit of armour against which witticism and innuendo broke themselves to pieces. Bit by bit the other became interested; he saw, or thought he saw, a chance to get three horses for two, three fairly good horses, too—and, perhaps, something "to boot."

Of course the presence of an audience helped Dick enormously, for the other was thinking as much of the figure he was cutting in public, as a trader, as of the trade he was making; and Dick's mind was on the trade only. He knew what the audience thought of him already, and he had the confidence of self-acquaintance. He knew that he was a better judge of a horse than his adversary or than any man present, because he had proved it on better men than they. At the same time, he never lost sight of the possibility of a new customer for his store and he did not want to drive a bargain that would leave any unnecessary ill will behind it.

The end came with a rush, as a man performing a card trick compels him to whom he offers the pack to take the card he wishes him to, without suspecting his own free will in the matter, so Dick forced the three horses he had himself selected upon the other. The Winter One did not know it, of course, neither did the audience know it; least of all did the man with whom he was bargaining know it. Only—when the business was over and the trade completed, did Bill, turning the herd down the road, lean over, as he passed the Winter One, with a grin.

"Dad swore yesterday he'd trade them there off this week!" he whispered. "Whoho!" he yelled aloud and vanished in a spatter of mud and snow.

"You got a good trade," I heard Dick telling his adversary. "There ain't three better cayuses for your work in the country. I'll be a poor man if I keep on like this."

"I suppose I ain't got stung so damned bad," was the complacent reply; and they all went in to bind the bargain in strong waters.

Before night Dick had sold that team for two hundred and twenty-five dollars, coming out of the entire transaction just one hundred and fifteen dollars to the good!

Some Old Citizens and a New One

At about this time quite a crop of new banks sprung up in the woods and crannies of the Cascades. In the eyes of a large part of the population, the bank exists for the single purpose of lending money. In the eyes of the more solid it is a semi-magical institution, and to possess a balance in it is a hall-mark of respectability. There is something to be said for both sides.

We had one bank and, as such nefarious institutions go, it was a very good one.[94] It was small and handy and its officers did really try to serve those with whom they dealt. We knew them, and they, though they probably laughed at us when our backs were turned, were friendly and affable, so that they came to have a definite place in the esteem of the country. With this esteem, to be sure, was mingled something of the suspicion with which necromancers and chemists were regarded in the middle ages, but this was only during office hours. Outside the bank, we knew each other by our first names, and we slapped each other on the back when we met. Even the fact that the officials were all total abstainers was hardly held against them, in view of the mysterious trade in which they were engaged.

Our education in the science of economics came later. It may have been good for us to get an insight into the machinery of money-making, for our ignorance of everything connected with the subject was abysmal. Be that as it may, our education, in the shape of a stout, middle-aged, rather red-faced person with an hypnotic eye and an extremely sociable nature, got off the stage one evening in the beginning of the long, long winter, and examined what was to be seen of the town from the steps of the hotel. He did not move for some time, but stayed there, regarding the shadows and lights upon the snow and the masses of dusky white beyond the river, chewing at an unlighted cigar. When he did move, it was in the direction of the saloon, where he remained for half an hour or more and returned to the hotel in the middle of supper, his face flushed a little, not unnaturally, but as though with the cold—and the hypnotic blue eyes a little brighter.[95]

When he began to talk a close observer might have noticed that he had the "patter" almost too well—but we were not close observers and we listened to him with pleasure, as to one who liked what we liked, and who saw, beneath the outer covering of rock and sage-brush, what we saw. Before supper was over we were talking as freely as he and in the same vein of semi-hilarious optimism.

For a week he wandered about, "looking the country over," as he called it—a phrase of ill omen, not often used in these days, since its deeper meaning has come to be appreciated—and then, at the corner of the street, there sprang up a real estate office, freshly painted, carefully furnished, carpeted and curtained. The town, like all its kind, was spattered with real estate offices already, so that this one did no more than excite a sympathetic respect for the belief in us which had called it into being, and a general stimulus to the flagging enthusiasm of all the other "real estates."

Our new citizen was a "hustler," too; nobody could deny him that. He seemed to be driving about all day long, and his office, now equipped with armchairs, an assistant, an inner sanctum, a typewriter and three telephones, never lacked for company. All visitors seemed to gravitate towards it as to a magnet. It had all the attractions of the saloon and more, for the whisky was of a considerably better quality and cost nothing. He seemed to be transacting real business, too, which was something that none of the rest were doing, and they came from curiosity to see how he managed it.

Time went by. Christmas came and went. Snow fell and melted and fell again. The "bad time" of January and February fell upon us, freezing up every centre of activity except the bank, the saloon and the new real estate office. The first whisper of spring whistled past us and fled northward, the branches of the trees became less distinct as the little woolly buds thickened and spread; the sun gave us a day or two of comparative comfort; carpenters began to get their tools together, farmers to put out their ploughs and horses; the earth to smile again, faintly, but still to smile; and while, like the bears, we were still taking our paws out of our mouths and yawning at the stupendous miracle of the coming of the spring, a new wonder rose up in our midst. The real estate office had become a bank.

"But," complained the officers of the old institution, "there is not room here for two banks."

"There very soon will be," replied the manager of the new one, "because I will make room. In the meanwhile, there are both sides of the street. When you feel me crowding you, let me know."

The speech fitted so well the sentiment of the place, and the *Frühlingslied* of the season,[96] that the objectors could find no adequate reply, and sheared off, laughing rather feebly. In the weeks that followed they took refuge in what Thackeray calls "the impregnable fortress of Donkeradam," contenting themselves with shoulder shruggings and dark sayings and veiled—but not too veiled—hints both of their estimate of those intelligences that were ready to risk their money in such hands, and of the treatment which they would receive when they returned in the near future to the bank of their fathers.

But the new bank and its office force laughed when these things were brought to their ears.

"You'd think they hated to see the place develop," said the genial one. "They've got into the habit of thinking of it as their own little private possession—and that threatening stuff isn't business! But there, what the hell do they know about business? Come on over the way and paint your noses!"

Here, said his supporters, was a man! He had not got any measley notions about whisky and he was free with his money, too. He did not put a man through any degrading "third degree" every time he wanted to borrow a couple of dollars; no, he took him on his face and let it go at that!

He was free, too: incidentally he was a delightful companion with a heart as big as a house, and a fund of anecdote which helped to pass many a long evening, when he came up the Valley to drum up trade. We liked him enormously; for he never failed to bring a laugh with him and he had a knack of getting inside of one and finding room for himself there as he had, in Twisp, for his bank.

It was a rich year that he had happened upon for his entrance and he made the most of it. "Anything that's got money in it is my business," was his motto. He had a finger in every financial pie in the place—always excepting the old bank, and even they seemed to be getting accustomed to his presence and smiled at him when they met. In truth, he had shaken the place up, and there was more going on in the town, on the land and in the forests than ever. He sowed promiscuously, of course, but some of his seed fell upon good ground and crops came up in barren places that had never seen them until then.

And his joviality grew and grew with his girth. That was his danger —the joviality, not the girth—and though he recognised it, he took no great pains to guard against it. His wife—for he had settled down among us, by now—began to wear that look of harried expectation which clergymen and workers in the tenement districts know so well, and seldom was he absent from his place at "second-drink time" in the saloon of his choice. But, in spite of that, he throve, and by the time the winter descended from Canada he was as much a part of the scenery as the hills themselves.

The winter wore through like all its predecessors, and it was well into the summer when the first distant sounds of the war that was raging beyond the Rockies came to our ears.[97] Having no acquaintance whatever with the fifteenth-century machinery of our national finance, these puffs of wind conveyed no message to us. We read the papers, and nodded, and pitied the inhabitants of the stricken East, as a people fast in the hand of an unscrupulous tyranny, whose machinations they had neither the wits nor the courage to resist. Perhaps we were not so very far out in our estimation. However that may be, we pitied them. As for ourselves, the crops would come up and the calves would grow, the cows would give milk and the forests lumber. The bickering and squabbling of the streets could not affect us.

The genial one "hustled" as hard as ever. Credit still seemed to be good—in his bank, at least—and with the smell of the freshly turned earth in our nostrils and the ploughing wind in our ears, we faced the year with even minds and unworried hearts.

Of course the whole story is familiar enough now, and the wonder is that it seemed so inexplicable then. It was the old, old thing, the hoary old cause of almost every financial fever that has ever attacked the country. We were all "over-extended"; it was not prosperity that we had been enjoying for the previous three or four years; it had been a debauch. We had been on a colossal "spree"; values of all sorts had climbed like the mercury of a thermometer in boiling water; in our cups we had looked upon these values as representing actual cash, whereas they represented nothing more than a tipsy dream. Then the spirit, already weakened by excess, was released from reason entirely, and the cowardly terror which we call panic seized us for its own.

As for the people of the Slope, they reverted to little children, trembling in the dark. Of the nature of the visitation they knew nothing; all that they did know was that money had ceased to circulate, that credit had fled, that old loans, which had become family friends, were suddenly called in and that even such cash as they had in the banks was locked up out of reach and that the key was lost.

The genial one's loans were of a general nature that defied collection. They had taken the shape of horses and machinery and teams and cattle and they refused flatly to change themselves into cash again. Then it was that, with his back to the wall, he began to juggle, and wonderfully did he keep his leaden dollars in the air. They came down to the ground eventually and everybody heard their fall and knew them for lead; but though he never got it, he deserved the greatest credit for his courage and ingenuity, and more gratitude than he ever got, too, for his great-hearted kindness to his fellow-men. He picked up every cent in the end, and we all have a very warm place for him in our memories.

Chapter 14

Feuds—Indigenous and Imported

The families around us were all so intermarried with one another that everybody, as it seemed, was related to everybody else. The Mackenzies, of whom Dick once said that they were a tribe and ought to have blankets issued to them like the Indians, numbered, at one time, thirty-five boys and girls, besides the grown-ups. There were six brothers, with their families; Dick's wife's two sisters and their families, and a sprinkling of cousins whom it would have been difficult to trace.

The wife of Dick, the chief of the clan, had a sister whose husband possessed a rather fantastic property, which he called a farm, on the very top of the hill at whose base we lived ourselves, and her we came to know better than most.[98] Her husband, known as A. C., was a most kind and happy-natured man, who had grown a little sad in the process of attempting to keep himself happy; but they were devoted to each other and rubbed along with no troubles except such as came to them from without. He made little attempt to farm his peak, but, instead, freighted the year through, which is a more philosophic and less jerky business. Besides all the other relations, the mother of two of the Mackenzie wives lived at the turn of the road, with her second husband, who was called "Dave" by everybody, and who was supposed to be something of a capitalist, for he owned the little house and garden in which they lived, as well as several "buildings" in the village.[99] He looked like a fat old New England pirate, chin whiskers and all, and, by the same token, he walked like one, though he always swore that he had never been to sea.

It was a clan bound up in itself, with its own politics, its own points of view, its own government and its own laws. Its members were always ready to discuss each other and they were seldom at peace. Yet, at a pinch, they would stand together and bear one another's burdens joyfully. As a clan they were at war with pretty nearly everybody, but as individuals they had many friends.

"Great oaks from little acorns grow," and one of the most expensive quarrels that our friend, A. C., brother-in-law to six Mackenzies, ever got himself into, arose from a little acorn—or rather two of them, called Helen and Frances, the step-grandchildren of the Lord of the Manor. It began with a piano, purchased by the father of Helen and Frances, upon that elusive instalment plan with which we are all so well acquainted.[100] The piano had been wandering about in the neighbourhood for years before it found a temporary abiding place in his house, and he, mightily pleased by the presence of it, determined to have the two girls taught to play. Their mother—a dear, well-educated little woman—was only too glad that the children should acquire some civilised taste, and a music mistress was engaged—the wife of the school teacher, as we remember.

Helen and Frances became swollen with self-importance, and, two days later, squinting with pride, they ran into A. C.'s daughter, Saidie, coming out of school.

"We've got a piano in our house," said Helen vauntingly, "and we're taking lessons."

"What in?" asked Saidie, looking at Helen's rather patched little face, "spots?"

"You haven't got a piano," retorted Helen, "and those ain't spots I got on my face—I fell on it."

"I don't wonder," remarked Saidie, "I'd do the same in your place."

"You haven't got a piano," shrieked Frances. "You can't get one, either—you're too poor—you're too poor!" she chanted, and Helen joined her. "You're too poor!" they chanted together, "poor! poor! much too poor!"

After an ineffectual chase, Saidie went home and appeared before her mother bathed in tears. The horrible taunt had gone home and, flinging herself upon her father, she sobbed out the whole story. A. C. listened, smoking.

"It's a fact, honey," he said apologetically. "Maybe if you had a better Pop, you'd be able to have a piano—but I'm all there is. Come to that, Harry's no better off than I am. He ain't as well off, but that don't help, do it?"

Louise ground her teeth, and said dark things of what she would do to the "little cusses," if she met them, but Saidie was inconsolable.

The next day she found the two sisters lying in wait for her, but in their excitement they neglected to take any precautions, so that Saidie, who was a well-built child, got a fleeting revenge by sending them back to their mother in tatters and with angry finger-prints on their faces.

This, of course, brought the mothers into the business, but the fathers still remained aloof. A. C. was busy, and Harry was in that condition which, with him, was an equivalent for it. It would not have taken much, otherwise, to start a fair-sized feud, for all A. C.'s easy-going temper. Atmospherical influences will affect the happiest-natured after a while.

Saidie, by this time, was immersed in pianos. She spoke of nothing else, and she thought of nothing else. She caught a cold, too, and lay in bed, chattering about pianos 'til it was pitiful to listen to her.

One of these waves must have travelled out of A. C.'s cabin door, up on the top of the hill, and must have hunted about until it reached the sensitised wireless station that was the piano agent's mind, sixty miles away, down by the river, for he hitched up his team and started up the valley, three weeks before his usual time. They call it "having a hunch" in our part of the world.

Then the mother of Helen and Frances told her little girls—calling from the house to the road below—to keep out of the way of Saidie and her brother, adding that they were little savages and no proper associates for "nice little girls." Saidie's brother brought the story home with him in the evening, and at midday, next day, who should appear at the door but the piano agent with a "line of talk" that would have held a steer.

The piano agent was cordial, sympathetic and explanatory, by turns. He was of the "Common People"—with capitals—and there was nothing that gave him such real joy—such satisfaction—such a healthy pleasure in his business—as to place a first-class instrument in the homes of his kind. That was what he lived for.

"That little girl," he said tenderly, "She's a good girl—she works hard—she ought to have a piano. She deserves a piano!"

He patted her head and waited for the poison to work.

"I can put a splendid instrument in for three hundred and fifty dollars," he murmured. "Pay as you can—every month—or every six months. We'll give you a square deal and treat you right."

Of course he got the order. If they had only known it, he had done that as soon as he had opened the door. Then he went down the hill on another piece of business—to the house of Helen and Frances, whose papa had not been keeping up the payments.

Had he whispered the news to Saidie's people, they would have been amply satisfied, and he could not have sold them a mouth organ. They wanted revenge—not music.

A week later, the same original piano, tuned and polished, was hauled up the hill and settled in its new abode. By this time Saidie had heard of the fate of the other children's piano, and she crowed. But not to them. Her revenge went much deeper than that. No, she sympathised with them and offered them hers to play upon if they cared to walk up the hill. She did it every time that she met them, too.

Then she got a music teacher, but the latter refused to climb the hill, and, having nowhere to put her own piano, lent it to the mother of Helen and Frances, so that Saidie found herself obliged to go to that hated place for her lessons. She would pass our house sobbing; for the two little friends had turned the tables on her completely now. She did not know a single note of music, and they were quite clever, both of them; so they would sit close by while she banged with her tired little fingers, and giggle at her—imitating her on the window sill. In a week Saidie was sick of the word piano, and A. C., working double tides, had three hundred and fifty dollars to pay—for, having bought it, he felt obliged to live up to the contract. He was not going to allow his wife to suffer the indignity of having it taken away; but he insisted upon Saidie's keeping up her music lessons, whether she liked them or not.

There are no such people for feuds as the Southwesterners. One entire community had emigrated to our part of the world from Texas, and, though they all travelled together across country for months and camped together and lived together, sharing everything, they brought their quarrels with them, as fruit trees are transplanted, with their roots wrapped up and hidden.

A typical Texan was old Mrs. Tiler—locally known as "old lady Tiler," the title of "lady" being conferred on all women of a certain age.[101] It sounded queer at first, but one grew rather to like it afterwards. It was the one outward mark of a deference to age, long since departed. A scion of a certain family, whose feud with the Tilers was of this evergreen type, fell ill. He had married a nice girl, but he himself was not a prepossessing person and there were grounds in his case for the old lady's dislike, as there always were for her judgments of people, since she was generous, charitable and just. To certain things—certain and, it is to be hoped, purely local—ways of treating women, one became, alas! accustomed, and though one did not condone them, they ceased to strike one very vividly. It was a mental attitude, and nothing could eradicate it; but in this young man it had become something worse, a fixed determination to do no single thing that he could help on his own account, and nothing whatever on hers. An hour before she had her first baby, she had to go down to the distant spring and carry back two buckets of water, while he sat on the porch and watched her!

He lived at some distance from the town, and when the news reached old lady Tiler that he had had a bad accident, hauling logs, nothing that anyone could say would prevent her going immediately to his assistance. It was pointed out to her that there were younger women a-plenty, but she tossed on her old black bonnet and drove off with her old white horse.

"That poor girl—'tisn't him or his ornery bones that I care about!" she exclaimed, "it's that helpless child of a wife he's got! She ain't fit to be left alone at any time."

The evening was well along by the time that she started and, though the doctor had been telephoned for, he was not to be found. He had many interests, good man, medical, agricultural and mineral—he was miles away. For hours the messenger sought him, and, at last, ran into him on the road as he was passing a house, after midnight, twenty-five miles off, with a tired horse and a tired body.

The old lady, in the meanwhile, had sent the weeping wife to bed, telling her that she made her nervous, and that she would want her strength in the morning. The decks cleared, she had cooked the patient a meal, washed up everything that she could find, swept the place out and then set herself to keeping the son of her enemy comfortable until help could arrive. He really was in rather a bad way and, though she would never acknowledge it, she was truly sorry for him. At last, towards four in the morning, the doctor came up, on a staggering horse, and the two of them set about the serious business of bone-setting and wound-dressing in earnest.

It was long after sunrise before they had finished, and the old lady, after feeding the doctor, went outside for a breath of air. She did not stay very long, though. "That horse of yours, Doc," she said from the door. "He's just about all in."

The doctor was fearfully distressed, but he had a reserve of strength within him, and he made no wail.

"It was in a good cause," he said. "He was a good horse—but we've all got to go, sometime—and it was in a good cause!"

She shook her head dubiously, and looked at the sufferer with a calculating eye.

"Maybe, Doc," she remarked after a while. "Maybe! I'm glad you think so—but if you was to ask me, I should say you'd killed a hundred-dollar horse for a ten-dollar man!"

We had spasmodic fits of morality (generally in the late autumn, after the crops were in), and though they occurred with a fair regularity, seldom took the same form two years running. One year it would be temperance—as that battered word is understood in the States. Another year, religion—of the Camp Meeting, come-and-be-saved, type; in another year it might take the shape of a hygiene campaign, but this latter was not of universal interest and rarely lasted into the snow. The "Temperance" movement, on the other hand, was always a popular one and generally kept us amused until the spring.

There were grounds for a movement; no one could possibly deny that. But the form which the movement took invariably led it into a blind alley before long, out of which it could never find its way.

So it was with us. The "cold water" army hurled itself on to the attack without the faintest idea of whither it was bound, and the noise of battle spread even to Olympia, the State Capital. Now it was perfectly true that several of the saloons were quite impossible, and that the sins of at least two of them cried aloud for retribution. We, the moderates, were quite ready to undertake the business of reform, and we had a little campaign of our own arranged which would have prevented sinners from getting their licenses renewed; but we gave no hint of this to the other "Reformers," because we knew that they would insist upon taking a hand in it and thereby ruin our chances before we could get a fair start. Our intention was to make such an example of the worst offenders as would leave a permanent impression upon the entire brotherhood, and insure to a tired man who had done an honest day's work, an honest stimulant when he wanted one. We began quietly among ourselves by inaugurating a "no-treating" league, which hit at the root of the trouble. We agreed, for the space of one year, never either to offer a drink to another, except for the most urgent reasons, or to accept the offer of one. We gathered together over a hundred and fifty men in this league. We then decided to send a memorial to the County Commissioners, praying them, in the interests of good order, to send over a representative who would take some evidence of the manner in which the offenders were conducting their places of business, and we mutually promised to stand by one another in the event of "trouble," from the offenders' friends and hangers-on, of which we anticipated plenty. They always have friends, and, since these are usually drawn from that element which has nothing to lose, they can be troublesome enough when their supply of free alcohol is cut off.

We continued to gather into this elastic and informal association most of the really influential men of the valley, and by "influential" is meant those who had a personal influence over others. Not the rich and stiff-necked, but men who worked with and beside other men and whom those other men respected personally and for purely personal reasons. Freighters, ranchmen, a stockman or two, one storekeeper, and two or three lumbermen. We steered carefully clear of the extremists, for we were attempting, to the best of our ability, to deal personally with a condition, and not to tinker temporarily with individuals.

But, alas! the volcanic forces under the direction of one individual, who went by the name of Brother B, broke out, just as we had got our petition ready and the very friendly commissioners were half pledged to grant our request. We, fearful of spoiling what still promised to be an effective move, retired, until the ground should be clear enough to allow of our maneuvering to some effect.

Brother B opened his campaign by visiting three saloon keepers with whom he was anxious to avoid quarrelling, and begging them to close their establishments on the following Sunday, so that he could capture the fourth, whose place would certainly be open, red-handed. The only result of this ingenuous policy was a roar of laughter from the profane, and the creation of a good deal of vicious sympathy for the intended victim. Perceiving this, Brother B set himself to combat it by speech-making and letter writing, in the course of which he accused by name several perfectly innocent people of fighting against what he was pleased to call decency, for the sake of their own depraved appetites—thereby adding a number of permanent members to the "For-the-love-of-Mike-give-it-a-rest" club—and he wound up by attacking the commissioners for letting such places remain in existence. Then, having done his best to hand over our last few rounds of ammunition to the enemy, he departed, vowing to start a prohibition fight at the earliest possible opportunity, thus driving us completely out of the field for the time being.

We had to wait six months before we "went after" our men again, but when we did we settled the affair swiftly and speedily. We ousted one, but Brother B's efforts were a bar to ousting the other. Still, we tamed him. He does not poison his whisky, nor empty pockets any more, nor does he sell liquor to Indians or children, so we did some good.

When the "reform" agitators began to show their teeth in earnest, and the miasma of a professional "Temperance" crept over our smiling country, its orators preaching the gospel of mush and water, at a settled rate per hour and those queer, but also well-paid adventurers, who call themselves Evangelists and who haunt the skirts of these hand-made epidemics, began to appear in the river towns, we of the upper reaches resolved to entrench ourselves behind one of the very few rights we had left, the right to call our souls our own if there were enough of us in one place to allow of its being incorporated as a town.

Our county had "gone dry."[102] That is to say, that the sale of liquor was prohibited outside the limits of incorporated towns, which still retained the right to judge for themselves on this important subject. To attain to that dignity and freedom it is necessary to show a population of six hundred souls, and Twisp, the metropolis of our sixty miles of Valley, had, so far, fallen short of furnishing the required number, even when all the land for two miles around was included in the count. However, it was the only place that seemed to offer a possible defense against cold-water tyranny, and we resolved to try for incorporation. The sympathy of the county authorities we had, in plenty, for what it might be worth, so we took stock.

The first count left us "shy" by something like two hundred, and we scratched our heads. We had no slightest objection to inventing names, but if, in the biliousness of defeat, some evil-eyed reformer should get it into his head to examine the paper—no, that was a risk. We did not want our Charter revoked.

"There's quite a few inhabitants comes to school every day," suggested one of the committee. "And if they ain't old enough to vote now, they soon will be. They got names, just the same, though, and that's all we want right now."

We began by taking those who were in their teens, but we ended by taking all—the last few petitioners, indeed, were hardly born, and one was only expected—but at that we were still fifty or sixty names short.

"Oh thunder!" said one, in desperation. "Throw in the cayuses—there must be sixty cayuses in town, and if there ain't, I'll swear there's sixty hens, anyway. Nobody's goin' to ask any fool questions—if they do, we'll ride them out of town on a rail!"

We took his advice. The emergency was our excuse, and we were at no great pains to keep silence about it. Our petition was blandly and instantly granted; the only hint we received of the authorities' amusement at our methods being the return of the document, as though by accident. We had the liveryman elected Mayor, and a properly sworn Council in office, within forty-eight hours.

When the "wet and dry" election came round we "went wet" by something over four hundred and fifty, and we had the intense satisfaction of reading what the "drys" thought of us, in heavily marked journals which somebody with plenty of time on his hands addressed to each of us individually.

Chapter 15

Progress—By Leaps and Bounds!

When Cortes, the Spanish conqueror, wrote home to his government, asking for colonists for South America, he said, "Only two exceptions I make. Send me neither Doctors nor Lawyers. I will not have them." Cortes had studied human nature. In the absence of lawyers and other lethal weapons, quarrelling is at the best little more than a pastime.

We had peace—not so stagnant as to be uninteresting, but still, peace—in our little township, until the lethal weapon already mentioned, in the shape of a qualified attorney, arrived in our midst, one winter's night just before Christmas.[103]

His terminus was the saloon. From the saloon, he wandered across to the post-office, when, having come for the mail of the house, we saw him for the first time. He was addressing a crowd of frightened but fascinated children on the subject of the season and the birth of their Redeemer, distributing nickels and peanuts all around himself as he spoke. His eye was glazed, but his voice was cheerful and he was inviting all the world to "loosen up" and "unbuckle." The dozen or so men and women who were standing around were much too well accustomed to sights of that sort to do more than smile at each other, but to the sounds they were not so used. Perhaps three of them may have been baptised, but the probabilities were that none of them had ever so much as heard of baptism.

The postmaster glared at him, and the postmaster's wife—who came from Kansas—sniffed at him. "Of course," she said to a woman near her, "out here in the West, everybody just laughs—but I assure you, Mrs.____, that back home in the East they wouldn't tolerate such a degrading spectacle for one minute!"

"Oh well," the other replied, pulling her shawl back from her head, "it isn't the poor man's fault."

"What isn't?" echoed the Kansas lady in a scandalised voice; "then whose is it, I'd like to know?"

"When men get up in front of a bar," her more tolerant sister explained, "this weather, fust it's one, then another—they get to treating each other," she waved vaguely. "They work hard—and it's like enough the only fun they ever get. It's a good man's fault, anyway!" she added.

Having concluded our business, we escaped. A day or two passed before we heard of him again, and then we learned that a cabin and few acres had been wished upon him by an enterprising real estate company, which had him in, and his money out, before he was more than indistinctly aware of the name of the place in which he found himself. It was what was known as a "relinquishment" that they sold him, if one can use the word "sold" in connection with the transaction at all. This, roughly speaking, means that a man, having taken up land, and having lived on it for some of the time required by law for possession, sells the rights he has acquired.

The real estate firm, having settled him in, would probably have forgotten all about him, had he not kept himself in their minds by ways of his own, and by the fact—every day more apparent to the entire community—that he was making towards delirium tremens. For a man who puts his back into the business, as he was doing, that race is never a very long one, and when, on one January afternoon, the elderly "old-timer," who had been induced to live with him as a precautionary measure, came shambling into the village, talking to himself until his three or four remaining teeth rattled like castanets, we were ready for his news—in fact, the experts had been waiting for it for a week past.

It took some little time to extract the details from him. What had happened? Uncurling himself from the barrel on which he had been sitting, he spat, and crossed the road to the more genial atmosphere of the saloon. Here he calmed down for a while and then suddenly flared up again; once more he relapsed into silence, and then, with a double-barrelled curse, broke out into a cackle of laughter.

After that he unburdened himself of his experiences.

He had been sitting, he said, looking out of the window—while his companion stood by the door. No, he had not said a blanked word to him—he had not even looked at him—when, just as he got up to see to the fire, the former pushed him aside and dived for his rifle, and the next thing he knew he was running through the snow to the accompaniment of a magazineful of thirty-thirties, the last of which had passed him just as he hit the road.

Hearing this from the old-timer, a group decided to visit the attorney. No sooner had the visitors come within sight of the cabin than its inhabitant, who by now had barricaded himself in, opened fire on them through the windows, and though his shooting was wild, it was close enough to send them back whence they had come, in something of a hurry.

They wasted no time in telephoning for the deputy Sheriff. We knew our deputy Sheriff, we had elected him ourselves. It was not, at that time, the brave and genial Charlie, but an older man, well-meaning, but rather too fond of himself, to our way of thinking.[104] Not that he had anything solid to boast of, or that he did any audible boasting, but he gave the impression of a settled and rather lofty conviction of the mental and moral distance between himself and the rest of his surroundings. He had an air which said as plainly as any words: "I do not often unbend, so you may consider yourself considerably flattered by my good-natured toleration of you!" He had a fierce face, too—which was also acquired.

The sun was drooping to the West when the guardian of the law arrived, and tied his pony to the hitching-rack. His mackinaw coat seemed to bulge a good deal as he came up the steps of the saloon, and we noticed a very business-like-looking Winchester on the side of his saddle. His features were stern, and we waited, hugging ourselves, 'til he stamped in and looked about him.

"Where is he?" he asked, looking round as though he expected us to produce him.

"Just where he was," the old-timer mumbled gleefully, "just exactly where he was!"

"Where he was?" the Sheriff repeated angrily; "where's that?"

"In his cabin—you just cross the bridge and take the river trail and keep right on 'til you get fired on. You can't miss it," the old-timer chirruped.

The Sheriff hunched his shoulders.

"Well," he said briskly. "I reckon we might as well get finished with it. We don't want to waste no time."

"You can't get him any too quick for us," another agreed. "Have a drink before you start"

The Sheriff drank, but his eye was troubled.

"Now," he said, wiping his lips, "which of you boys is coming? Let's be getting along."

Nobody answered, and presently the old-timer spat at the stove. "Hell!" he exclaimed, "there's only one of him!" He was enjoying himself thoroughly now, since, on account of his age, he could not possibly be dragged into the mess.

"But—ain't any of you boys goin' to help?" asked the Sheriff. "It's gettin' dark."

"It is," spoke up one, "and some of us has got to get home over that trail while the light lasts. What's keeping you?"

The Sheriff shook his head unbelievingly.

"I wouldn't have believed it!" he exclaimed. "Not if anyone had told it to me! If anyone had said that—"

"Nor wouldn't I!" said an onlooker. "You mean to say you want a posse to gather in that thing, do you? Oh, come on, fellows," he said, turning to the others. "Let's go and get him for him."

In response to this invitation, half a dozen wrapped themselves up and unwillingly followed the speaker outside.

"Anybody got a good rope?" he asked. "We'll take that buggy; we'll need it to bring him back in."

The Sheriff, feeling that he was losing his place in the picture, offered his guns, saying that he had a rifle himself, but the offer was rejected—kindly, but not without a little mirth.

"A good rope's all we want," said one. "I'll bet he's asleep by now, and if he's got the horrors good, he'll be as harmless as a calf. I've handled fellows with the horrors before this!—Shoot? Man, he couldn't hit a farm the way he is now—if he was to aim at it!"

An hour after the buggy returned, and a howling thing wrapped up in a blanket was tied to the seat.

"Give him a drink," said one. "It'll quiet him. It's an awful mean thing to have—and we got to get him to Twisp."

They gave him four, pulling his head back and pouring them into his mouth, after which they got under way and disappeared into the murk.

The winter was being smiled out of existence and the world was turning and murmuring in its sleep. The cattle looked up at one with genial joviality as one rode past them through the bunch grass, and a stray lark or two found courage to sing its matins and even-song. It was only another spring to us; but it was the most splendid and noteworthy event in the minds of the birds and beasts.

It was a good spring that year, and, as it opened its hands wider and wider, the familiar sounds of hammer and nail and saw rattled through the clouds of ploughing dust like small-arms fire. The place hummed with affairs. The little local paper delivered its annual address upon the probabilities of a railroad invading us, and recorded joyfully the "sales" and "real estate transactions" of the day. One read that so and so had disposed of his holdings in town lots, for prices that made one blink, until one saw that "the beautiful town dwelling of Mr. (the other party to the deal) in Twisp entered into the deal," when one smiled again, the "town house" being an old friend. But though one might smile at their "sales" oneself, in public one nodded as gravely as any, for these things were taken as seriously as the Gospels—in fact much more seriously—by the neighbours.

One evening in that delicate season that flits between spring and summer, the Winter One was once more walking home from the post-office, when a horse trotted up beside him and a cheerful but modulated voice hailed him.

It was the Justice of the Peace—and the modulation was a compliment not to the Winter One himself, but to his women kind, and, also, to the office which the J. P. was holding. He was schooling himself, in response to suggestions, tactfully given, by the "Comrade," that a person in his responsible position, with a grown-up daughter and a growing boy, not to mention a district of that size to preside over—a prominent citizen, in fact, of his calibre—should be an example socially to the country side.

"Well, well, well," he said, clapping the Winter One on the back, "and how's things?"

"Fine, fine as silk. How's the world treating you, Judge?" replied the latter.

The horseman's face twitched with pride and pleasure—he had not been elected long and his honours still lay heavily upon him.

"I haven't a kick coming," he laughed. "It's treating me as well as I'm treating it. Breaking even, breaking even! Say," he stooped a little and spoke confidentially, "say, have you heard?"

"Heard what?"

"He's back. Yes, sir, he got off the stage at the hotel!"

"Who's he, Judge?"

"The lawyer fellow, the one that got took to Medicine Lake last fall. You remember, don't you?"[105]

"Come back?" The Winter One stopped in the road and stared up his amazement. "That man—come back here?"

The J. P. nodded, and a look, half of amusement, half of approval, came into his bristled face.

"He's certainly got his nerve with him," he blinked. "What do you reckon he means to do, now he's got here?"

"Maybe he's going to open an office—ought to be quite a help to you, Judge!" the Winter One jested.

The other nodded. He seemed to have something on his mind, and the Winter One waited for it to come out.

"Maybe," he pushed back his hat, "maybe he ain't such a bad sort of a cuss—when he's on the water-waggon."

"Why, yes—no reason on earth he shouldn't be as good as they're made. It's a narrow place to sit, though—and a mighty rough road."

"He just needs a grip—eh?" the J. P. laughed again, but rather nervously. "Say," he went on in a lowered voice, as though afraid of being overheard. "It won't do any harm to help him catch a hold, will it—not a damn bit of harm. It ain't as though none of us had ever had a jag—we've all been there."

"Not quite there—glory be! But of course we'll do anything we can. Will it help him any to have him up to the house sometimes?"

"That's just what I was a-coming to," he said joyously. "Talk to him—give him something to hitch his mind to—he's an educated fellow and a mighty bright one. I got talking to some of the boys after I seen him get off the stage and they'll do their piece. You speak to him when you see him, will you? I tell you a man's got to have something to him to be able to come back to a place where he's cut up once in that style. Goodnight," he cried, as he cantered off. "Give my love to the ladies!" he called over his shoulder.

So contagious is the force of a charitable idea, enthusiastically undertaken, that, in a short time, the object of the J. P.'s sympathy became the fashion, and man and woman, warmed by the heart fire of a kindly deed, and anxious to be "in the movement," fairly swamped the man under their beneficence. He was a welcome incident in the early summer, and we watched the development of the man who had crept out of the shell of the hopeless "case," with interest.

We had not much "law business" because, until his arrival, we had never appreciated the extreme easiness of the process known as "going to law." Even now, though we felt a natural conceit at having a full-fledged attorney among us, we preferred to look at him, rather than employ him. He was like the parlour china—a thing to boast of and to contemplate, but not to touch. Nor did he invite us to use his professional services; but when a question of one man's right to another man's consideration arose, he would give an opinion offhand and with a smile.

It was not long before the more advanced members of the community began to speak, without any seeming awe or hesitation at all, of the chances of certain long-standing issues which they would "take into court if something wasn't done about it." The leaven was working. A month later, the printing press of a long dead rival to the local paper was bought by the real estate company and set up with a flare of trumpets in the "Eagle Building," which consisted of half a former hotel, no longer usable as a living place owing to age and insects, and which had been split into pieces and distributed over the northern end of the village. Contemporaneously with the birth of the newspaper, a "Commercial Club" was formed, with the lawyer for a president, and our spring "land boom," which had been delayed by these preparations, came out like a giant refreshed with wine.

Chapter 16

A Prosperous Season

We were coming into our own, the earth smiled upon us, and upon this current of cheer and well-being we were borne into summer.

Now the apartment which our friend the lawyer had selected for a legal office had passed through many hands and vicissitudes. It had been, as we have said, an hotel; but it had also been a schoolhouse, and, at one time in the dim past, a saloon.

The Paper's first appearance came with the ripening of the corn.[106] It was the most deliciously intimate journal that we have ever beheld. A whole page was devoted to correspondence, another to our doings. It was starred with advertisements from the stores, who had no need of advertising. It was all about ourselves, in fact, and concerned itself with nothing and nobody outside of our acquaintance.

In the natural course of things it fell foul of the other journal, which was edited in Twisp some ten miles away, and we would not have had it do otherwise.[107] The latter referred contemptuously to it as the "leaflet" of the real estate company, and spoke of the "squeak which we received Monday from the 'Eagle.'" The "Eagle," in reply, started a guessing competition, with an old saddle for a prize, on the origin of the other paper's name. "Why," it asked, "is it called the 'News'?"

After a month or so the two papers really warmed up to their work. I arrived at the office one morning just in time to tear from our fiery editor's hand a challenge in due form—"shooting to kill"—which he was posting to his rival down the Valley. An armed peace was preserved for a few weeks, but alas, all good things must come to an end, and though our little lawyer carried us well over into the New Year with interest, he was approaching the top of the hill of his self-control by September. It was absolutely impossible for him to get anything stronger than lemonade in the saloon, or in Twisp, and, becoming possessed by pity for himself, he began to recount his dreadful experiences in the columns of the "Eagle" as a warning to his readers, and as an appeal—though he made no mention of this—for sympathy.

The owners of the sheet—up to now his firmest supporters—deprecated these articles as being both foreign to the spirit of the paper and infernally depressing, besides. For three numbers they ceased, and then, in extra-large print, came a leading article dealing with "the Demon Rum," in a familiar but very lurid fashion.

The owners—the real estate firm—shrugged their shoulders and tried to appear unconcerned, but the cold-water element of the place raised a paean of joy. This was what they had waited for all these years, they wrote. On with the good work! Let the scoffers scoff and the unregenerate grind their teeth—forward!

This mention of the "unregenerate," of course, referred to the real estate company, and all their friends—for the "better element" seemed to include everybody who did not approve of them or of their habits. It took a day for this to sink into the owners' minds, and an hour more was needed for them to appreciate the fact that they were under a contract to pay the man for editing abuse of themselves, in their own paper, for twelve months to come. They did not expostulate, this time: they walked up to the "Eagle Building" in a body, and informed the Editor that they were not running and didn't propose to run a temperance tract, that the "Eagle" was their property and that he could either behave himself or get out. He said nothing, but sat staring at them, until their nerves gave way under his eyes and they left him alone, slamming the door behind them.

"That'll hold him for a bit," said one as they made back to their committee room in the saloon.

"And if he gets fresh in the next number," remarked another, "we'll take the son of a—she wolf and heave him! Contract? Hell, ain't we got one, too? He was to edit the paper for us, wasn't he? For us!—not for a sore-eyed—" Words failed the speaker when it came to describing the water drinkers, and he growled in his beard.

The lawyer was suspiciously quiet and polite for the remainder of the week, and when Friday came, it was generally agreed that he had taken his medicine, and that the next day would see the authority of his employers fully restored.[108]

We must turn for a moment to the mirror of complete respectability—too far removed, as yet, from the stir of this ruffle to do aught but smile at the antics of the combatants—the Bostonised, Harvardised Owner of the sawmill and the larger of the two stores in the town. It was generally understood that he owned also, either for himself or for others, a large share in the saloon, and this was the general reason given for its really excellent liquor and still more excellent conduct. It was a model, and, since there was an obvious need of the institution, it was unanimously admitted that it was lucky for all that it was in such good hands.[109]

That year the County Commissioners had taken it into their heads that the licenses of the saloons were altogether too cheap, and they had, consequently, raised them by two hundred dollars. The Lord of the Manor had refused to recognise the right of the commissioners to this added two hundred dollars, because, as he said, the notices had not been sent out until after the first of January. So, with a letter of protest, he had forwarded the amount of the old license, and was still waiting for an answer from the commissioners, who had, by now, forgotten all about it,—when the Friday alluded to arrived.

The "Eagle" was not due to appear before nightfall; so such of us as were interested in the proceedings waited in the saloon or the post-office until the boy—the sole medium of communication with the editor's office—brought the bundle down for distribution.

The Winter One opened his paper with pleasurable anticipation, which was amply justified by the first words that met his eye. One short sentence, printed in red and black, entirely filled the top half of the first page. "Booze champions, beware!" And below it, in an article crammed with italicisations and exclamation marks, the editor informed his supporters that their own champion had taken heart from their kind encouragement and was about to start in a crusade against all the Rum Shops within reach, beginning on the one which now defaced their beautiful city, and which was, at that moment, being conducted, without even the vicious formality of a license, by the Lord of the Manor—whom he named—and the bartender—whom he named several times. He would start proceedings at the earliest possible moment, and he would see justice done upon the offenders if it was the last thing he ever did!

Without waiting to read any more, the Winter One tucked the paper into the pocket of his mackinaw for the entertainment of his evening, and made his way to the Lord of the Manor's office in the gloomy, half-lit depths of his cavernous store. Silence deep and unbroken was upon the place, and, gliding between boxes and counters and saddlery, he sat himself down upon a convenient packing-case and waited for something to come through the wire netting behind which the Lord of the Manor was engaged in reading about himself.

Presently the Winter One scratched a match upon his overalls, and the figure behind the partition straightened up.

"Ah-ha!" he said, in friendly fashion. "How are you? Lovely weather for the crops."

"Lovely," replied the other. "Any news in the 'Eagle'?"

Without answering a word, the Lord of the Manor crumpled up the paper in his hand, and striding over to where the great stove gaped cold and empty, flung the offending thing in and clanged the door to with his foot.

"I told those men," he said severely, "that they were crazy to take that fellow up. They've done it—and now they can pay for it! He ought never to have been let out of the asylum!"

"Well, he can't do *you* any harm," replied the Winter One soothingly.

"Harm! No—but he can spread these—these hideous fabrications of his. These people will believe anything!"

"Yes." The Winter One knew nothing as yet of the affair of the County Commissioners. "But you've got your license and everybody knows it. He can't start an election."

"As to the license—why, that's not my fault. I've done the right thing about it. They had no business to go raising them after the beginning of the year—no business in the world. I've paid them what they ought to have—and, though they haven't sent us the paper—you see for yourself how—oh, damn the whisky-sodden fool, and the fools who let him loose—and the other fools who kept him here!" he broke off.

"Well, he can't do anything after tonight," the Winter One assured him, "because they're going to throw him out tomorrow, bright and early."

"Hm!" snorted the Lord of the Manor. "Why the devil didn't they do it last week, if they were going to do it at all?"

"Because they've got such tender and sympathetic natures," said the Winter One.

"They've got tender heads," remarked the Lord of the Manor. "And I'm not so sure about their throwing him out—the fellow's a murderer —or he's got the face of one."

Supper time being long past now, the Winter One took himself off, and left the troubled little town behind him.

The Lord of the Manor may have drawn his bow at a venture when he spoke of the lawyer's having the face of a murderer, but the events of the next morning showed that the doubts he had expressed about the expulsion of the lawyer were founded upon a fairly accurate idea of the capabilities of the ejectors.

When, again in a body, they marched up to the "Eagle" building on Saturday morning, having ascertained that he had not left the place the night before, and demanded admittance to their own property, they were received by the muzzle of a Winchester through a barricaded window, and the voice of their tenant, threatening the instant annihilation of anyone who attempted to walk in.

One cannot argue with a frenzied eye that is looking at one down the sight of a Winchester, and the Committee retired hurriedly. From a glimpse which they had had of the interior it was evident that the insurgent had provided himself with plenty of food against a siege; but his only water supply came from a pump just outside the back door. He could not last long without water. They would, they decided, creep up to the pump at dusk and remain there until he came out, when they would fall upon him and throw him into outer darkness.

But he anticipated their decision, and when they came, cautiously and from the rear, two whistling messengers of his vigilance knocked up the dust on the bank behind them, and once more they retired—this time at a run.

It began to look as though the comedy of the Sheriff would have to be repeated, but one of the Mackenzie brothers, bolder than his companions, offered to go back and attempt a parley.[110] There was still plenty of light, and he advanced upon the fort from the village street, thus demonstrating a good deal of sense, for, if he were fired upon, the bullet, which would certainly miss him, would take the general direction of the store, the hotel and at least two dwelling houses, in which case the town would have to concern itself with the capture.

The garrison was waiting for Mackenzie, but, even in its exaltation, it recognised the tactical conditions, and allowed him to approach.

A long conversation ensued, through a crack in the door that separated two armed men, but the garrison was firm. It had cultivated the impression of its own right to do what it pleased with the paper and the office, and nothing could shake it. Things had come to a deadlock.

The Editor got out three "extras" in those three days, and, by some means or another, contrived to have them sent to the post-office for distribution; but, human nature being no stronger than its weakest inclination, and food failing him, he stole out on the evening of the third day, after scattering the type out of the windows and putting the press out of business, and went to bed in his law office.

The feelings of the Real Estate Company may be more easily imagined than described when they saw the wreck that he had left behind him, and, without delay, they took out a summons and hauled him up before the bar of justice, in the person of our dear old friend, the J. P.

Now the latter was a farmer, pure and simple, and he lived, with the whole of his family, in a two-roomed house, by the river. He could, at a pinch, contrive a scrawl of handwriting, and he could, with an effort, read; but that was as far as his scholarship went. Of law he knew less than nothing at all. The rebel had not been idle in the meantime, either, for, by the time that they had one summons out, he had started no less than seven legal actions—and all on criminal counts. The entire Real Estate Company and the veteran German he charged with fraud in the matter of the relinquishment which he had bought from them; against the Lord of the Manor and the bartender of the Duck Brand he laid a complaint of selling liquor without a license.

By now the snow had fallen and the roads were all but impracticable, so that the business of conveying the various criminals to the county seat—sixty miles away—for a preliminary hearing, was a difficult one! The entire male rank and fashion of the village were arrested and bailed in succession, by a dazed Sheriff, all except the Mackenzie, who refused to give any bail, and who, in default of a cell, had to be followed about by the town constable[111]—a soft-natured, soft-headed old fellow, whose ambition it was to be everybody's friend, and who could not have kept a child in custody except by bribing it with candy.

Neither would the Lord of the Manor give any bail. His first rage spent, he had recovered his poise.

"But, Mr.____!" the poor Sheriff implored him. "I'll go bail for you myself—just say it!"

"I would prefer not to," he replied, with a cold smile. "I have no quarrel with you—none at all. Go ahead and arrest me. I want to go to Conconully, anyway, and I am delighted to go at the government's expense."

The venerable old German—a veteran of '70 and of Metz, the story of which he would relate over and over again—who had grown fat and prosperous and highly respected, with a large family of children and grandchildren—was found by the Sheriff, painting his roof, and when informed of the former's errand, he pushed his spectacles up on to his head and gazed down at him, red-faced.[112] He refused to believe it at first, thinking it to be a practical joke, but he was compelled presently to descend and, spluttering German oaths, to go through the process of bail-giving. He perked up, though, when he understood the company in which he found himself.

"Oh, well!" he said, shrugging his shoulders, "if Mr. ___ (the Lord of the Manor) can stand for it, maybe I can! Don't let me keep you, Mr. Sheriff. You must be a busy man these days!"

The preliminary hearings complicated matters still further by bringing a charge of perjury upon the head of the Mackenzie, but, taking the season and the roads into consideration, the trial was put off until the spring, when everybody would have his ploughing done, and there would be time in which to go into the affair thoroughly. The Mackenzie, still without bail, returned to our midst, and continued to be shadowed, in a dreary and dispirited manner, by the constable, who had made arrangements to visit a daughter on the Sound and who could find no one to take over his duty.

Now the turn of the lawyer-editor came. His offences were set forth on several pages of foolscap, and they ran all the way from taking unlawful possession to threatening to kill. The Winter One read the accounts of them in the Judge's milk-house one Sunday afternoon.

"It will be spring," he said, "before you are half-way through."

"I'm studyin' up on the thing," replied the Judge vaguely, turning the handle of his separator. "I'm studyin' up."

"Stay with it," said the Winter One. "It will cheer up the evenings, if it does not do anything else!"

Our own impression was that, in the event of his being called upon to give an opinion, the Judge had his verdict all ready long before the court ever opened. The same opinion was prevalent in other quarters.

The Judge's butchering business precluded any operations of justice before half-past four in the afternoon, and when the hour struck, the court room was so full that the stenographer had to use her elbows to keep herself on her chair.

The Sheriff, breathing heavily, leant against the constable, who was also breathing heavily. It was a cold day and a wearisome business, so that they had their excuse; but the rest of the audience was intensely interested. The Lord of the Manor sat near the rostrum, saturnine amusement upon his face. The veteran of Metz sat near him, gazing at the defendant, his arms folded over his capacious chest, and a beam of rancorous mirth shining through his spectacles; he, too, had taken precautions against cold and weariness, but he had stopped while they were still in the stage of precaution. The defendant, pale but at his ease, shuffled a heap of papers, and looked carelessly at the plaintiffs, who sat in a row, four of them, with two lawyers from Twisp flanking their position; over all, carefully out of the way of the light, the Justice of the Peace, bent forward with his head supported by his hand. His pose was perfect, austere, composed, apart, the shadow of Justice. In that dim light, behind his rampart of books, he loomed over the court.

He had very little to say or do on the first evening. The defendant and the plaintiffs' counsel began to quarrel before they had well taken their places, and, knowing of no way in which to bring their squabbling to an end, and seeing that it was entertaining his friends and neighbours enormously, the Judge allowed them to run on, unhindered, until hunger and exhaustion put a full stop to the performance.

Then he rapped upon the table with a tack-hammer.

"The court," he said solemnly, "stands adjourned until tomorrow," and, before the contending parties could get their second wind, he had left the building. Reluctantly the audience dispersed. They had had a splendid time. Both sides had done themselves thoroughly well; and the next day was looked forward to with eagerness. It was better than a dance; with the saloon in full swing on the other side of the road, nothing was lacking at all.

"You did fine, Judge," said the Winter One warmly, as they walked home.

"Think so?" the Justice of the Peace asked in a pleased voice. "It ain't so blamed difficult as I thought it would be."

"Just like a dog fight. Set 'em on to each other and leave 'em be, eh?"

"I ain't goin' to get between 'em 'til I'm sent for," he laughed.

The green and red and blue of the winter sunset were merging into the velvet purple of the dusk the next afternoon, when the sleighs, containing the attorneys for the plaintiff, the Sheriff, and the plump and tireless court stenographer, drove in from Twisp. The Sheriff was still rather somnolent, but, refreshed by a visit to the Duck Brand, strode into the court room, from which the Judge was carrying his chopping-block, and leant heavily against the desk on the platform. There was a whispered colloquy between the two, before the mass of the audience arrived, during which the Sheriff nodded and twisted his moustache fiercely.

"Sure! Sure!" he was heard to say. "I don't reckon there are any, but we'll make sure!" He stealthily patted his hip.

The court began to fill.

"Gents," said the Judge, rapping with the tack-hammer, "before the court opens, there's a word or two I'd like to say. I ain't accusin' any of you of such a thing—but when gents get to tongue-fightin' like they did yesterday, they're liable to get mad before they know it. We don't want any more trouble in this court than we got already, and, as presiding officer and responsible for what happens in here, I must ask any of you gents that have got such things on you to hand your artillery to the Sheriff. They will be returned by the constable when you leave the room. Mr. Sheriff, go round and collect, if you please, and we'll get down to business,—honest, fellers," he concluded, "it's against the statutes, made and provided—honest to God, it is!"

"Pass 'em up, boys," said the Sheriff. "No ill feelin', but I got to do what the Judge says—pass 'em up!"

In the next ten minutes, amongst scattered dust-storms of protest, two old but still serviceable forty-fives were taken from the plaintiffs, a baker's dozen of all sizes and calibres from such of the crowd as were jammed in too tightly to escape and were impatient to see the curtain rise; while the defendant, still smiling palely, was relieved of an automatic thirty-two which he was carrying in a holster under his arm. This restored the good humour of everybody and the court was opened.

There was never such a court and never such a case before, even in the United States, where the administration of justice, civil and criminal, has sunk to a lower ebb than in any other spot on the face of the civilised and half-civilised world. The witnesses would contradict themselves a dozen times in a dozen minutes; and every question from both sides was frustrated almost before it was spoken.

Still the Judge continued, calm and impassive as ever, resolute not to betray himself. When the "I protests" began, never a word said he, but, knowing the instant wrangle that would follow, left them to settle it for themselves. The defendant, smiling and good-tempered over his witness at one moment, would suddenly hurl himself from his chair and walk up and down, shouting and waving his arms, but never an eyelash did his Honour blink over it.

Night after night, for three weeks, the examination and cross-examination continued, and there is no saying how much longer it would have been dragged on, had not the defendant, while mooning about his office one morning, discovered a trap-door in the floor, underneath an old piece of oilcloth. Having nothing else to do until the afternoon, he set himself to prising it up, and succeeded after a while in pushing it open, when he got a chair and lowered himself into the depths below.

It will be remembered that, in days gone by, the building had once been a rival of the Duck Brand. It had not much of a name at any time, and, towards its end, it was a pretty deadly sort of place for a man with any money in his pockets to venture into. There were several such places in the Valley—there are yet, or there were a few years ago. The liquors sold in them are made up of cheap whisky, strengthened with corn alcohol, coloured with tobacco juice and, when the occasion requires it, reinforced with "dope," which latter does its work cheaply and expeditiously, and leaves the unfortunate who swallows a small glass of the vile concoction helpless in ten minutes.[113] After that his pockets are emptied, and he is laid out in a corner to sleep it off.

The "dope" is very cheap, and a barrelful of it costs next to nothing, so that when the proprietor of the defunct place of refreshment left, he did not take the trouble to remove the stuff from his cellar, and there it had remained, tainting the already none too clean air, ever since. The poor defendant, torn with worry—for, by now, he was almost penniless and no future presented itself—his nerves jangled to pieces, thinking and dreaming, of course, of the one thing he could not have—a nervous and physical wreck, sighted the receptacles of poison in the corner and found one of them half full.

That night there was no defendant, for he was lying totally unconscious beside the fell barrel, beyond immediate help of restoratives. His door was locked, too, and no one, remembering his previous exploits, felt like breaking in.

For two days he remained alone, and on the third night crawled back to his cabin, which had been left untouched since his last occupation. He stayed there alone for three or four days, and then, as we sat at supper, the disheveled figure of a man rushed into the house, crying that the lawyer was running up and down the road shooting off his rifle at everything he could see or hear.

He had broken out in an entirely new place this time, for, while he called out at the top of his voice—"Look out, booze-fighters—here comes the temperance movement—watch out for the Hand of God, you rum-swillers!" he would also yell—"It's the red one! Keep him off!—The red one—the red one!" And he was shooting in the air, not as formerly, upon people and horses. He wanted to call attention to himself and, if he could collect a crowd, preach a sermon.

He was amenable to gentle handling, though, and we got his rifle away without much trouble, and took him down to Twisp, where he vainly implored the doctor to give him something to quiet him before he went completely off his head. But the doctor, who had taken a violent dislike to him, refused flatly, so that the task of getting him off to the asylum was none of the easiest.

Of the journey we cannot speak, first hand, for, once we had delivered him to the Sheriff, we left the pair to their own devices. Suffice it to say that the latter hauled him out four days later and returned to us, looking, as it seemed to us, a little thinner and less fierce than of old.

We have continued to get along without a lawyer ever since.

Chapter 17

The Land Boom

There came a year when we had a real land boom. The crowds—for crowds they were—who found themselves too late for the fair, further South, flocked up to us and bid against each other heartily for such land as was already planted and producing. A "buyer" from the "outside" is regarded up there in the same light as an American in Rome or Paris. No one doubts that, if he is not a rich man himself, he represents rich men, and his good faith is never questioned. As a general rule, this is a sound principle, for a man would hardly undertake such a journey without a genuine reason for it. But these land-seekers were as crazy as stockholders and imagined that they had only to get options on orchard land from the unsuspecting natives and wait for the rest to fall into their laps. They did the natives a grave injustice if they imagined that such acquired smartness as they themselves possessed was enough to get a stick of wood, for nothing, from our people.

The weakness of these gentry was that they could not tell a real buyer from an option sharp, and presently the lower of all the buyers— an Englishman—passed through Twisp, where the real estate agents had made their headquarters, without a soul being the wiser. He came up, wise man, in overalls, and though he could not disguise his accent, he did very effectually disguise his identity. He had somewhere in the neighbourhood of a hundred thousand dollars to spend, but he looked like a lumber hand out of a job. The local "Real Estate Company" made no such mistake when he landed in our little village.

They were pleasant—that was the Mackenzie "end" of the business —and ready to "take him round" and let him see the country for himself. In the hands of the Mackenzies, it may easily be understood he was not likely to see anything of the tracts, the options upon which they had already sold. They had kept back ten or twelve of the best lots in their own hands, and these they exhibited carefully, going over every inch of the ground, showing the fruit that the same land had grown the year before and asking what seemed like a reasonable price.

There is no need to go into that transaction in full; suffice it to say that they took twenty or thirty thousand of his dollars away, simply and painlessly, and, upon the strength of the sale, which they advertised far and near, sold such remaining and less satisfactory options as they still possessed, for famine prices. Another land-hungry Englishman was dumped on our doorstep by a Mackenzie[114]—the one who "brought in the buyers"—at ten o'clock of a certain October morning.

"Here, Colonel!" he called up from below. "Here's another Englishman; come down and speak to him!"

It was a very tall, very nervous man, speaking with an accent that smelt of Cheapside; and he smoked cigarette after cigarette, as he talked, rattling on as though afraid of our asking questions if he stopped.

Mackenzie had discovered him in Wenatchee, and had sniffed, with that sixth sense of his, a probable "mark," and the stranger was only just coming out of the trance into which Mackenzie had thrown him.

He had brought a friend with him, he told us cautiously; a deserving young man whom he wished to see settled out here. For himself he did not know whether he would go back to England or not. If the country suited him he might stay.[115]

We regarded him with kindly pity. Did he really think that the "Land Company" was going to let him out of its grasp now that it had him?

"I say," said one of the family, attempting gently to warn him, "you mustn't believe all these fellows tell you about the country, though don't say I said so, because they're all friends of mine—but put a pound or two of salt on it—eh?"

"Me?" he laughed. "I'm rather too old a bird to be caught by the likes of them! Don't you worry about me!"

"Sure! sure!" we agreed hastily, "but they're pretty bright—in their way—and it may not be your way, that's all."

We did not see him for two days after that, but we heard of him, through the Mackenzie who had been "showing him" over the country. He had given him some excellent shooting, and a bird's-eye view of various farms. He had talked "fruit" to him, too, and when the new arrival came to supper with us on the third day, the first half dozen words he spoke told us that the poison had "taken." For an hour he ambled on, and we listened, politely, hoping to find some tactful means of warning him against the trap into which he was moving with such perfect confidence in his own ability to deal with our flint-brained friends!

But he had passed the stage when warnings can take effect, and the few careful words we spoke were received with an impatience that we understood perfectly. He was half in, already, and any kind of moral brakes that we might attempt to apply merely rasped his own good opinion of himself. We talked of other things, but since he could see only that one, we presently abandoned the pursuit of our own interest and allowed him to pursue his monologue unchecked.

The friend whom he had brought was a typical little cockney, and one of the very dearest men it has ever been our good fortune to meet. He saw perfectly well what was coming, but professed not to care one way or the other. The only thing that he did resent was the confidence his patron reposed in Mackenzie, which seemed to him like an insult to his own intelligence. But, since his opinion was not asked he kept it to himself. He had been, it turned out, a clerk of the other's, and still preserved the "master" and "man" attitude to a considerable extent. We, conceiving this to be no kind of spirit in which to succeed on the Slope, chased it out of his mind, and before long his chest began to swell, his head straightened itself on his shoulders, and he began to walk like a free man. He began to behave like one, too, somewhat to the other's annoyance, the first signs of the new freedom in his cockney soul taking very definite shapes.

"Oh, don't talk rot, my dear fellow!" he remarked one day to his former employer. "This ain't the blinky old office. Give it a rest!"

"I don't know what the devil's got into that chap," said the employer to us, later in the day. "He was as quiet and respectful as he ever was in London, a fortnight ago. The last day or so he's been getting simply insolent. I believe he's been drinking!"

He had; but we did not tell his employer who had put the bottle to his mouth.

It is hardly necessary perhaps to say that our new Englishman soon came under the fell but ingratiating influence of Mr. Hasketh, and when we heard of the additions and improvements which they had mutually planned for the farmhouse with which Mackenzie had provided the stranger, we laughed long and loud, in the woodshed. Mackenzie had found out just how much money our friend had for immediate purposes, and fitted him with a hundred and sixty acres, and a ramshackle house, at a price which gave the seller an adequate commission while leaving enough to insure Mr. Hasketh a steady job for the fall.

As far as we could, with hints and advice, we strove to help the tenderfoot get his house in order for the ordeal of the winter, but he was not easy to help. He wanted to build open fires, even though we assured him that they would be of less than no use to him, and that he would freeze to death in front of the biggest that he could design. Everything was to be English!

"What I call a free-handed gentleman," said Mr. Hasketh, who relapsed into the Essex retainer as soon as our front door was closed behind him and he felt himself safe from alien influences. "There's a winter's work ahead of me, I can see!"

The Lord of the Manor took one of his violent fancies to the new arrival, and aided him by advice and a ceaseless stream of tools and materials from his store. A little later he gave him some more assistance on the farm by handing his son-in-law over, on a contract for a year. The son-in-law was a lymphatic soul, and, tiring of the dull life of plough and harrow, induced the Englishman to open a Real Estate Office.

"Thunder! If them fellows can make it go, you ought to be able to! Why, you're a real business man—you've been in business. You can't help making money at it."

The ex-clerk scowled and growled, but this only drove the Englishman on.

A span of mules and a "hack" were needed next to "travel around in." The Mackenzie family were on deck and they fitted him out—the mules for three hundred and fifty dollars, and the "hack," hastily painted and redecorated by Dick, for sixty-five.

"Don't you tell any of these fellows what you want," the Real Estate Mackenzie cautioned the Englishman. "They'd soak it to you every way they could. I'll fix you up and I'll take care of you. Feel responsible, you see. I brought you in, and if any of them coyotes was to get to you, I'd never forgive myself. You'd better get yourself a good horse, too. There's a lot of ranches around here you couldn't reach with a hack. Ill feelings? Just because you want to make a bit of money? Why, I want to see you do it! There's room for both of us, and maybe, in time, we can get together and hitch up! Anything we can do, call on us. I'll give you a list of places we ain't touched because we've got all we can handle!"

Generosity oozed from him, and he swung off towards Dick's abode, in a hurry.

"Get a move on, Dick," he said when he met him talking to the Winter One. "Hustle out a gentle-lookin' cayuse for the Dook! Come on, now, or somebody else'll smell it out!"

"Cayuse?" replied Dick. "Go and take your pick. The place is lousy with 'em."

"Here's one that might do," said his brother, pointing to a fat and peaceable-looking pony with a mild eye. "What about it?"

"He might if he was drugged," replied Dick. "He's done his damn best to kill everybody who ever got on to him."

They settled at last upon a big, racy-looking black.

"He's good-tempered, for a cayuse," said Dick, "but he's full of bunch-grass."

The Englishman's idea of running a real estate business was to "list" all the places that he came to and then to sit up on the hill and wait for something to happen. The little Cockney, though, had ideas of his own.

"What one ought to do," he said gloomily, "is to go and sit on the porch of the 'otel at Twisp and get our hooks into the suckers before those second-story ones down there drag 'em off the stage. A 'ell of a business we'll do this way, I don't think."

Then came the fruit boom.

"Nutty!" cried the little cockney clerk, "that's wot—balmy! Lord love a duck! They think all they got to do is to stick a twig into the ground and watch it grow—and the value of their land with it. And they're getting ready to tear up all that good alfalfa—wot can be sold sometimes, for something! I ain't got patience with 'em—honest!"

In his rough-and-ready way he had touched the real reason of the sudden popularity of the apples. Anything new was quite sure, with us, of a certain favour, on account of its novelty. As we have seen it expressed in a serious American journal, "A new thing is always better than an old one, even if it is only just as good!" It is the spirit of the country—the spirit, in fact, of that "brain-storm" which we call Progress. It is a fool of an idea, without foundation either in reason or in history, in a country where the writings of Tom Paine are taken infinitely more seriously than Scripture.

To return to the apples. The chief reason, apart from the novelty, which started us upon their cultivation, was that fruit land would be more valuable and more easily marketable than alfalfa or corn land. In our much advertised part of the world, every ranch, one may almost say, is for sale. Everybody swears loyally by the country, and everybody, with the exception—(and that only a possible one) of the saloon keepers, is ready to leave it at ten minutes' notice.

We planted apples—all kinds of apples—principally the wrong kinds. What was wanted was a show apple; the others are a drug upon the market, but we did not know that, then. We saw a world with its mouth agape for apples, and we set about trying to fill it.

Notwithstanding that it bore all the earmarks of a "hand-made" boom, the fashion took a violent hold upon us, and when it was heard that apples from our own Valley had been sold in London, the seal of respectability was set upon our efforts. The fact that those apples were picked specimens of a very choice fruit, carefully tended by professional hands and grown upon trees which had stood in the same place for at least ten years—they were six inches in diameter, and they brought a shilling apiece—was lost sight of. Fruit trees meant land values and land values meant salvation.

The Lord of the Manor got the fever badly. He had planted orchards some two years before,—but orchards of a quarter of a mile each way!—and he preached the gospel ceaselessly.[116]

"Transport?" he would cry. "Why, we shall have a railroad in here in two years!"

"Shucks! I've heard that every year since I came," one told him. "This isn't the season to pull that old gag, either."

"Oh ye of little faith!" he laughed. "It's coming—it's coming. My reward is at hand."

"I've got a notion that it'll stay there for quite a while to come," said the other. "And I'd like to have you notice in the meanwhile that the Valley, acre for acre, isn't producing as much by a third as it was five years ago—and the Lord knows it wasn't producing any too much then."

"Croaker!" he replied, unperturbed.

"All right. I'll croak, and you go ahead and plant apples. I'd a blame sight rather get a sore throat croaking than trade places with you."

Chapter 18

Quite Another Story

When the hills are baked brown, and the long day is a burning fire, there are two seasons in each twenty-four hours when, if a man has a talent in that direction, he may forget all the rest. One is in the early, early dawn, when the breeze creeps up, fresh as a baby's breath, and the earth and the trees are still wet and sweet with the dew. Then the quaking-asp thickets are fluttering gardens of mystery, and even the scorched sunflowers and the dried-up sage-brush exude something of the hopeful childhood of the day. The other comes a little after sunset, when the glow is still upon the mountains and the vast tired world sinks sighing to its rest.

It was on such an evening that Hughie, having been left to himself, sat on the porch of the crazy little cabin on Desolation Hill, and smoked, watching the colours change in the skies and the eyes of the world close themselves slowly, in sleep. Remembering how he had longed for solitude before he had known the meaning of the word, he was both surprised and annoyed at a craving for company which had been growing upon him all the afternoon. As has been already said, one cannot gaze at the appalling for any length of time with comfort, and the study of the stupendous, after a while, weighs upon the soul.

To the North, a man might have made his way into British Columbia without encountering a living soul, or coming across a human habitation; to the West, he could have come almost within sight of the Pacific, unseen and unheard of any.

Given the proper conditions, there is something very soothing in the contemplation of mountain tops—as in the study of other inaccessible things. One's eyes are lifted from the earth and the antlike things that crawl upon it. It is like fingering a raised letter copy of the Bible to follow the lines of crag and precipice and green hillside. The wind in the trees, there, was like the prayers of all the lovers in the world passing up to the Mother of Love: the only sound of earth to be heard was the ceaseless song of a late lark and the contented purr of grouse or prairie chicken.

When the light begins to die in the skies, and the colouring in the West darkens to bronze over the furthest range, and the frogs and the crickets intensify the solitude with their chattering until one can hardly bear the weight of it, there comes one of the moments that pay for all, for then the elves of art and memory come out in the gloaming and fling their magic on the laden air, and the night, like some mighty organ, accompanies their song, but so softly that one hardly feels the presence of the music at all.

A sensation of utter insignificance had taken the place of exaltation in the watcher's mind, and he knocked out his pipe, resolving to go to bed and sleep while there was yet anything of his dwindling self left. His bed, in those days, was in a deserted corn crib, the cabin being impossibly stuffy, and hither he pulled his bedding.

He had made one journey and was returning to the cabin, when the sound of heavily shod feet clinking on stone and gravel came to him from beyond the western edge of the hill, and he halted indecisively. He had not been in the country for long, then, and in spite of his loneliness, he was by no means sure that, as a companion for the hours of darkness, a stray native would be altogether welcome. Besides, the fire was out and the wanderer would certainly expect to be fed. It was the Winter One's first summer, and he was very new indeed to the country!

So he stood and waited, divided in his mind between an instinct for hospitality and an instinct for comfort and convenience, while the footsteps came nearer and nearer. But he had left a lamp burning in the cabin, and, realising that escape was out of the question, advanced upon the approaching nuisance with the best grace that he could muster.

"Come in," he called as a shape rose out of the gloom. "Had any supper, yet?"

"Why, thank *you*," replied an unexpectedly clear voice—the voices of the people are not clear, as a rule. "I've had something that I thought was going to be my supper. Don't you light the fire up again for me."

"I don't reckon it's out yet," said the host, warmed by the reaction of relief. "All alone?"

"All alone. I've staked my horse out down by the Creek. Say, honest, I ain't a bit hungry."

There was a note of courtesy in the voice—of almost formal courtesy, indeed—that made the listener's heart beat with real pleasure, and he led the way into the cabin joyfully, and pulled out its only chair.

"Well, this is fine!" the newcomer exclaimed, swinging in and dropping his hat upon the table. "I didn't know there was any human beings around here."

"There's only me. Make yourself at home while I get the fire to going."

"But I have eaten," the other tried to protest. "Well, that's awful kind of you. Canned tomatoes don't make a man-sized supper, and that's a fact."

He was a tall, thin, fair-haired man, who came into the lamplight, with bright blue eyes, just saved from steel by kindliness, with a back as straight as a drill sergeant's, a close-cropped moustache curled upwards and the long thin jaw, delicately square at the end, that is only carved by breeding. His right hand rested on the table, and the Winter One noticed that the forefinger had been taken off at the base and that a broad scar ran down the back of the hand to within an inch or two of the wrist.

As the bacon spluttered and the water began to boil, the newcomer talked, politely and with animation, as a man talks to another man in the latter's house. Not an expletive passed his lips, and when he ate, he did so slowly and with an air of self-deprecatory interest in the Winter One's remarks.

But the latter was really interested before long, and his manner must have shown it plainly, for, though the courtesy of his guest never diminished, a friendly warmth crept into his voice, and his expressions became, gradually, more direct.

"I didn't ever come here," he said, rolling a cigarette. "I just happened. I dropped here and I didn't move on. There was four of us started from Montana—I'll tell you why, some time—and we headed for B. C. We made it, too, but there didn't seem to be anything doing in our line—oh, there was cattle, and cayuses, and a range, but we knew their winters too darned well; we'd had one in Montana, and that was plenty. We were Southwesterners anyway. I haven't got right used to the cold yet, but every time I start to go South, some damn thing comes along and I get staked out again. I've forgotten what it is to be foot-loose. Well, we got in here and camped, where the store is now. The summer was just about gone, and the next morning, when we went through our clothes, we had just seven and a half dollars between us. Seven dollars is no good to four men and not much good to one, but it's better than a dollar-fifty, so we sat her up and played a round of poker hands for her. Nebraska took the pot, and beat it, and we three sat looking after him and wondering what next.

"We fished a while, and slept a while, and along towards evening the other two saddled their cayuses and hit the trail out of here after Nebraska. Hoppy said he'd most rather work than freeze to death, and Arch didn't say much, but he lit out with him. So there was me and old Pieface left looking at each other. Pieface wouldn't work at anything but a saddle, and I didn't know how, but I learned—gee—I learned!"

The speaker shivered dramatically.

"I found an old shack with a lean-to, and I put Pieface in the lean-to; then I—yes, I fell from grace and went to work, and I've been working ever since. I ain't a cent better off than I was when I got here, either."

He smoked for a while with one eye shut.

"Oh hell!" he said presently, beaming upon the Winter One, and flicking the end of his cigarette through the door.

"Why don't you start for the South now?" the latter asked sympathetically. "The summer's only just started."

"I've forgotten how to drift—that's why. I've got so that if I don't get my meals and my shaving water regular, I can't sleep. Ain't it awful, the habits a man gets into? Pieface is getting old, too, but he hasn't lost his self-respect—he hasn't had to work. I've tried to persuade him to, but when he looks at me and just asks me if I'm going to do him dirt in that way after all the years we've known each other—he won't, anyway, so it's no use asking him. But he'd carry me back home at the drop of a hat. Well, it's a hell of a trip from here to New Mexico, for one horse! You never been there? No? They say the Lord made it out of the leavings of Hell when He was feeling economical." There was no irreverence in his tone at all, nor did he even smile. "And to judge by some of the things you see there, you'd say it was no bad guess. There's parts of Texas much the same, in fact the Southwest is like that all over—the parts of it I've known—and the people. But I like them better than the folks up here. They got manners down there, or they had in my time—they had to have."

The blue eyes hardened over for a moment like glass blown upon in frosty weather.

"There's a lot of Swedes up here," he said ruminatively, "that wouldn't be alive ten minutes after they hit Nevada or New Mexico, though they're quieter places to live in than they used to be. There was money down there—there is yet, and you can get it without having to work like a flunkey or a cayuse for it. You can do a man's work and get a man's pay for it, and when you and your boss have had enough of each other's company, you can part like men and not like skin-itchy children."

The host nodded.

"I reckon you've travelled some," the other went on agreeably. "Well, then, you know what I mean. I went there from the East, the blankest tenderfoot ever you saw—when I was twenty—and I'd hate to say how many years ago that was. How old should you say I was? Well, I'll put you out of your pain," he laughed. "I'm forty-six. Yes," as the Winter One shook his head incredulously, "thank you. Your idea is appreciated—but wait 'til you see me in the light of day. The Southwest was full of misfits then—men that couldn't have made themselves comfortable any place—and that wouldn't let anyone else be comfortable, either. They didn't last awful long, as a rule—the real ones, but they certainly did shake things up while they were at it. Say, you stop me, if you want to go to sleep."

"What in thunder should I want to go to sleep for?" the Winter One demanded. "Go on. I'm enjoying myself for the first time since—I don't know when! Go on."

"Sure! I don't often get the chance to shoot my mouth off like this nowadays," he jerked his head over his shoulder with a grimace.

"Well," he continued after a pause, during which he stared down the Valley with one eye shut as though calling up memory across the miles and the years. "If you think you'd really care to hear about it, I'll tell you about the first of the misfits I met up with, if it's only to pay for my supper. Sitting here, talking and smoking like this, in that," he nodded at the twilight settling like a slowly sinking ship into the darkness, "sort of brings it back to me. There wasn't any hills to speak of there, but the sky was just the same, and that lady"—he pointed with the glowing end of his cigarette at a tiny spangle of silver in the lake of the milky way,—"she saw it, too. I was looking at her just before It happened, and she and I have been good tillicums ever since.[117] It was this way—when I first hit God's country—that part of it that looks so like Hell—I got a job with an outfit that took me on because I looked so darned helpless and they thought I might amuse them—which I did before I got through. It took about eighteen months to make a job of me, but when I was made, I was made! And then, I was sent out for the first time on night work—we were short-handed. Up 'til then I'd been helping wrangle the horses and doing any old job that was lying around.

"There ain't nothing particular about night work, except that you have to keep awake, but, for some reason, I know I thought a heap of myself when I went out with the others that time.

"A grand blue night it was. The herd seemed to spread all over the earth, I remember, like a great black jelly with lumps in it. There was a teeny little breeze blowing—Gee! I can smell the wind, the cattle and the water now! There were only four of us—we were a bit short-handed, as I said—and after a bit another fellow—whose name I don't remember —and I, got together on the far side. The cattle were quiet and we had been singing to 'em, though they didn't need it because we'd pushed along pretty hard that day. Well, we got off our horses for a bit and he asked me for the makings and rolled himself a cigarette. He stood there pulling away at it—it looked like a tiny bit of a red lamp in the dark— and we got to talking, in whispers. Why does a fellow always whisper in the dark?

"He'd got a girl somewhere here and he started to tell me about her, but I wasn't listening to him and I didn't hear much of what he was talking about. I'd a girl of my own—two of them—one three thousand miles away and one fifty, and a kid of twenty-one doesn't pay much attention to another kid's description of his girl on a night like that, though twenty-one wasn't so gosh awful young in that country! There were kids of twenty-one down there who had a killing to their name for every year of their age. Well, as I was saying, we stood there, talking about ourselves when we heard a man get off his horse and come towards us. We didn't move, thinking it was one of the others, but he was close beside us before we turned round and got a look at him. He was a kid like me, an open-faced kid with a big mouth and laughing eyes. He looked from one to the other as if he expected to recognise us.

"'Howdy, boys,' he said.

"'Howdy,' says we.

"'Who are you riding for?' he asked.

"'___,' says we.

"'Oh, are you,' says he in a gentle, surprised sort of voice. 'Well, then.' Before we could lift a finger, he's got his gun out and us covered. 'Then there's your pay,' he says, and shoots the fellow beside me through the head. 'And you,' he says to me as the fellow's body straightened out under my feet. 'You tell ____ that I'll shoot a man of his for every five dollars that he owes me until the account is settled—see?'

"All the time he was talking he was backing off, still smiling, just like he was asking me to have a drink, but the muzzle of his gun was looking at me between the eyes and his left hand was hanging over the hammer, all ready to start fanning. Back he went, creeping like a cat, and I just stood with my tongue out, staring at him. The last thing I remember of him is the steel on the muzzle shining in the mist and the scraping of his boots on the grass. If I'd been a little older—a few years later—I might have taken a chance on him, I don't know. There's men who would have, I daresay. But the whole thing had been so hellish sudden, I was phased. I didn't rightly understand what had happened until I come to in time to hear him galloping off, laughing to himself. Yes, sir, he was laughing and singing as he went—like a happy-hearted girl!

"Then I woke up and saw what was lying there close to my feet. I hadn't ever known him well, but it didn't seem real! I thought I'd been asleep and dreamed it—I did, honest. There were the cattle, just where they had been, except that they were making a bit more racket, now—and there was the night—just the same quiet, peaceful night with the breeze still a-blowing and that lady star up there still a-looking at me—and there was me. *His* cayuse had moved off a piece, but it wasn't far from me, and mine hadn't even shifted. It doesn't seem at these times as though the world could go on—without batting an eyelash, does it? You'd think it must have seen what had happened and would just stop for a minute to look, wouldn't you?

"I bent over and took a look at him. His mouth was wide open—his eyes were open, too, and there was a hole in his head you could ha' put your hand into, and I don't remember to this day just what I did do after that except that I yelled and yelled 'til someone come along and cursed at me for startling the cattle.

"The fellow that did it? He had a heap of names. The Southwest was lousy with bad men, but he was the worst of them. He wasn't twenty that night—he wasn't much more than nineteen, and he'd killed fifteen or sixteen men then. He was the only man I have ever heard of who owned up that he killed because he liked killing—he liked seeing them wriggle—that's what he said—wriggle!"

It was late before the host turned into his corncrib that night, for his visitor's appetite for talking had grown with eating. Here, there and everywhere his reminiscences darted like a searchlight over the night of the past. He had lived through the roaring "eighties" and always in the very centre of the whirlwind. The whole story of the crimson days of Texas and Nevada and Colorado and New Mexico and Montana and Wyoming and the Dakotas will never be told because the men who created it left behind them no word of their doings. Many of them still remain; young men still, and parts of the Slope and the Southwest have not yet lost all their colour, but the heavy, ceaseless tide of civilisation is creeping over Montana and Wyoming, and the bits of wreckage that the waters have flung over the Rockies have burrowed deep into the hiding-places of the still new lands, to heal themselves of their hurts and dream of the years when all the world was young.

"What happened to him—the fellow who did it?" the host asked.

"I never saw him again," said the other, "though I heard a heap about him. He rampaged around for two years after that—but they got him in the end all right, all right—and the man that got him was got himself a year ago. He was a quarrelsome son of a she wolf, too. I worked for him one time. I knew him well, and I got the story of my gentleman's finish from him—so did everybody else who ever met him, I guess. Have you ever noticed," he lit a fresh cigarette and leant across the table, "that the braver a man is in cold blood the more he shoots his mouth off about himself when he's warmed up, and when he's got a reputation like that fellow had (and he'd earned it, too; he had a good solid right to it—no three men could have done what he did, no, sir) the more mule-tempered he gets?"

The guest stopped talking, and looked out at the white, broken track of Goat Wall. Neither man spoke for a minute or two. As the grey purple of the mountains deepened and sank, and became immersed in the velvet dusk, it seemed as though all creation were standing still, watching something. Not a leaf stirred; the late lark ceased its whistling, only the crickets and the frogs croaked and chirruped to each other. The smoke from the two cigarettes hung trembling in the air and, far away down the Valley, there came out a tiny pinpoint or two of light.

"It's home to them," said the guest. "I guess, maybe, those people down there haven't ever seen a real home—but it's home to them."

"Just as well for them if they haven't," said the host. "They've got plenty to be discontented with, already."

"That's something else that they don't know," returned the guest. "Maybe they're better off so, like a cow's better off—yet if it comes to that, it'd do some of them a damn lot of good, a little discontent would."

"Some one's got to live here," suggested the host, "if they can't contrive to live anywhere else."

"That's right. That's right," he laughed, his momentary ill humour vanishing.

The host, after disposing of his guest in a sort of stretcher which he had manipulated out of two quaking-asps and a piece of canvas, lay for a long time staring up at the quiet, aloof stars, that picked out the blue, blue curtain of the sky. The frogs and the crickets still kept up their monotonous concert, the night wind blew fresh and clean from the ends of the earth, bringing on its breath the faint scent of sage-brush and rock, for rock has a scent of its own in the stillness and the dark, as the dull vain facts of existence come out into the mind when one is alone with the night.

How like it was, he thought, to another night millions of years ago, among other hills and other rocks! Under different stars—there was no Southern Cross here—but how like! Gazing sideways at the mountains, he could almost hear the rushing of a great river beneath, and smell the ashes of the camp fires, dead or dying around him. Five had sat together round a flat rock that night, and that was the last time that four of them had seen the sunset. Morbid? One gets morbid at times, thank God. A person who has never been morbid has never been anything.[118]

When the host got back to the cabin next morning he found his guest half hidden in steam and smoke before the stove, his sleeves rolled up, and the collar of his flannel shirt tucked in.

"Making breakfast's hell," he announced. "I don't mind getting dinner so much, or supper, but having someone to cook breakfast's one of the things that would reconcile me to married life! For the sake of Mike don't come any nearer!" he exclaimed as the Winter One offered to help. "It's enough for one of us to get all stunk up at the beginning of the day. You go outside 'til the smoke clears off and we can see to eat!"

"Shut your eyes," he said when all was ready. "Eat it quick and think about something else while you're doing it!"

The meal and the horrible business of dishwashing over, the two sat down once more upon the porch.

"Home?" he said presently in answer to an interrogation. "I haven't got any home! I've got a homestead and a hundred and sixty acres of greasewood that I wouldn't have taken the trouble to farm if I'd been in my right mind. I've ploughed and harrowed and cleared for years, and I've only a rheumatic shoulder and a crushed foot to the good. There ain't anything makes me feel so damned helpless as having to grow my own food. Work like a blanky burro just so as to drag enough out of the blanky ground to keep myself alive! And if I could get where I belong I could get forty-five a month and my grub and live! I am a good cowhand and I can handle horses and—oh hell," he smiled, "what's the use of kicking?"

Chapter 19

Miner's Luck

The only time of year when we saw the Indians in any numbers was when they came to attend the annual fair in Twisp. The main attractions for them were the races, and the chance, always a good one, of getting whisky. Now whisky affects an Indian as it does no one else. Half the Indian troubles in the past originated in whisky, and most of their troubles at present spring from the same source. Anyone who gives whisky to an Indian ought to be hung, but since that is, alas! impossible, he ought, at least, to be sent to prison in Alaska for life. No other punishment is at all commensurate with the crime. But since Indians have a knack of collecting good horses from heaven knows where, and whisky is cheaper and goes further than cash, they were usually royally drunk on the evening of the second day. They were not dangerous then, only cheerful; an Indian goes mad when he comes to after a bout rather than during one.

Dick Mackenzie was a hardened sinner in this direction (the "community spirit" was not strongly developed in any of the Mackenzies), and, in the matter of horse-flesh, a gipsy has fewer principles even than a Siwash.

One Fourth of July, when the excitement of the second afternoon's "exercises" was at its height, Dick and "Pete," he of the bag of feathers, went into one of the saloons, and, after refreshing themselves, filled their pockets with half-pint flasks of the cheapest sort of whisky, saying that since the Duck Brand had retired from its office of entertainment, it would be quite a while before they could get a drink again and that they proposed to "stock-up" against the draught of the morrow. The impression they gave—and meant to give—was that they were contemplating reselling their supplies at greatly advanced prices to the sufferers whom they would certainly find in their own town in the course of the next day. It was a shrewd idea and an immediately popular one—with the saloon keepers.

From there they meandered on to the race-course, their coats tightly buttoned and stuffed with paper, so as to prevent the flasks from clinking. They stayed for a while looking on, and then, talking and chewing, they made in an aimless fashion towards the Indian camp, which had been set by the side of a stream, a quarter of a mile or so from the town. No one saw them go—nor did any see them return. It was getting towards twilight when they walked into the "tepee" and began to inspect the horses that were picketed there. The young men and most of the squaws were on the race-course still and would, as they knew, remain there 'til dark; only one old man and an aged woman or two had remained behind. Old as the man was, though, he was not too old for a horse-deal, and Dick, producing a "wad" of perhaps a hundred and fifty dollars, principally in one- and two-dollar bills, very soon had one or two horses picked out. What happened then one can only conjecture; but an hour later, Dick and Pete started for home, by a roundabout way, with eight or nine horses, including two really splendid animals, each of which was worth what they had paid for the lot; and they were far out of reach before the bucks and squaws returned, to find their elders hopelessly drunk and the camp denuded of all the animals of any value at all. By that time Dick and Pete had the horses safely pastured, and that night they went to bed laughing. Dick says Pete laughed in his sleep.

The next morning, however, when they went to look at their prizes, the two good ones were missing, and it was reported that three squaws had been seen in the dim virginal light of the early morning driving some horses at a rapid pace northeastward. In twenty minutes Jim and Bill were a mile out of town, galloping like demons, but never did they see those two horses again, though they met the squaws. The squaws laughed softly, but neither of the boys could get anything in regard to the missing horses out of them. They knew, of course, that the squaws had taken them, and they searched every hiding-place that they knew of, but all without result.

It was not often that anybody boasted for any length of time about a victory over those two, and Pete spoke soundlessly to the skies when the boys returned. One can see him now, his head thrown back until the rim of his battered hat balanced itself on the collar of his shirt, his hands in his pockets, his jaws, beneath their thick stubble, moving luxuriously around the words which he was mouthing to himself. Dick swore until even his wife protested, and Ruth went out and sat on the chopping-block and beat her fists against her bare little knees with delight. "Perhaps Pop wouldn't think himself so blamed smart after this," she chortled. "Anyone who could get chewed up in that style by a soused Siwash," she added, "couldn't trade with a blind Baptist, let alone a grown man—and he oughtn't to be allowed about alone." At which her mother fell upon her from behind, and, the dogs joining in, the atmosphere was cleared up in a riot that could have been heard on the other side of the river.

It was the next spring when Dick and his family, with Pete, started out to find the pot of gold at the end of the rainbow, taking with them as big a "grub stake" as four pack-horses could carry, together with Sarah, Ruth, Bill, Alice,[119] a shaggy individual who answered to the name of "Hen," all the dogs, and old Senator, the family mule. Hen, it was understood, was to manage the horses and do the serious part of the cooking when Sarah and Ruth struck, which, as Dick had been forewarned, might happen at any time. They had not the slightest idea of whither they were bound, or what they would find when they got there; nor at that moment did they care. The mountains were full of gold, and why should they not be able to come upon it, as had so many others? There are few conditions of mind comparable to the true Westerner's delight in such an ideal combination as fine spring weather, a sufficiency of food for a couple of months, and a search for a mine in prospect. The dull warnings and reproaches of such consciences as a few years of superficial contact with the soul-deadening common sense of a busy world may have given them, are silenced by a glance at the full packs and the full confident voice of their hopes.

For weeks they wandered hither and yon, far away from any human trails, eating the young grouse and killing an occasional bear, 'til on an evening towards the middle of July, they arrived at a place to which they instantly gave the name of "Horses' Heaven," on account of the bunch-grass which grew waist-high, and here they pitched their camp.[120] Here, too, or within half a mile of it, they came upon the supposed object of their search, for Pete "struck gold" in a hollow of the rocks, and in the general jubilation that followed, "claims" were "staked-out" in every direction, until, among them, they owned several acres of rock, each with a grander name than the last. And there was gold too—real gold; the fact that the veins ran hither and thither like a drunken man trying to find his way through a barbed wire entanglement, and that they had a habit of "petering out," just as they seemed to promise best, made no difference to the feelings of the future millionaires. Somewhere in them, they were sure, the real "Momma Vein," as Ruth called it, lay, and once they touched that! No one could attempt to paint the pictures that danced before their eyes, until their picks weighed no more than feathers during the day—pictures that followed them into their sleep and out again, at night.

They built a rough log storehouse, and the provisions getting low by this time, Dick departed to bring back the three necessities of existence, flour, beans and giant-powder,[121] while Pete and Hen dug and scratched madly after the will-o'-the-wisp vein. Dick returned towards the sunset, a week later; how he found his way nobody but himself can explain. "I just reckoned that was the general direction," he said, "and I followed it up!" No born woodsman or plainsman ever can explain how he finds his way, any more than a cat of our acquaintance who was taken away from home into the next State on a train and who was found, a week later, on the porch steps, licking itself, could have told how it had come back three hundred miles over a road which it had never travelled before, in seven days!

Long and late they talked that night, and the next morning when they woke, they began again enthusiastically. They had a cook-stove, a largish affair, that they had "packed" with them, and this they had set up at one end of the store-house with the stove-pipe stuck through the wall. Hen was cooking that morning, and he had put the beans on to boil the night before, so that, with one thing and another, the top of the little stove was covered to its capacity.

It was raining and the whole tribe was "sitting around" waiting for the biscuits to bake and the water to boil, but the wood was rather wet, and Hen became impatient. Near to the stove, but at a safe distance from any sparks, was a mass of dry brush and kindlings, and Hen, picking up an armful of them, pushed them into the fire, and then, opening up the draught, placed himself before the glare, rocking to and fro upon his feet, his hands behind his back.

Dick had not seen Hen's movement, for his back had been turned, and now hearing the cheerful crackling, he looked around.

As he did so, the stove seemed to lift itself bodily from the floor, and part in the middle, the bean-pot sailed in an arc across the room and crashed against the door. Hen came through the air in a melee of bacon, coffee and frying bear-paw,[122] a deafening explosion and a blinding flare drowned the yells of the women, and a new doorway appeared in the wall, through the smoke at the back of the cook-stove.

It had all happened so suddenly that Dick could only stumble up from his knees, murmuring faintly, "What the hell—" and Pete, on whom the larger part of the scalding beans had landed, wiped his face mechanically as he crouched against the wall, until Sarah, with a culminating howl, made for the pile of brush.

"Leave it be!" yelled Dick, now thoroughly aroused. "Leave it be! That's where I stored the giant-powder last night. What's happened?"

"Hen," replied Pete, grinning again. "The fire sulked and he reckoned to warm her up. It's a wonder you didn't store that powder in the oven, while you were at it, Dick!"

A deep and ominous silence followed.

"Goda'mighty!" muttered Hen in an awestruck voice as he realised. "Giant-powder—in the fire—and me standin' on the top of it—Goda'mighty!"

There were three sticks of the infernal stuff in the fire and yet no one was killed or even badly injured! Is it any wonder that they grew reckless after a while?

And they were all the same! The risks that they were in the habit of taking as regularly as they took their coffee must have accounted for any number of less hopelessly careless people. They played with destruction as a child plays with a top.

One we knew—another Bill—made a business of digging wells, in which he was allowed to have something like a monopoly. Firstly, because well-digging is an arduous business, and secondly, because Bill was supposed to be somewhat feeble-minded, and, at the same time, to have the gift of "feeling water." He and his cleft stick were in great request on this account. Having mysteriously located the desired spring, he would dig down to bedrock and then and there blow his way into the earth with repeated charges of dynamite, which he exploded by means of a home-made "time-fuse," the only kind of fuse that he could be induced to use. He would set his charge, light the fuse, and then be pulled up the twenty or thirty feet, with death simmering beneath him. Once when he was digging a well for a friend of ours, he repeated this performance five times in one forenoon, until the former, who was a tenderfoot and had consequently a decent regard for risk, remarked that he had tinkered with his life often enough for one morning, and suggested that, since they had to use giant-powder, he would feel considerably happier if Bill would condescend to use a professionally manufactured fuse, of which he had several, in the afternoon.

Bill was rather indignant at the implied lack of confidence in his own fuses, but agreed, since the other seemed to be really worried over the business, to do so. First, though, he had another charge to set off, and this he proceeded to set, grumbling to himself. A ladder had been lowered, so that Bill could climb up the first fifteen feet or so, but the rest of the way he had to be hauled.

He started up, and stopped half way, squinting into the depths. The fuse was sputtering, and the tenderfoot, in an agony of nervousness, danced on the top and implored him to hurry.

"I wonder whether I set that fuse right," Bill wondered aloud, "seems like—"

"Well, for God's sake finish your wonderings up here!" the other besought him; "while there's still something left to wonder about!"

"Gee! You are a nervous cuss!" remarked Bill scornfully, and started to scramble up the rope. He was just on the edge of the hole, half in and half out, when his doubts about the fuse were solved, for the charge went off and he rolled over and over on the ground, shouting indistinguishable words, with half his overalls taken off as though with a knife. His face was full of pebbles and his hair was singed when he got to his feet twenty yards from the well and felt for his hat.

The only thing that really seemed to offend him was the loss of the hat. It took a month to get the pebbles dug out of his face, and he looked afterwards as though he had had a bad attack of smallpox, but about that he cared not a whit. Later he developed a fixed idea that he was a British nobleman in disguise, but he kept on digging wells, and he was still alive when we left. He will probably long be spared by a merciful Providence, because he could dig wells, and he was a handsome warning (or, at least his face was) to anybody who saw him.

There was another case of the same sort, in which another of the

Mackenzies was concerned. An old and rather peppery farmer, having acquired a house and lot at the corner of the street in Twisp, wished to dig a well, and with Charlie's assistance (he who was afterwards the deputy Sheriff) dug a hole about ten feet deep, close to the house. Here there were indications of water, and Charlie, who was a miner, advised the proprietor to sink a small charge of nitro-glycerine to clear the way through what might be pure rock. But he advised him to wait for his (Charlie's) return and not to attempt the job himself. The old gentleman flared up at this and remarked that if he hadn't got enough sense to do a little job like that for himself at his time of life, he'd go without any blamed well.

"Just as you please," said Charlie, "but I'd go easy with nitro-glycerine, it's awful tricky stuff—but just as you please—it's your own blamed hole! I'll be back in two days," and with that he left him.

The old gentleman, conceiving this to be in the nature of a challenge, but having, in truth, very little acquaintance with any other explosive than black powder, wandered into the town, where he hoped to be able to get some advice on the subject. He got that, or a substitute for it, at the first saloon he came to, and from there, he set out on a search for nitro-glycerine. This is not an easy thing to come by at any time, for even our people draw the line of common safety somewhere. But he found it. In his condition he could not fail to find it, of course; though he might have searched for half a year had he been perfectly sober. He brought home with him a five-gallon can!—and an ounce bottle would have held more than he needed. How he got it home is a secret between himself and his overworked guardian angel, but he did it, and, with what he conceived to be infinite caution, lowered the charge—which properly placed, would have blown a city block into atoms—into the hole.

Then, still with caution, he maneuvered a rock to the brink of the deep cavity, and, providing himself with a long pole, lay down, as far off as the latter would reach, and prodded the rock over the edge.

When he came to himself, and the remains of the hole, the house, the sidewalk, and two or three small trees had ceased falling from the skies, through the dust he heard the yells of many people—far off, as it seemed in another world. He could see nothing through the fog of dust, nor could he move from the place where he lay. But the yells came closer, and, as the clouds settled, he pulled himself into a sitting position and saw a great crowd bearing down upon him, pulling what looked like a high cart with them. A minute later he came to in real earnest, for a stream of water smote him and flung him over while three or four demons leapt at the burning wreck of his house, with hatchets, yelling madly.

"Get him out!" he heard one yell; "get the old fool out! He was skinful a while back, and he's likely sleepin' it off!"

In his efforts to answer this insult he rolled over and over, but the words would not come. His mouth was full of earth and smoke, and as fast as he attempted to clear it, the more hopelessly choked up did it become. Finally he gyrated through the remains of the fence and crawled across the street, unseen, when instinct guided him to a saloon in a corner of which he dropped. It was empty. Even the proprietor had rushed out to join the crowd, and our friend staggered behind the bar, where he collapsed again, but within reach of refreshment to which he helped himself liberally—from the bottle.

The work of destruction came to an end when it was seen that there had never been any need of it, and the fire company, mopping their brows, rejoined the crowd.

"Blowed hisself up," said one. "He must ha' had some giant-powder—Charlie said they was diggin' a well."

"He's done it good and plenty, anyway—Bert has," remarked another. "There ain't a sign o' hide or hoof of him!"

Regrets were expressed; unknown qualities of Bert's came to light while the crowd stood near the yawning chasm that marked the spot where Bert's well had once been.

"Mean stuff that giant-powder," said somebody.

"When it's as old as a man it is," volunteered another; "not otherwise! What in hell do people want to sell condemned truck like that for? It's against the law—by—it's against the law!"

"Where did he get it from, anyway?" asked someone, and there was a note of threat in the voice.

It began to look as if trouble were brewing for some storekeeper, and a general move began to be made in the direction of the only place where such things were to be purchased.

By now, the proprietor of the saloon where Bert had come to an anchorage had remembered the defenceless condition in which he had left his bar, and he scurried back. In the door he stopped to see if anyone had been taking liberties in his absence, and a sound of breathing, heavy but irregular, came from the far end of the room. In righteous wrath he strode across and dived down upon a recumbent form beside the ice tank.

"A man can't get a breath of air," he vociferated, "without some damned soak comes in and steals his—what the hell!"

He dropped the collar he had been grasping and reeled backwards.

"Bert!" he whispered, and then, advancing a timid hand he shook the old man gently; "how—how did you get here?"

"Got here?" mouthed Bert. "I dropped in—that's what I done—jes' fell in here—how you comin'?"

"Fell?" the other gasped, looking up involuntarily for a hole in the ceiling. "Fell in here—did you say you fell in here?"

"Sure!" Bert hiccoughed. "Lemme sleep! I ain't got nowhere to go—house—everything—all gone to hell—lemme sleep!"

"Ain't you—ain't you hurt?" the mystified man asked. "Are you sure you ain't hurt, Bert?"

"Norrabit—lemme sleep!"

Once more the saloon keeper ran outside, and found the crowd, now much thickened, about the steps of a general store, half way down the street.

"Bert's all right, fellows," he shouted, "he's in my place—says he fell in there—he's up to the guards with booze, but he's livin'—an' says he ain't hurt!"

Bert was far beyond explaining himself when the crowd followed to look at him, nor, ever afterwards, was he able to tell with any certainty how he did find his way into that bar; so the legend or half legend remained.

Horrible things—cases, that in gentler climes would have turned one sick to think about—seemed to lose some of their horror in the arms of the lovely, melancholy-haunted mountains. One came to realise the true value of a civilised training, up there, for even if it be shorn of any religious teaching, it is impossible altogether to keep it from the influence of the religion which is all about it, and it adapts unconsciously that religion's social ethics even if it knows nothing of the reason for their existence. There is just so much provision for the journey in each man's pack: some employ it and give thanks to the Provider, some employ it mechanically, giving no thanks at all, and some are totally unaware of its existence, but all who do know of it, through teaching and example, employ it because without it they will not be able to live on friendly terms with their neighbours, and man is by nature, as we know, a sociable person. But when there is no need to live on friendly terms with any neighbours, and there is no knowledge of the provision, man reverts to the animals.

One, living alone with his wife and daughters in a fold of the hills, ten miles or so from us, committed an indescribable crime,[123] and the doctor came to us after attending to the victim, his lips twitching and his eyes frankly streaming. He could not speak at all for a long time, and when he told us where he had been, he did not seem to realise, in the least, the chances he had been taking of being killed, for the man had been on the place when he arrived, and had, as we learned afterwards, threatened to shoot anyone who appeared. Our little hero of a doctor would have done just the same had he known it, but he did not.

We got the deputy Sheriff on the telephone and explained as best we could, the job he had before him; and the Sheriff, for once roused out of the individual in whose shape he lived most of the time, swore, by all his gods and several other things, that he would have the man dead or in jail before night. This was at about midday, and we turned with what appetite we could to dinner.

We were still sitting about the table when the telephone bell jangled and the voice of the Sheriff asked for the doctor. The latter with a light in his eye sprang to the box and glued his ear to the receiver.

"Got him, did you?" he called. "Good for you, old chap! I hope to God you killed him, though death's too damned good for him!"

His face grew puzzled as he listened. The Sheriff had not "got him." In fact the Sheriff had been chivied off the place, and though he had stayed long enough to send half a dozen bullets at his man, he had missed him and had been forced to retire under a hail of lead. Would the doctor kindly notify Charlie Mackenzie, if he were to be found? It was two men's job, anyway. The doctor would. In half an hour he had notified everybody whom he could call up, and Charlie was half way to the spot before the former had finished. Others were on their way to the spot, too; it looked, in fact, as though the ruffian were going to be lynched.

Charlie found the deputy Sheriff in the road, a mile away from the scene of operations, and leaving him there to keep off anyone who might try to follow him, made for the farm. In a thicket of quaking-asps, he left his horse, and proceeded to reconnoitre.

In open contempt of the Sheriff, the farmer was ploughing on the hillside some five hundred yards away, but, as Charlie's keen eyes recognised, with a Winchester strapped to the plough. Between Charlie's hiding-place and the house was an open space of perhaps a hundred and fifty yards, the whole of which was under the eyes of the man on the hillside, and within easy range. Not that Charlie minded much about that. What he was afraid of was that the man might see him, unhitch one of the horses and escape before Charlie could get after him. A long, stern chase is no joke in that country, and Charlie's cayuse was a borrowed one in which he reposed no great trust. He might both lose his man and lessen his chances of ever becoming a Sheriff himself. Charlie pondered. Would the man come back to the house, or was this ploughing a piece of pure bravado? He might, of course, be able to bring him down from the thicket, but there were two cogent reasons for not attempting this. If he missed, the man would be warned, and if he did not miss—there was trouble enough in the house already! So, like a wise man, he threw a scarf over his horse's eyes and waited events. It was a long wait, but since the man was hot with ploughing he would probably grow thirsty before long, and the fact that the Sheriff had not returned would probably inspire him with confidence to go back to the house for a moment.

While waiting Charlie laid his eye along the sight of his rifle once or twice and inspected the magazine.

At last, after what seemed like aeons, Charlie saw the farmer straighten up and look around, and his heart leaped within him. Then, as he watched, he saw him unstrap the rifle from the plough-handles and, after a little hesitation, start towards the house.

Closer still Charlie crouched among the bushes. The man coming down from the hillside paused once or twice and peered in the direction of the road whence Charlie had come. Shading his eyes with his hand, but seeing no sign of anyone, he came on more boldly and presently entered the cabin from the far side, still carrying his rifle.

There were two windows overlooking the open space between Charlie and the cabin, but he maneuvered himself along between the trees until he arrived at a point opposite the corner, when he stooped as low as possible, and ran, never pausing until he dropped under the closed windows, safe from sight, when he edged himself to the entrance on the far side and looked round the corner.

The door was opened—away from him—and he could hear the man moving about inside. Though Charlie had been in tight places before, it is doubtful whether he was ever in quite such a narrow fit as he found himself in then. If he were seen from the window, he would be dead before he knew it; if he were seen from inside the door, the odds were a hundred to one against his being able to get in a shot before his adversary, and, even if the latter walked out of the door, it would be with his rifle in his right hand—and cocked, to a certainty. He was sure of a long, long time of imprisonment already, and, complete savage as he was, his nerves gone utterly to pieces, he would kill without hesitation.

A cramp of the other world descended upon Charlie, now, and he squirmed feebly in its grip; the uncertain shuffling of feet came nearer to the door as he writhed, and he heard the rifle clink against a chair with a steely clang, while his sweating fingers closed over the steel and the trigger of his own. Then a dim noise, as it seemed to him of voices, came from the far distance, and the man apparently heard something, too, for he stepped out hastily and brought his rifle to the "ready," his head turned towards the road.

That was Charlie's moment.

"Put 'em up!" he hissed softly. "Dod gast you!" as the other spun around; "drop that gun and put 'em up!"

Between cramp and excitement, his eyes had a ferocious glare in them, and the other, after a second's mad stare at him, he did as he was bid. Charlie's muzzle was not five feet away from his head, and his own was pointing towards the hillside.

"Turn round," continued Charlie, "and walk—and keep a-walkin', if you want to keep on a-livin'—hurry along!"

To say that the Sheriff was glad to see Charlie would be to bleach that worthy's emotions. Had he been a Continental, he would have fallen on his neck and kissed him on both cheeks.

"That's the boy!" he murmured brokenly, as he festooned the prisoner in ropes and handcuffs. "That's the boy. You're a ring-tailed posse all by yerself, Charlie, damn your blanky old eyes!"

"You keep him, now you got him," said Charlie, wiping his face, his heart beating a tattoo of self-gratulation, "'cause we," he added magnanimously, "*we* mightn't be able to get him again!"

"Closer than a brother," the Sheriff promised him, putting a final touch to the decoration he had applied to the captive's hands, which were tied to his neck, so that, if he moved them, he would throttle himself. "He'll be my Siamese twin 'til I've got him behind the bars. Good work, Charlie—I won't forget who done it!"

"No," said Charlie to his Winchester, "I don't reckon you will. I'll see to it myself, if you slip up on it!"

The Sheriff, borrowing Charlie's cayuse, secured his man to it, hand and foot, and ambled away in the direction of Twisp, while Charlie shouldered his Winchester and marched home, singing an endless song, with a dirge-like refrain, to himself.

The Sheriff kept his word—so well, in fact, that when the prisoner arrived at the county seat, he could neither walk nor stand nor sit with comfort, for the Sheriff had tied him to the bed during the night, and tied him to the horse during the day. He had wasted no time on the road, either, and it is a poor enough excuse for a road at any time. The County Sheriff being abroad on his arrival, he had locked him in himself, and left him in company with two horse thieves, a cattle rustler, an arson case and an attempted murder.... He would not trust anyone with his jewel. He "allowed" that he would have the County Sheriff's personal receipt for it before he let it out of his hands.

But the County Sheriff, who was engaged upon a more or less harmless case of bigamy, was in no hurry to return, and two days went by during which the deputy hovered around the gaol, like a boy with his first puppy, looking in every hour to see with his own eyes that his treasure was still safe in its cage. He grew haggard and pale with the continued anxiety, and his conscientious abstinence from whisky during the period of waiting began to tell upon his temper and his nerves.

On the third night while he was turning restlessly in bed, wondering when he would be able to return to the comforts of a natural life in his own town again, the prisoner, who had been permitted to take the stiffness out of his limbs by chopping wood in the gaol yard, relieved him from the necessity of further self-sacrifice by lifting the gaol-door from its hinges and vanishing into the night, together with the rest of the State's guests, except the "attempted murder," who had a charge of buckshot in his right leg, and who related the story of the escape to the gaoler in the morning, with yells of laughter.

But the poor wife, in the lonely cabin, nursing a three-days'-old baby, did not laugh when the news was brought to her.

"He'll kill me!" she moaned; "he swore he'd kill me—he'd have done it that day if it hadn't been that he was lookin' out for the Sheriff! I know he'll kill me!"

Since it was impossible to move her for at least a week, Charlie and his brother camped in the place, one by the door, the other at the back, and slept turn and turn about. Then the deputy, cursing in a fashion which anyone not acquainted with the everyday conversation of the country can only dimly imagine, started out with three others to scour the country. And they scoured it, too—thoroughly—but their gentlemen had left no trail to discover, and at the end of a fortnight, they gave it up, arguing, with reason, that the main thing that mattered was to be shut of him, and that they reckoned they were!

Chapter 20

The Unforeseen

Socially, the two most important events for our people were funerals and dances, and to the first they would flock as thickly as to the second, whether they had any acquaintance with the deceased or not. The "bone-yard," as they called it, had a strange attraction for them at all times, and the main feature of the annual festivals of the Lodges consisted of a visit there, accompanied by the bands of both villages and headed, if such a reason could be found, by an old soldier—generally the veteran of Metz—carrying the sword of office with which he would wave us a graceful salute as he passed.

A very young Congregationalist, the nearest thing we possessed to a qualified parson, officiated and, indeed, officiated very well, upon these occasions. He had what is known as a "moving address" and, being naturally emotional, he contrived some splendid effects. The audience, too, were emotional, and easily moved to tears, so that altogether it was rather a tax upon the nerves to take part in these affairs. It was expected of one, however, a large following being supposed to have a soothing effect upon the relatives, as giving a decent appearance of general regret. The feeling is, of course, universal but the conditions were not. Some of the participants used to drive fifteen and twenty miles with the thermometer at fifteen or twenty degrees below zero. It was one of their few opportunities of meeting and talking.

"Old Lady Tiler" was a very regular attendant, and her old white horse figured in almost every funeral procession that we saw, though her ideas of spiritual comfort for the mourners were those of the early, early Puritan Fathers. Her creed was a mixture of many "persuasions" overlaid with a perfect trust in God, which carried her over some very bad places. But that trust was compressed within the bounds which her early training had placed about it. When a neighbour's baby, playing about in its father's workshop, swallowed a screw and died before help could get to it (accident! accident! it dogged our steps day and night!) she came, when the funeral was over, and sat on our porch for a while, blinking at the summer afternoon.[124]

"A tough deal!" she sighed. "Not that she hasn't others—and more than she can handle for that matter—but it's a tough deal for all that! She come to me just now when we was on the hill"—the rusty crepe bonnet shook from side to side—"baptised? no, 'twas only six months old! How could a baby of six months old take religion?—and she asks me what's going to happen to it where it's gone"—she shrugged her shoulders. "What could I say—I had to allow it was going to hell."

Nor could anything shake her belief in that merciful dogma. That He who said, "Suffer little children to come unto me!" should be capable of hurling a helpless baby into a bonfire seemed to her perfectly natural, and the horrible and unspeakable cruelty of it perfectly compatible with an infinite Love and an infinite Justice. Yet she loved and trusted the conception which she had of God, and when her own children died she did not even murmur. "He knows best," she said, over and over again; "we've all got to go sooner or later, and maybe it's better they should go while they're still fit to!"

It is a world of contradictions, and it is the contradictions that make it the splendid place that it is. Dear "Old Lady Tiler!" She is dead, now, and has joined her children two years since—but her memory is very tenderly cherished by some of us. No great lady was ever possessed of a more perfect dignity than she could muster up at a pinch, nor has any woman, of whatever degree, ever been capable of a more selfless sweetness of soul.

Once, in the spring of that summer when all the world turned suddenly young and green, for two of us drove down to Twisp with "Dolly," near as venerable then as her mistress.[125] They drove carefully, as always, for Dolly was not to be hurried. Going down she was even more lazy than usual, but they paid her very little heed, for they were alone with each other in the 'teens of a year whose adolescence was to see the most wonderful event that ever happened. The narrow lanes were each a separate nosegay, the hills were green and covered with sunflowers, the soft air had a tang of salt water in it, like a whisper from an old friend, and they lazed along too happy even to talk.

They had several things to do in the little capital and it was well after five o'clock before Dolly was brought out and hitched up again. There was an uncomfortable look in her eye and a listless flop to her ears. The livery-man said that she had eaten too fast for her teeth, but that a little gentle exercise would probably settle the trouble. The Winter One, though, noticed the presence of grains of oats and a good deal of "slaver" about her muzzle, and he hesitated. She was a glutton, as he knew, and, if she had swallowed her oats at her usual pace and had been fed too soon after watering, it was possible that a damp ball of congealed oats might still be lingering in her pipes. So he treated her, pouring water into her ears and rubbing her throat downwards until she shook her head and seemed to breathe more freely.

"We'll go slow, anyway," he said to his companion. "There's nothing to hurry for."

So they started off, the Comrade driving, and he smoking peacefully and in perfect accord with the perfect afternoon. Up hill and down dale they loitered, until they came to the top of a rise, when Dolly, recognising her whereabouts, pulled herself together and started for home at a good round trot. Over the incline she went, steadily enough, until she arrived at a turn of the road, high above a farmhouse yard, when she stopped, stood for a moment, and then, without warning, came down in a heap, turning, as she fell, towards the frail wooden fence that divided the road from the yard. This gave under her weight, and the Winter One, lifting the Comrade from her seat, unhooked the tugs and dragged the bridle from the mare's head. Thus freed, she slid, head over heels, down the bank, taking most of the fence with her, and rolled over into the yard; once more she struggled to her feet, and once more she sank, the blood flowing from her nostrils.

It was over in a second, and the two in the road looked down, dazed at the suddenness of it. It was like losing an old friend and a valued friend, and for a minute or two neither spoke. Then they noticed that it was getting dark: they had still several miles to go.

But the buggy, full of parcels, recalled them to themselves, by commencing to slide over the edge of the bank, and after pulling it back into the road again, the Winter One mopped his forehead and looked about him. The house to which the yard belonged was dark, and so was the growing night. They had still five or six miles to go, and, sorry though they were for the fate of poor old Dolly, they could hardly stay there to mourn her all night.

A ray of light came from a house a quarter of a mile or more away, and, leaving the Comrade to guard the buggy, he set off. He had not the slightest idea of who lived there, for he knew that the place had changed hands several times in the past two or three years, but he trusted that the indwellers, whoever they might be, would have a horse on the place capable of being driven single—a somewhat uncommon thing in that country.

As he expected, the family were utter strangers to him, though anything but strangers to his rather desolate condition. They were at supper, and he apologised for disturbing them over that semi-sacramental meal.

"Our old horse," he explained, "petered out coming home—she quit us at the bottom of the hill back there—and rolled herself into somebody's yard, whose name I don't know. We'd be awful grateful for the loan of something that could take us back home."

"Well, think of that!" exclaimed the wife sympathetically. "You got your woman with you?"

The Winter One blushed slightly, and she laughed.

"That's meaner still, ain't it? The old blue horse'll go single when he's feelin' good. Won't he, Paw?" she asked her husband whose sympathy, 'til now silent but expressive, found words.

"Sure. I'll go and bring him in. He's out in the woods somewheres. Where's your rig?"

"Just under the hill—what's left of it," replied the Winter One. "It's mighty good of you to take all this trouble."

"Trouble, hell!" he said genially. "Did you say that she'd rolled into the yard back there! I'll get her planted tomorrow."

"It's a new way of introducing oneself," said the Winter One, "to throw a dead horse into a man's yard—"

"Anyway's better than none. And a little matter of a dead horse in the yard ain't nothing—oh, this is the bounding West, all right, all right!" he chirped as he disappeared.

The Winter One went outside and watched him slip a halter onto a young horse and jump on its back.

"I'll bring him right away!" he called, as he galloped off. "You go back and tell your woman it's coming!"

It was pitch dark by now, and the Winter One trudged back, cheered, in spite of his depression, by the contact with human kindness. Where else, he asked himself, could such things happen? Nowhere. It was all a part of that medley of tragedy and good humour and sheer comedy which is known as the West. There were so many things that had to be taken seriously that people became economical of anxiety and sorrow, only dribbling out their emotions when it became absolutely necessary.

He found the Comrade sitting in the buggy, smoking a cigarette. She too could be a stoic.

"What is, is," was their joint philosophy, "and it never lasts for long. Since it is, there is no use in trying to pretend that it isn't—but since it never lasts there is no use in fussing about it!"

"The old lady'll have a fit when she hears about Dolly," he remarked.

The Comrade did not reply for a moment, and he moved a little nearer. Even in the gloom he could see she had been crying.

"I went down and patted her good-bye," she said. "It was all that I could do—and the old lady will be just as sweet as she can be about it—you see if she isn't. I know her! It's funny," she went on, "but this road seems to have a perfect hoodoo on it for us, these days. We won't try it again—something always happens!"

This was true, but it did not seem a good time to pursue the subject.

"We'll break that presently," he assured her. "It's only trying to prevent us getting married. It's jealous of me, that's all."

It was one of the longest drives, that short five or six miles, that either of them remembers. The night had come down for good, they had no lamp, the "blue" horse was distinctly sulky at having been dragged away from his bed and his supper, and he was balky and "jumpy" by turns, and before they had left the lights of the friendly farmhouse well behind them it began to rain. Why does it always rain on these occasions? The road, bad enough even in the light and with a horse that they knew, became a thousand times worse in the dark, with a justifiably incensed cayuse whose acquaintance they had still to make.

Now at a foot's pace, now at an unwilling trot, now at something not far removed from a hand gallop, they made their way along the indistinctly "blazed" trail, for the most part in silence, until they swung on to the wooden bridge with a rattle that seemed to spring every joint and nerve of the long-suffering buggy. The bridge was crossed by tacks—for the "blue" horse was suffering from nerves by now—and when the ladder hill from the road up to the house appeared, he braced himself firmly on his legs and refused to budge at all, humping his back and switching his tail, and flinging every threat that his experience had shown him to be effective in the past, at his driver.

But the latter was in no mood for "bluffs" and after exhausting every means of moral suasion he drew the reins through his fingers and caught up the long rawhide, balancing it to get the right reach and draw.

"I'm going to light into him," he said to the Comrade; "I don't give a hoot whose horse he is, if he was reared a pet. Do you want to get out?"

"Not much," she replied, grasping the seat and speaking between her teeth. "I'm ready—keep his head straight!"

Down came the rawhide over the obstinate hump and a shiver of mingled pain and rage went through him, but he stood fast. Then the cataract descended, and when it was over the worst of the hill had been covered in a series of bucking spasms. On the easier grade, he put his head down and fled, and, once at the top, he made the garden gate in two slides and a convulsion. Then he stopped with the tip of the near shaft comfortably jammed in the fence.

"Well," said the driver, "here we are—I wonder where the old lady is. Don't go in 'til I've got him tied up. We'll face the poor old girl together."

But the Comrade was already inside, and when the Winter One arrived upon the scene, he found her with both the old lady's hands in hers, on her knees, telling the story. An ogre could not have resisted that appeal, and the old lady nodded kindly, though her face was working.

"Don't you worry, my dear," she said. "I had a kind of hunch something was going to happen today and—don't you worry! It wasn't your fault, dearie. She was due to go almost any time—don't you worry!"

Nor would she leave the house until she had seen the Comrade eat her supper and had assured herself that she was not going to grieve too much over it. Nor would she hear of any payment for the damage. Her principal idea seemed to be to comfort the Comrade; of herself she had no thought at all. Yet, she was, by all accounts, a hard old person where money was concerned, and she could drive a bargain with any man.

When her daughter died and her son-in-law[126] handed over his boys to her keeping, she worked them so unmercifully that one evening the eldest one was discovered, after hours of searching, curled up in a neighbour's barn, hidden deep in the hay. The poor child was half demented with heat and labour and prayed to be left to get a little rest.

She had the old ideas about youth. If it was not worked half to death and kept without pocket-money, it would fall into the hands of the devil; and, by the way, calmly as she had assented to certain damnation of her neighbour's baby, she had never taken any steps to get any of her many grandchildren baptised.

Her heart, at seventy-four, still yearned for the old, savage life of the waggon and the plains. Heaven knows, life was savage enough in the Methow in our time, but it was altogether too "settled up" for her. She was a born rover and, two winters before she died, started down to New California to join a sister spirit, who had emigrated with her from Texas in her youth, and who, to her joy, had discovered a country so new as to be absolutely uninhabited.

"It was fine!" she said when she came back; "but I'm gettin' too old—I ain't old, but I reckon I'm gettin' too old to really enjoy myself anymore!"

Chapter 21

Wedding Bells

When good Father Luyten[127] began to visit us at regular intervals and say Mass in our house, we discovered that there were quite a number of Catholics scattered about in our district; that is to say, within a radius of some fifteen or sixteen miles. The most faithful were those who lived at the greater distance, the dear Germans who had settled up at Mazama. In all weathers, starting at five o'clock and coming over the snow-choked road, fasting, and nearly frozen with the bitter cold, they never failed. One old Bohemian peasant always walked both ways and could scarcely be persuaded to partake of the little feast which we prepared for our friends on these occasions and to which they always contributed by bringing the most wonderful cakes and dainties. In time the congregation quite outgrew the narrow limits of our cottage, and we all decided that, come what might, we must manage to build a Church.[128]

The first step was to secure a site, and this the Judge most generously presented. Then funds had to be raised for the building, and the Comrade, trading on the well-known fact that nobody could ever refuse her anything she asked for, started on the campaign. She covered many miles in her buggy, driving a very young buckskin mare, during the next few months. Her methods were as Catholic as her object; in one day she got subscriptions from two saloon keepers—unknown to us, of course, for we could have done that for her, though not half so well. She called them out of their establishments and harangued them from the buggy, and so pleased were they at being treated as human beings by the little exquisite that they gave more than anybody else and gave it with a hearty good will.

Saloon keepers are, for some mysterious reason, always more generous on these occasions than anybody else, and the better the object for which they are asked to give, the more freely do they give. There is often more real human kindness in a publican than in a prophet; the absence of any conceit of virtue in themselves makes them desire the contact with it, and they are pleased with the thought that real virtue is not in the least above meeting them on the level ground of their mutual humanity.

Two of us, at least, had an ulterior object in view when we built the little Church. The Comrade would have a Church in which to be married, if she had to build it with her own hands. "They shall have a chance to see one Christian wedding, if they never see another!" she remarked.

And they did. There never was such a wedding before—never! Apart from the service itself, every single item was absolutely unique and inimitable, and the service itself had several quite original features. It is not in the nature of some people to do anything as anybody else would do it, and we are among the number of those elect. The whole affair was complete, too. There was nothing missing when we had finished. The excitement began weeks before, and it lasted for days afterwards. The fact that it was a Catholic wedding gave it a "cachet," and surrounded it with delectable mystery.

"Why," said one outsider to another, while the Church was building, "can anybody come into one of their churches while the service is going on?"

"I think so," said a brother Pythian. "That's what I understand. The only thing they keep to themselves is what they call the High Mass. They won't let anybody in to that!"

The bride and the bridegroom had decided, when the great ceremony should be over, to leave in one of the two motor cars which the countryside boasted—belonging, it is perhaps unnecessary to say—to one of the Mackenzies.[129] He had very little else in the world, and how he became possessed of a forty horsepower car is something which only he could explain. He used to transport land seekers and others up and down the Valley in it, at prices which he generally disclosed to them when they were at the top of the Valley and consequently helpless.

This we chartered, Ben assuring us that between such friends as we were the charges would be farcical, and all attempts to get a settled price out of him were unavailing. Absolute sobriety was also promised. That was sine qua non.

We had a small organ in the Church, which we had bought from Louise at a moment when a passing piano salesman had entangled her errant fancy, and on this the wedding march was practised by a musical neighbour of ours, until the pedals weakened; and, when the moment arrived, the organ squeaked feebly for a while and then settled down in dumb anger and despair.

In the gloaming of the evening before the ceremony Father Luyten arrived, and we heard him practising the Kyrie Eleison and the Gloria at the bottom of the hill as he drove. He went on practising, too, most of the evening, until someone asked him what was that melancholy thing that he was singing, when he laughed and ceased.

"You don't like music, no?" he asked. "We will see how it sounds tomorrow."

When the morning broke, a more nervously miserable man than the bridegroom never walked the earth. He felt sentimental, too, which did not help matters, because no one seemed to notice his presence at all. He moved about like a shaking ghost, while Old Lady Tiler caracoled around the kitchen, and armies of whirling figures haunted the house.

He tried the front, but an ominous stir sent him flying back to the still safe refuge of his own room, and here he stayed peeping out of the windows nervously and smoking endless cigarettes for half an hour or more.

Then he pulled himself together and went down to the Church, where thirty or forty men were already gathered, and he shuddered at the sight of them.

"Damn it!" he cried, at last, in vexation of spirit. "Everybody seems to be getting married today, except me!"[130]

The men nodded to him and spoke a word or two of sympathetic greeting, but they felt stiff in their store clothes, and he wandered away again, settling, at last, upon a bank from which a view of the road from Twisp was obtainable.

Time was passing, but there were no signs of Ben or of the car, in which the bride was to be conveyed to the Church, and a real nervousness began to impose itself upon the irritation which had been tormenting him 'til now. Supposing—? A dozen horrible possibilities ran gibbering through his mind, and he made for the house and the telephone. It would be a real relief to have some definite object to swear at, anyhow.

Forcing his way in, he called up Twisp and enquired if anyone had seen or heard of Ben that morning and, if so, was Ben sober? He tried the post-office, the hotel, the newspaper—forgetting that the editor was on the church porch already—and finally, what he should, of course, have tried first, the saloons, one after another. It was at the second of these that he got news of him. Ben had been in about half an hour back.

"Did he say anything about where he was going?"

"Why, no. Who is this?—Oh, it's you, Colonel?" the cheerful voice went on. "Well, well—I reckon he's headed for your house like all the rest of 'em. Was he what? Who—Ben? Depends. He was—happy, if that's what you mean. No, I reckon he's got a good start—he's sure got that!"

The miserable bridegroom dropped the receiver and regained the road. Of course! He might have known it! He wondered how he could poison Ben when he did arrive. And in this festal state of mind, he went back to the Church again. Here he found one valuable friend in the person of the Justice of the Peace, and him he dispatched back to the house with a buggy which someone had left by the fence.

"It's a hell of a thing to bring her to Church in," said the J. P. disgustedly, as he surveyed it. "You hadn't oughter have placed any damn reliance on what a Mackenzie said to you. A thing like this," he kicked the wheel of the buggy, "is plenty good enough for some people—Well, we can't help it, now. Main thing is to get her here, ain't it?"

By now the little Church was filled to its capacity and the grassy space in front was crowded far beyond it. Through this the bridegroom sweated, and into the Church, where he sat down under the eye of the lady organist, feeling like a lost puppy on a cold night and hoping that no one would come and turn him out. She paid him no attention whatever.

"The thing's gone and laid down on me!" she wailed in a whisper to a woman near her. "It's the pedal," she went on; "it's come unhitched some way!"

"Where's the man?" asked the other.

"What man? Oh, him? Search me. How on earth am I to get this thing to working before she comes, is what I want to know!"

The bridegroom sat quite still, he had evidently not been recognised. He was intimately aware of the horrid moment that was coming, when he would have to walk up the aisle, alone, and take his stand in front of the altar rails. For perhaps the second time in his life did he know what real loneliness was. That sensation is not to be found in solitude—the shrinking up of the whole personality until one feels like a long dried orange. Then the brain calls in vain upon that other self, that stands, as a rule, rock-like behind the flinching spirit which is accustomed to turn to it when all the earth is leagued against it. Then, in the echoing emptiness of the soul, the mind becomes a cave of winds and the sweat comes out in a cold drizzle.

All this and more swept over him in wave after wave, until, in sheer desperation, he pushed himself to his feet and squared his shoulders. The lady organist looked round with a start.

"What you doin' here?" she asked. "I never seen you come in."

"I don't know," he answered truthfully. "If I did, I'd tell you."

The insult spurred his self-respect as far as the top of the aisle, where he sat down, only to spring up again instantly as the sound of buzzing wheels came from out-of-doors, and through a fog he saw a white thing, which he took to be the Comrade, followed by eight little white flowers of bridesmaids, advancing up the path, supported on one side by his brother[131] and on the other by the indefatigable J. P., whose honest face, shining with soap and pride, brought the first comforting ripple of mirth which the victim's dreary being had felt that day. Before he knew it he had sniggered aloud in the face of the congregation, who, anxious to show that they knew how to comport themselves upon this or any other occasion, were gazing straight in front of them with set, funereal expressions—the women, that is to say; the men were all standing at the back—and then, hearing the snigger, sniggered too out of pure sympathy with a friend in affliction.

This had the result of taking the lady organist's mind off her business for the moment, and the opening bars of the Wedding March which she had forced from the protesting instrument, trailed off haltingly into silence, when she turned with a scandalised face to the men nearest to her, and, bending almost double, flung herself upon the organ again.

After that, the bridegroom was in a cloud. People moved near him, voices spoke to him: Father Luyten loomed up in front of him, bidding him repeat certain meaningless words, during which the Comrade gave him her left hand and refused to change it.

". . . Wilt thou take this woman to be thy wedded wife?" he was asked, and he cleared his throat.

"Sure!" he replied with a ghastly smile. "Sure!"

Gripping the ring, he seized the Comrade's finger, like a doctor performing an operation. Now he had tested that ring the night before to make quite certain, and it had slipped on and off comfortably. It was a huge ring—a knuckle-duster of a ring. "I don't want any mistakes made about us afterwards," the Comrade had said. "I want something that's built to last!"

It stuck—of course it stuck. It had been meddled with in the night by the fairies, like everything else, including the motor car. It stuck hard and though the bridegroom set his teeth and pushed, it stayed at the knuckle.

"Put it on," Father Luyten whispered hurriedly. "Put it on!"

The Comrade set her teeth hard too, and nodded, and, the fairies tiring of the joke, it slipped over the knuckle as easily as a leaf falling on the softest turf.

The bridegroom sat down, wiped his forehead and glanced cautiously at his bride. The bride hid a little yawn with her hand.

The Mass went on quietly, and a solemn silence fell upon the congregation. It was soothing, after the mental racket of the morning, and the restored bridegroom began to feel a grateful glow of manhood creeping over him, as he realised what had been happening. It was done; the waiting was over: a little while now and they would escape from the semi-Pagan rites in the house—well for him that he had no idea then of what they were going to be like!—and drive off, he cared not in what, through the summer day towards the river. They would go over the summit, he told himself decidedly, yes, they would go over the summit; through the dear whispering pines; through miles and miles of woods and moss and silence. It was worth enduring a little longer for!

Suddenly the murmuring quiet was rent asunder by a voice from the altar, and the bridegroom grasped at the altar rails for support, while the congregation rustled its amazement behind him.

Father Luyten was intoning the Kyrie Eleison!

He was a little out of practise, but he was not out of heart; he stood with his feet planted steadily, his head thrown back and his chest out, emitting an enormous volume of sound that tore through the little building leaping and falling like a happy gale.

On it went, occasionally breaking a point, but rising victoriously above the mischance, until the last word of it whirled out of doors and Father Luyten shook out his elbows like a man who has done his duty well.

He had, too. The congregation were all craning forward intently, thoroughly interested and waiting for him to begin again. The Congregational minister, standing half in and half out of the door, suddenly discovered that his mouth was wide open, and shut it with a snap, the while he stared at Father Luyten with envious eyes. To be allowed to let go like that during service; to open the chest and shout like Jeremiah when the people began to get apathetic—and all by himself! That was to be something like a minister! He told us afterwards that it was one of the most impressive things that he ever remembered to have heard! Having got under way, Father Luyten was not one to shrink from the full performance of the Marriage Mass, and the onlookers got their full "money's worth" before he had finished with them and us. He also gave a friendly, but very direct little sermon, addressed to us, but aimed at them, on the subject of marital responsibilities, which reached its mark sometimes, to judge from the coughing and foot scraping that told of a shot gone home. He had them where they could not get away and he "browned" them thoroughly. He wound up with a few remarks on the subject of divorce which cast a distinct gloom over several people in front of him. And then the "wouf! wouf!" of the wedding pedals began once more and a dirge-like march played us into the open air.

Then, for the first time, we learnt the story of Ben and his motor car. It had been precipitated, with three people in it, over a two hundred feet drop—but none of them had been seriously hurt. Ben had not been in it for once—of course not! how could he have been? We found him in the house, a quarter of an hour later, but he was very vague about it—vague and tearful, with alternate bursts of heroic gaiety. He had sent for another car, though. He had thought of that before he began to console himself, and, with its owner, had covered the twelve miles in something under twenty minutes.

His car, when rescued from the bottom of the cliff where it had fallen, was found to have sustained no more damage than a crushed lamp!

We hurried into the car after the wedding ceremony and mass, and the J. P. pushed himself in, unasked, beside us. He was very much worked up. He had a genuine devotion for the Comrade, and remarked over and over again, as we bumped toward the house for the reception, that this was the proudest day of his life. He was in tears, too, by the time we got indoors, for emotion is always rather lachrymose with us—and we dropped him into a chair on the verandah, putting a glass and a cigar into his hand.

The bridegroom, then, turned to his own needs, which were simply and easily satisfied. He had no appetite at all for solids, and he tore off the high stiff collar with which he had been torturing himself, the instant that he had shut his door behind him, and just in time to escape the first and worst rush.

There must have been two hundred people and more in and around that little house, and, over all, came the strident voice of Old Lady Tiler from the kitchen, enquiring, acidly, how much that gang of coyotes reckoned to eat, before the old people could get a mouthful.

Knowing our guests, we had hidden the whisky—or we thought we had—but there was wine enough for them to swim in had they been so minded—which they were. Only the intense difficulty of moving about at all, prevented them. They ate—heavens how they did eat! And their voices grew loud and jovial.

The Kansas lady, with pink ribbons in her hair, had stationed herself beside one of the tables, and gazed with haughty complacency at the crowd.

"I suppose one has to," she said to one of us. "It's a lot of trouble, but it's expected. You'd think some of them hadn't eaten for a week, wouldn't you? Hold on, Willie, that's your thirteenth plate of ice-cream. I've been counting them!"

Willie, a lad of fifteen, grabbed the piled-up saucer with both hands and went back to the privacy of the thicket behind the house, where, as a friend told us afterwards, he had consumed all the preceding ones, lying flat on his stomach among the trees.

The Kansas lady was still talking when a youth, the son of a Texan friend of mine and a most promising young ruffian, elbowed towards us. He had had the grace to leave his chaps outside, but in his hurry had forgotten to take off his spurs, which were not adding to the comfort of the people near him.

"Darn you, kid," said one girl, rubbing her foot. "I should think you'd have had sense enough to leave them horns of yours outside! What do you think this is anyway? A corral?"

"You're doin' fine, Colonel," he cried to the bridegroom. "You're doin' fine. This is the real thing, this layout of yours. When you get married—you get good and married, don't you? And you want everybody to know it—nothing mean about you—no, sir." Then he saw the Kansas lady, and he raised his dripping glass.

"Hallo, Sis!" he greeted her. "How'se you comin', old-timer?"

Her eyes gleamed and her mouth opened quickly, but, with splendid self-restraint, she closed it again and turned her head away.

"You can't keep them out," she remarked, "but they ought to be put in a barn by themselves."

"Not me, lady," he retorted cheerily. "The barn ain't built that could hold me today. Push it across, fellows; push it across. The roof's off!"

The Comrade, by now, had got to her room, hoping to be allowed to change her dress, and she stepped in, shutting the door smartly behind her. A figure started up from a chair and stood apologetically. It was Ben. He shook his head sadly at her.

"No fault of mine," he said. "You know that. Smashed—all smashed. Poor old Ben—"

She waited to hear no more, but ran for assistance. She had been tried high enough that day, and Ben in her bedroom was a little more than she was prepared to put up with. He was evicted gently and set down in the hall, talking to himself. The bridegroom explained that the whisky was lost, but offered him wine, a bottle of which he placed beside him. He was really sorry for Ben, but he was a good deal sorrier for the people who would have the job of getting him off the place later on.

At last, after ages of noise and dust and delay, the Comrade was inducted into the motor car and we got under way—as we hoped—alone. We were wrong about that, though, for we picked up a passenger in the village, another Texan, of the black-coated, black-hat type, the sort that could play stud poker for thirty-six hours at a time without fatigue. Then we did start in real earnest, and the Comrade clung to the side and the bridegroom to his hat.

"We got quite a way to go," the driver explained between tense lips, spitting out dust as he spoke. "And we got to hit'er up when we can, y'know."

"This is the way to travel," whistled the Texan between his teeth. "Open her up—don't mind me!"

It was the first time that either of us had ever tried those roads in a motor car, and it seemed as though somebody had been digging them up in the night. We thought we knew every rut and stone and bump in that stretch, but we felt like perfect strangers then.

Presently, however, the road forced the pace into a moderate fifteen or twenty miles an hour and we breathed more freely. The bridegroom even contrived to light a cigarette.

We stopped to pick up the driver's married daughter, a rather cold-faced lady, who forced herself into the seat with us.

"It's your car for the day," said he to the Comrade, "but you won't mind her, will you? She's thin, and it's a good big seat!"

We couldn't help minding her, but under the pale hypnotic eye, we crowded up and made the best of it. She started a little and stared when the Comrade began to smoke, but she said nothing, and we lumbered up the mountain side peacefully enough.

"You want to go careful up here," said the Texan. "This trail's full of snags."

"I know every snag from here to the river," replied the driver. "I've got so I got names for 'em now."

Once on the summit, he "opened her up" again and we flew through the pines. Alas for the pleasant loitering dream! We did not jolt in the back seat—we bounded. A motor car is a horrible conveyance at the best; at the worst—which that uneven, rocky, snag-haunted road was—the memory of it is a thing to haunt the dreams!

We were getting pretty deep into the woods now, and the trail was little more than a half cleared jungle, but the speed continued unabated, until we turned a corner sharply and the inevitable, which had been pursuing us ever since we cleared the rise, arrived. We were going at forty miles an hour, or more, when a snag rose up out of the ground and hurled itself at the crank.

The Texan left his seat abruptly and knelt on the floor gripping the brass-work with both hands; the car dived off into the woods with a sickening lurch and brought up in a tangle of young pines. The Comrade fell against the other woman, with a "There! Didn't I tell you so?" and the bridegroom, who had banged his knee against something and was swearing softly to himself, got out.

"Which was that one?" he asked cynically. "Mabel or Ethel?"

"It's a fact, I did forget that one," the driver confessed, hanging over the crank.

"She's got a nasty, jealous disposition," remarked the Texan. "She didn't forget you."

After twenty minutes of pulling and hauling and cranking and bad language, during which the Comrade and the driver's daughter took themselves thoughtfully out of the way, the car was rolled back onto the trail again; but she breathed heavily and seemed to be disgusted and hurt. She started, indeed, but it was evident that the body blow had knocked her early vigour out of her.

Groaning and wheezing, she pushed along, until we came to a bare scorched area that lay in the middle of the smiling woods like a wound. On one side of it, deep among the scorched trees, stood three of four buildings, one of which a few days before had been a saw-mill.

A clutter of iron and steel was scattered around, and, in the door of a frame dwelling house, miraculously preserved from the flames, was a young, fair-haired woman with the inevitable baby in her arms.

"Swede outfit," remarked the Texan with a pleasure at the sight of the ruin which he made no serious attempt to conceal. "The woods are lousy with 'em!"

We joggled up to the gate and then the car, finding itself in congenial surroundings for a breakdown, coughed languidly and came to a walk.

"I reckon," said the bridegroom to the Texan, "that we might as well call it half a day, and hunt up a rig."

"I reckon," the Texan agreed. "Maybe there's folk living around here some place. I'll walk down the trail a piece and look."

"She'll go all right in a while," the driver assured us. "She just wants coddling. She often gets like this. There's no call to go hunting rigs."

"So? Well, I'll stretch myself anyway," said the Texan and walked off briskly.

"I'll go and sit in that house," said the Comrade, "and wait for something to happen."

Half an hour went by, but the car still sulked, and, no sign of the Texan approaching, the bridegroom went in search of such men as the ruins might be concealing.

It was not the sort of place where a buggy would be likely to grow, but a waggon of some sort they would be sure to have, so he peered about and came upon a man in scandalously torn overalls, sitting on the remains of a boiler.

Yes, they had a waggon—to the river? It was a long way to the river. It was a longer way to tomorrow morning, the bridegroom argued, and he had no camping materials. Also it would be just as far in the morning as it was now. Also he was prepared to pay well for it. He would have to, as he knew, in any case, and he thought he might as well have the moral advantage of that understanding beforehand.

When, at last, it was put together—the term is not inept—he and the Comrade went back to the spot where they had left the car, and, as they turned into the road, they came upon what seemed to them one of the most pleasant sights they had ever beheld, for a good, roomy buggy, drawn by a team of stout greys, hove in sight, and the boy in charge of it announced that he had been sent by our good Texan who was waiting for us down the road.

The motor man looked up, and wiped his face with his sleeve. There was calculation in his eye.

"She just needs sparkin' up good!" he observed. "Now if we had a rope—I got one."

We were in the buggy by now, too pleased with our luck to listen very carefully, and the motor man had his car secured to the back rail of the buggy while we were still congratulating ourselves.

"Now then, sonny," he called, seating himself at the wheel, "start her up!"

The near cayuse looked around nervously, and then said something to his trace-mate, who tried to look round too, so that when the buggy started, neither of them was attending to their business, and the ear-splitting yells of the engine as the buggy pulled the car forwards, caught both of them off their guard.

The near one got up on his hind legs and tried to crawl out of the harness, while the off one put his head down and bucked. The boy, a little white about the gills, but full of grit, hung on to them, his hands twined through the loops of the reins, and the Comrade, clutching the rail at the back, shrieked at the motor man to stop his indecent performance and hire a team for himself.

"Why, you ain't scared, are you?" he called jestingly.

"Me?" she cried back. "Not a bit—I love it! I'd like to stay here all night and watch you—but we've got to get to the river, and the harness won't hold forever. Oh, for pity's sake stop it!"

It was eleven o'clock that night when they reached the river and went on board the steamerette which was to start at 4 a.m. on its trip downstream to the railway station. And it was just eleven o'clock the next night when they brought up at the dear old Pedicord Hotel in Spokane.[132] The restaurant was deserted, but for the night waiter, a fatherly old fellow who stared almost incredulously at the Dresden china girl, who blew in, fresh and exquisite as if she had just stepped out of a florist's band-box, and at the severely correct, blue-serged Britisher who carried her bag.

"Supper? Sure! Right away! Say," he leaned over, as he pushed in the bride's chair, and enquired in a confidential whisper, "Professional people?"

That was their greatest triumph. They had not been taken for honeymooners, but for strolling actors!

The secret came out the next day, however, when the bridegroom came in and placed a cushion in the chair prepared for the bride.

"She ain't come down yet, Mr. Newlywed," called the blooming waitress from behind the counter. "How'd I find out? Laws! That cushion give you away!"

Chapter 22

God's Country

Oh, but there are times when the heart turns to the sun-splashed, ice-floored memories of that country! To the natural lanes that ran in and out around the great lake behind the hills, where we bathed and fished in the summer and shot duck in the dazzling autumn afternoons. The lake was alive with birds. We have seen again and again mobs of six or eight hundred, swift-flying splendours of duck, near as large as geese! Rarely did we come away with less than four or five brace after half an hour's stalking—aye, stalking; none of your cosy overhead work for us. We walked them up in gum-boots and rarely got more than three shots apiece.

Both barrels, one after another, and if one had judged it well, a third, which reserve sometimes was held between the teeth. Then, numb but happy, we would climb back onto the buggy and let the patient old cayuse whom we always employed on these occasions loaf along through the gold and crimson of the trees, with the clear, frosty blue overhead deepening into violet and purple, on over ruts and stones and sagebrush, while we smoked and sang songs and felt like gods transplanted from Valhalla with a god's power on earth! There is nothing quite like it to be found in any other place. England, of a sharp November evening, may remind. The veldt at certain moments may suggest, but something is lacking in each. England cannot give the sense of space—no, not even on the moors, for where in England can you watch the sun set over mountains a hundred miles away, and that yet seem to be no further than the garden gate? And Africa has no "tang," no frost and no twilights. In both countries, too, one feels "small," a mental illusion which does not affect one on the Slope.

Nor can anyone arrive at a just estimate of human values if his physical view is limited by the other side of the street. The houses are the work of man and they will crumble away in time with all the rest of man's work, but the hills and the mountains and the hundred-mile valleys are not the work of man and they stare in silence across the ages. A lifetime passes across them like the shadow of a cloud, and if one is not afraid to stare at them, one may catch a glimpse of that at which they are staring. And then man's pride, man's glory, man's ambition will be seen for the dreary, empty, melancholy objects they are, so long as they begin and end with man alone.

And then the rain!

It is one thing to watch a garden or a street in a shower, it is another to stand under a deep, deep verandah in the open air and see a world being washed, to watch the storm sweep at you from British Columbia in a grey mist of lances, and then to look southward and see the sun shining in a cloudless sky over the Cascades. Even when one is outside, without any prospect of shelter, the fear of it is tinged so strongly with wonder, one's own insignificance is so caught up in the exultation of one's soul when the avalanche comes and the earth is blotted out, that one seems to be seized in the arms of a great, happy giant, and one laughs into the teeth of the wind and the wet, rejoicing mightily. There is nothing sad or dreary in our Methow rain storms; they go roaring with laughter from one end of the horizon to the other, like some hero king of mythology, while the pines bend in high and dignified courtesy, the cotton trees stoop awkwardly like clowns caught suddenly in the Presence, and the little quaking-asps huddle giggling together like young girls, shy, slim, sweet and self-conscious. Oh, it is a court that the rain king has!

Sometimes the lightning joins in, but he is a mad, careless, destructive condottiere, striking as he passes for the sheer pleasure of striking, roaring drunkenly the while.[133] He dances on the peaks, leaping from one to another, laying the clouds open with a stroke, flicking a blow among the trees, now in one quarter, now in another. Then the cattle huddle together, and the grazing cayuses gallop about wildly, and the dogs and the cats run for shelter with cries of angry fear. It is a country for lightning, that. Every piece of rock is impregnated with metal of one kind or another, and the fire seems to bounce about in the mountains like a ball. Considering the ferocity of our storms, however, we had singularly few accidents. If a man who has lived in the open all his life persists in taking shelter under trees at these times, it can hardly be called an accident when he is killed. It is deliberate suicide and nothing else. When the Sheriff serves a warrant stuffed into the muzzle of his gun, upon a man, and the man refuses to take it, there is no jury in the West but would return a verdict of "suicide while of unsound mind," in the event of the formality of an inquest being necessary.

How tame and flat and "Sundayfied" everything looks when the riot has passed and the hills laugh it goodbye! A stillness, almost like that of winter, settles on the hollows and ploughland, while the birds are still undecided as to whether they shall take their heads out from under their wings, and the cattle and horses have not yet the courage to separate and graze.

One imagines that the Great End will come in some such a fashion. First a whisper from the North, then a cloud, then a swirl of lances, a hurricane of wings—a rent in the skies and then the voice of God pealing from height to height and from cliff to cliff, echoing among the "draws" and through the canyons.

In the late autumn the country is not a good thing to look at. Burnt brown in the summer, the roads by the end of November are either trails of black mud or else are converted into frozen ruts, feet deep in places, on which no horse that was ever foaled can keep his footing. Cold, barren and inhospitable, one sees the day decline with joy, and the dark is welcomed with relief and delight.

Then, one morning, one wakes up and looks apprehensively out of the window, while the stove chuckles over its breakfast and the dogs and cats hump their backs and glide round it and pass the time of day.

Then a contented sigh breathes through the house, and "Here she is at last!" one cries.

It is difficult to describe the first sensations with which one greets the return of the snow. The physical relief has something to do with it, there is an excitement, a *joie de vivre*, a spiritual elation—but how can one take one's feelings to pieces and spread them out?

As the thick, heavy flakes sift and settle on the ragged hills, one is reminded of nothing so much as a tired, worn, scorched or frozen heart that has found its own peace, instantly and completely, as that peace is always found. In the evening every tooth of pain stands out and the unhealed edges of the wounds sting and ache, but in the pure, cold ghostly dawn every scar is covered, every wound buried in balm, and what was an eyesore overnight becomes a miracle of light and beauty in the morning.

And with it comes that soft, musical silence, which muffles everything. People walk and drive and ride, but their very voices are softened and mild until they seem little more than whispers.

It shuts one in, too. After all those months of space, it is pleasant and cosy, that heavy curtain between oneself and the outside world; as the carpet thickens and thickens, until the tops of the fence-posts are covered with a solid turban a foot high, and the levels of the windows are reached, one feels more and more the reason of winter; one understands it for what it was meant to be, a time of the year for man to lay aside his labour and betake himself to a spiritual retreat where he may think and pray and cultivate his mind, and praise God for the possession if he can.

Few people can place a finger on a certain spot on the map and say, "I was never anything but perfectly happy *there*!"

Notes

1. Washington State was admitted to the union on November 11, 1889.
2. In addition to the Columbia, the largest, Washington has many major rivers, including the Snake, Yakima, Pend Oreille, and Skagit. It is not clear which ones Fraser is referencing.
3. Samuel L. Hill, who married the eldest daughter of railroad magnate James J. Hill, owned land for a time near Pearrygin Lake in the Methow Valley. Speculation that the Great Northern Railway would come through the valley was strong in pioneer times. (The same last names of Samuel and James were coincidental.)
4. Oregon Territory was established in August 1848. Washington Territory, part of the original Oregon Territory, was established in 1853.
5. The four were Mrs. Hugh Fraser (the author, née Mary Crawford), Hugh Crawford Fraser (the author's youngest son), Katherine Lucy Wray (her future daughter-in-law), and John Fraser (the author's eldest son).
6. Guy Waring, the Harvard graduate from Boston who platted Winthrop, is referred to by the nicknames the "Owner" and the "Lord of the Manor" throughout the book.
7. Hugh Fraser was a lieutenant in the Royal Scots Fusiliers in the Second Boer War, 1899–1902, in what is now South Africa. He was twice wounded and came to the Methow Valley to recover, according to the *Okanogan Independent* newspaper. He would later die in World War I.
8. Mrs. Hugh Fraser's eldest son, John "Jack" Fraser, traveled later to the Methow, bringing his brother's betrothed, Katherine Lucy Wray, referred to in the book as "Kitty" and the "Comrade." Katherine Wray would marry the author's younger son, Hugh, in the Catholic Church in Heckendorn on June 29, 1911.
9. The Butler Hotel stood on the corner of Second and James streets in Seattle.
10. Wildfires are a fact of life in the North Cascades. In the summer of 2014 when the editors were writing this footnote, the largest forest fire yet recorded in Washington State—the Carlton Complex—was started by lightning from a storm over the Methow Valley. This mark was exceeded by the wildfires that burned in the state in the summer of 2015.
11. The author arrived at the train station in Wenatchee.
12. The Columbia River, not yet dammed, still ran freely, including its rapids. By modern roads, it is 100 miles from Wenatchee to Winthrop, Washington.
13. The author disembarked at the confluence of the Methow and Columbia rivers, at the town of Pateros. Her trip in a wagon up the Methow Valley, along the Methow River, was considerably bumpier than her steamboat ride up the Columbia.
14. When the author refers to a "rig," she means a wagon, not a boat. "Rig" is a term still used in the Methow to refer to trucks, cars, wagons, etc.

15. Cayuse is a word used in the American West, generally referring to a poorly bred horse.
16. The author likely dined in one of the mid-valley towns of Carlton or Methow, or perhaps Silver, which no longer exists.
17. "The Preacher" was likely Reverend O. W. Mintzer, who was an active Methodist in the valley from 1903–1911.
18. The first Winthrop creamery was downstream on the river side of Winthrop's main street, near where the pedestrian bridge now crosses the Methow River. The creamery was opened in 1906 by Lieutenant Evelyn Aldrich. Other creameries were established in Winthrop farther upstream, also between the river and the road.
19. Hugh Fraser's cabin stood on Riverside Avenue near Winthrop's lower bridge, where Highway 20 crosses the Methow River.
20. Melachrinos were a popular brand of Egyptian cigarettes.
21. Waring's Methow Trading Company was the largest building in downtown Winthrop. The building no longer stands.
22. The author settled into a house owned by Mrs. Martha Ann (Bacus) Filer. It stood near what is now Filer Avenue, at the same level where it hooks into Castle Avenue above Heckendorn, on a bench of Stud Horse Mountain.
23. The author is likely referring to cottonwood or aspen trees. There are few native alders near Winthrop.
24. The author is referring to the Sawtooth mountain range in what is now the Lake Chelan-Sawtooth Wilderness.
25. Edgar Bertram Filer, Martha Filer's youngest son, was born in 1875 in Dallas, Texas. He died in 1909 in Bellingham, Washington.
26. "Parky" is British slang meaning snappy and pleasant but chilly in describing a person.
27. Lieutenant Evelyn Aldrich of the British Navy. He is later referred to as the "Admiral."
28. The North Fork of the Methow River is the Chewuch River.
29. Hugh Fraser arrived in Winthrop in the winter of 1904–1905, hence his nickname the "Winter One." Mrs. Hugh Fraser, his mother—nicknamed the "Summer One"—arrived in Winthrop on July 30, 1906.
30. The stage driver was likely Frank Witte, who ran stage services into the valley during the book's era.
31. This is likely not the Goat Wall that we know today, which stands up-river of Mazama. The author may have been referring to Lucky Jim Bluff, which rises above Big Valley Ranch and can be viewed from Winthrop.
32. "Watson" is the author's nickname for Edgar Allison, who married Clara Thompson on March 1, 1905.
33. Mrs. Filer's granddaughter was Laura Emily Dibble.
34. Mrs. "Hudson" was Anna Estelle (Moore) Hotchkiss. Mrs. "Hasketh" was Margaret Mussett.
35. "Twickenham" is the name the author uses for the Heckendorn family.
36. The "judge's boy" is Clarence Heckendorn. "Dick Mackenzie" is Chauncey "Dick" McLean.
37. Lilac is a syringa.

Notes

38. Fraser is referring to arrowleaf balsamroot, which blooms profusely across the Methow Valley hills in spring and early summer.
39. The author's comments in this paragraph echo historian Frederick Jackson Turner's idea that American civilization is made distinctive by the pioneer experience, even as civilization overtakes the American frontier. Put forward in 1883, the Turner Thesis had significant popular appeal in the early twentieth century.
40. Irrigation ditches were increasingly important to Methow Valley agriculture in the early part of the 1900s and remain key to it today. Some open ditches have been replaced in recent years by pipes to reduce leakage and improve water pressure.
41. When the author refers here to the Methow River, she includes the "North Fork" of the Methow, now known as the Chewuch River.
42. "Judge Twickenham" is David Eugene Heckendorn, also referred to elsewhere in the book as "the Judge" and the "Justice of the Peace" or "J. P."
43. The "Nebrasky Outfit" refers to the McLeans. Some had come through Nebraska on their way west and had married Nebraskans.
44. Dick McLean's brothers were Frank, George ("Hungry"), Charlie ("Baldy"), Ben, and Bert. Dick's wife, Sarah (Smith) McLean, also had sisters in the valley: Anna married Bert McLean, Louisa married A. C. Luther, and Mary married Daniel Robbins.
45. Winthrop eventually won the contest between the two towns. Heckendorn is now a neighborhood in the down-river part of Winthrop.
46. Dr. C. R. Mackinley, of Brewster, apparently travelled throughout Okanogan County to treat patients.
47. Three McLean infants are buried in Winthrop's Sullivan Cemetery. One grave includes a year: 1904. The other two graves are not dated.
48. Maude and Millie McLean were the two sisters of Dick McLean who came to the Methow Valley.
49. Ruth McLean married Ira Van Buren in the fall of 1911.
50. "Pete Malloy" is Pete Bryan, who was a long-time friend of Dick McLean. He is elsewhere in the book referred to as simply "Pete."
51. Tom Wills was the Winthrop postmaster.
52. "Granma" was Sarah (Smith) Hall. She was married to David C. Hall, her second husband. Previously, she was married to Michael Smith and had five daughters: Hattie Smith, Anne Smith (married to Bert McLean), Sarah E. Smith (married to Dick McLean), Louisa Smith (married to A. C. Luther), and Mary B. Smith (married to Daniel Robbins).
53. Mr. F___ was Frank M. Fulton.
54. A white schoolhouse opened in 1903 on Castle Avenue not far from what is now the Shafer Historical Museum in Winthrop. By 1906, the student body had outgrown the school.
55. "Dutch Bob" is Robert Oertel. His daughters were Frieda and Anna. Part of his land eventually became the Bear Creek Golf Course.
56. In 1908, the first high school classes were taught in the valley. In 1913, construction started on a school for grades 1–12 in Winthrop. Meanwhile, high school classes were held in the Methow Trading Company store and even in the Duck Brand Saloon building.

57. Edgar Allison was likely the teacher referred to here as Watson.

58. "Mr. S" was likely W. L. Singer.

59. The McLean store stood northwest of the corner of Main and Center streets in Heckendorn.

60. The "Mehalahs" were the Sisters of the Pythias, an auxiliary organization to the Order of Knights of Pythias, a fraternal order founded in 1864.

61. "Mr. H" was Samuel Hotchkiss, who lived near the author and had seven children: sons Reuben, Leonard, Calvin, and Edgar, and daughters Olive, Ann, and Adelia.

62. "Mr. Hasketh" was Henry Mussett. The 1910 census lists Mussett as seventy-one years old, born in Essex, England, and first married to Rhoda Partridge. His second wife was Margaret, according to Winthrop's 1920 census.

63. The Oration in the Grove was part of the commencement ceremony at Amherst College. Winthrop locals referred to the area around what is today the Winthrop Barn Auditorium and Mack Lloyd Park as "The Grove."

64. "Beehardt" was the author's name for Frank Biart.

65. "Hudson" was the author's name for Samuel Hotchkiss.

66. "Maw" was Louisa Sullivan, David Eugene Heckendorn's mother. She convinced David Heckendorn, a son of her first marriage, to come to the Methow Valley to help care for her invalid second husband, James Sullivan. After Mr. Sullivan died, she deeded the land that became Heckendorn to David.

67. Clarence Heckendorn was David Heckendorn's son.

68. "Jack" is the author's oldest son, John Fraser. See Note 8.

69. "Grantly" likely refers to Harry E. Marble, the editor of the *Methow Valley News* in Twisp.

70. "Laura Dibb" was likely Laura Emily (Dibble) Hutchinson, who was Martha Filer's granddaughter.

71. "Luther's Hill" is now known as Stud Horse Mountain.

72. Today the lake is spelled Pearrygin and is part of the Pearrygin Lake State Park. The lake was named for Benjamin Franklin Pearrygin, who was in the Methow Valley by 1890.

73. Coyotes still live in the Methow Valley.

74. Officially, the hottest temperature recorded in Winthrop is 106° Fahrenheit on July 27, 1939.

75. Louisa (Smith) Luther, sister to Mrs. Dick McLean, married a Methow Valley man, Asa C. Luther. The author calls them the "Larkins."

76. Mrs. "Hill" was apparently Laura Wills, the wife of Tom Wills, the Winthrop postmaster.

77. "Desolation Hill" likely refers to a place in the Rendezvous area between the Methow and Chewuch rivers.

78. The author apparently meant cottonwood trees, still abundant along the rivers.

79. In the nineteenth century, traveling salesmen were called "drummers."

80. Walter Frisbee built a wire-cable river crossing not far from where the pedestrian bridge now spans the Methow River in lower Winthrop.

81. C. E. Briggs, who was age thirty-eight (not seventeen or eighteen, as the author reports), went with his father to the Duck Brand Saloon on June 3, 1906. Leaving his father in the saloon, he went to an out-building and shot himself.

82. Ferd Haase, Sr., emigrated with his family to the United States after being in the military in Germany. He had six children and lived in a house behind what was then the Duck Brand Saloon in Winthrop, now the Winthrop Town Hall.
83. Joseph S. Baker was the manager of the Duck Brand Saloon in 1906.
84. "The Owner" was Guy Waring. See Note 6.
85. Before it was moved to town, the sawmill stood about five miles up the Methow River near what is now the Big Valley Ranch.
86. Siwash is a Chinook Jargon word for native peoples derived from the French "sauvage." It is now considered a derogatory term for Native Americans.
87. The "Comrade" and "Kitty" were the author's nicknames for Katherine Lucy Wray. See Note 8.
88. "Mother," in this case, refers to the author, Mrs. Hugh Fraser.
89. Saltpeter is a name for potassium nitrate.
90. "Robinson" is the author's name for Clarence M. Davidson, who was president of the Winthrop Percheron Company.
91. Florence McLean and her husband, Harry Tuttle, were stunt riders for a time in the early movies.
92. The author is referring to Winthrop and Heckendorn.
93. "Spavin" is osteoarthritis in a horse, which causes swelling.
94. The Methow Bank in Twisp, later called The Commercial Bank, was established before Fraser arrived in the Methow Valley.
95. The author is likely referring to J. O. Ostby, who in 1906 opened the Methow Valley Bank in Twisp, not to be confused with the Methow Bank in Twisp.
96. *Frühlingslied* translates from German to mean "spring song."
97. Fraser is referring here to a financial crisis that occurred in 1907 during what was already an economic recession in the nation.
98. Louise and Asaph Colgrave Luther owned land on Stud Horse Mountain above Heckendorn.
99. The mother of the Mackenzie wives was Sarah (Smith) Hall. Dave Hall was her second husband.
100. Harry Greene, Guy Waring's stepson, had two daughters, Helen and Francis, with his wife, Florence.
101. The author here refers to Martha Ann (Bacus) Filer, who married Jacob Conrad Filer (Sr.) in Dallas, Texas, in 1861. They had ten children in Texas before they started west in 1883 in a wagon train that included other families that eventually settled in the Methow Valley: the Stones, the Dibbles, the Fultons, and the Thurlows. Martha Filer's husband, Jacob, died in Pendleton, Oregon, in 1883. She then moved to Ellensburg, Washington, and finally to the Methow Valley.
102. Okanogan County "went dry" in June 1910. The only unincorporated areas that voted—unsuccessfully—to "stay wet" were Conconully, Loomis, Chesaw, and Molson. The Oroville vote was tied: eleven votes to eleven votes.
103. The attorney was George W. Goode.
104. Two deputies who served before Charles H. "Baldy" McLean were Walter Metcalf and H. H. McNeil.

105. In 1909, George Goode spent time at the state psychiatric hospital at Medical Lake, Washington, near Spokane. Eastern State Hospital still provides psychiatric care at Medical Lake.
106. *The Winthrop Eagle* was published in Winthrop for one year beginning in May 1909.
107. The *Methow Valley News*, founded in 1903, is still published today.
108. *The Winthrop Eagle* came out on Friday night.
109. The Winthrop Town Hall is now in the building once occupied by Guy Waring's Duck Brand Saloon.
110. The author here refers to Frank McLean, who was part of the Winthrop Land Company.
111. The constable was Charles W. Dibble.
112. The "venerable old German" was Ferd Haase, who fought in the Franco-Prussian War of 1870, which included the Siege of the Metz.
113. The "dope" is likely laudanum, an opiate, which was not regulated in the early 20th century.
114. Frank McLean was an energetic Methow Valley promoter and salesman.
115. John S. Chapman emigrated from England to the United States in 1909. His "friend" was Robert Alfred Hodges, who also came in 1909. Both are listed in the Methow Valley census for 1910.
116. Guy Waring's Land 5 orchard in the Rendezvous area proved to be a business disaster, though a few apple trees are still alive today. Other orchards in the Methow Valley, once they were irrigated, proved more prosperous but were severely damaged by the freeze of 1968, which set an official state low-temperature record of -48 degrees Fahrenheit. Commercial orchards are a small part of the valley's economy today.
117. "Tillicums" is a Chinook Jargon word meaning friend/relative/tribal member/family member.
118. Hugh Fraser is recalling his army days in the Boer War in Africa.
119. Sarah was Dick McLean's wife. Ruth, Bill, and Alice were three of Sarah and Dick McLean's six children.
120. "Horse Heaven" is an avalanche-path/meadow high on the West Fork of the Methow River.
121. The Giant Powder Company was the first company in America to produce gun powder. Giant Powder dynamite was sold at most merchandise stores in the country.
122. "Bear-paw" likely refers to an earlier version of what became today's "bear-claw" pastry.
123. George Stuckey was charged with incest in October 1911. *The Okanogan Record* reported his escape in its November 3, 1911 issue.
124. *The Okanogan Record* reported on June 17, 1910, that 18-month old Ralph Albin, living near Winthrop, choked to death on a screw.
125. The two who drove down to Twisp with Mrs. Filer's old horse, Dolly, were Hugh Fraser and his fiancée, Katherine ("Kitty") Wray.
126. Mrs. Filer's daughter Anna married Mathias "Sie" Walter. They had four boys—Archie being the eldest—and two girls. Anna died in 1910.
127. Father Luyten preached at the Catholic Church in Heckendorn. He came from Waterville, WA.

128. The community leaned on Mr. Heckendorn, who had earlier donated land for a Methodist church, to provide land for a Catholic church, which was built along Filer Avenue in Heckendorn.
129. Ben McLean owned an Everitt-Metzger-Flander—an E.M.F. 30—which was also called an "Every Morning Fix-It" or "Every Mechanical Failure" or "Every Miss-Fire."
130. The wedding was reported in the June 20, 1911, issue of the *Methow Valley News*.
131. Hugh Fraser's older brother was John "Jack" Fraser.
132. The Pedicord Hotel stood on Riverside Avenue in Spokane.
133. A condottiere is the leader of a band of mercenaries.

List of People

Abe Sourdough	Unknown
A. C.	Asa C. Luther
Admiral	Lieutenant Evelyn Aldrich
Alice	Alice McLean
Arch	Unknown
B____	Unknown
B.	Unknown
Beehardt	Frank Biart
Ben	Ben McLean
Bert	Unknown
Bill (well-digger)	Unknown
Bohemian peasant	Unknown
Brother B____	Unknown
Brunton	Unknown
Chapman	Unknown
Charlie (driver)	Unknown
Charlie (lumber mill)	Unknown
Charlie (lawman)	Charles McLean
Clarence	Clarence Heckendorn
Cockney clerk	Robert Hodges
Colonel	Lt. Hugh Fraser
Comrade	Katherine Wray
Dave	Dave Hall, Sarah (Smith) Hall's second husband
Dutch Bob	Robert Oertel
Ed	Unknown
Father Luyten	Father Luyten
Frances	Frances Greene, Guy Waring's step-granddaughter
Frank (driver)	Frank Witte
Granma	Sarah (Smith) Hall
Gene	David Eugene Heckendorn
German veteran	Ferd Haase Sr.
Grantley	Harry E. Marble
Hasketh	Mussett family—Henry, Margaret
Helen	Helen Greene, Guy Waring's step-granddaughter
Hudson	Hotchkiss family—Samuel and Anna had seven children, Reuben was the oldest
Hen	Unknown
Hill	Wills family—Tom Wills was Winthrop postmaster

Hugh/Hughie	Hugh C. Fraser, Mrs. Fraser's youngest son
Ira Van Piets	Ira Van Buren
Jack	John Fraser, Mrs. Fraser's oldest son
Jenkins	Unknown
J. P.	David Eugene Heckendorn
Judge	David Eugene Heckendorn
Justice of the Peace	David Eugene Heckendorn
Kansas lady	Possibly Mrs. Tom Wills, the postmaster's wife
Kitty, Miss Kitty	Katherine Wray
Landlady	Martha Ann (Bacus) Filer
Larkins	Luther family—Asa C. and Louise
Laura Dibb	Laura Emily (Dibble) Hutchinson
Lo(u)ise	Louise Luther
Lord of the Manor	Guy Waring
Martin	Unknown
Mackenzies	McLean family: Chauncey "Dick," and Sarah had six children—Jim, Bill, Ruth, Chan, Alice, and Florence. Dick had five brothers—Frank, George, Charlie, Ben, and Bert—and two sisters, Maude and Millie. Sarah had three sisters—Annie, Louise, and Mary—and their mother was Sarah (Smith) Hall.
Maw	Louisa Sullivan
Metz veteran	Ferd Haase Sr.
Mother Flanagan	Unknown
Mr. F	Frank Fulton
Mr. H	Samuel Hotchkiss
Mr. Kelly	Unknown
Mr. S	Probably W. L. Singer
Mrs. Dick	Sarah McLean
Mrs. Hill	Mrs. Wills, married to Winthrop postmaster Tom Wills
Nebraska	Unknown
Nebrasky outfit	McLean family
Old Lady Tiler	Martha (Bacus) Filer
Owner	Guy Waring
Parsons	May have been E. H. Parkinson
Pete/Pete Malloy	Pete Bryan
Preacher	Reverend O. W. Mintzer
Robinson	Clarence Davidson
Sadie Lawrence	Unknown
Saidie	A. C. and Louise Luther's daughter
Sarey	Sarah McLean
Selena Scaraway	Unknown
Summer One	Mrs. Hugh Fraser, the author
Texan	Unknown

Tilers	Filer family
Tom	Tom Wills, the postmaster
Twickenham	Heckendorn family—Eugene "Gene" and Catherine, children Violet and Clarence
Veteran of the Metz	Ferd Haase Sr.
Violet	Violet Heckendorn
Watson	Edgar Allison
Will (ice cream)	Unknown
Winter One	Hugh C. Fraser, the author's youngest son

Photo Credits

1. Mrs. Hugh Fraser – From a front page of *A Diplomatist's Wife in Many Lands* (Dodd, Mead 1910)
2. Hugh C. Fraser – Shafer Historical Museum, Ernie Cotton Scrapbook
3. Steamboat "Columbia" – Shafer Historical Museum, Melvin Risley Collection
4. Frank Witte stagecoach – Shafer Historical Museum, Dick Webb Collection
5. Creamery in Winthrop – Shafer Historical Museum, Badger Boesel Family Collection
6. A bird's-eye view of Winthrop – Shafer Historical Museum, Wink Byram Collection
7. Heckendorn canning house – Shafer Historical Museum
8. Methow Trading Company store – Shafer Historical Museum, Badger Boesel Family Collection
9. Two men in alfalfa field – Shafer Historical Museum, Badger Boesel Family Collection
10. White school house – Shafer Historical Museum
11. Ethyl Haase – Shafer Historical Museum, Haase Family Collection
12. Duck Brand Saloon – Shafer Historical Museum
13. Guy Waring's sawmill – Shafer Historical Museum, Jordan "Butch" Sullivan Collection
14. Winthrop bridge collapse – Shafer Historical Museum, Carroll Family Collection
15. Harry Greene – Shafer Historical Museum, Heckendorn Family Collection
16. Hay derrick – Shafer Historical Museum, Badger Boesel Family Collection
17. Guy Waring – Shafer Historical Museum, Louise LaRue Moore Collection
Cover: Postcard, "Burke-Lehman Tract, near Twisp, Wash." – Shafer Historical Museum
Frontispiece: Steamboat "Selkirk" – Shafer Historical Museum, Ernie Cotton Scrapbook